# LOW INTERMEDIATE
# Workbook

ACCOMPANYING MEDIA

# OXFORD PICTURE DICTIONARY

## CANADIAN EDITION

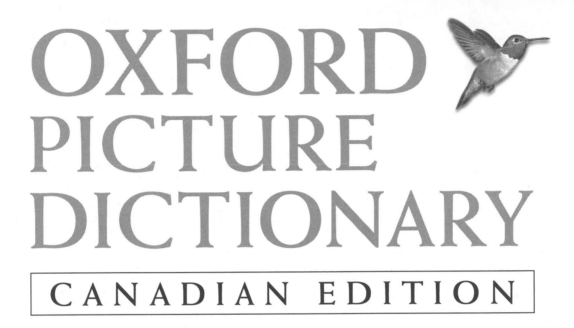

Marjorie Fuchs
Margaret Bonner

# OXFORD
UNIVERSITY PRESS

70 Wynford Drive, Don Mills, Ontario  M3C 1J9
www.oupcanada.com

Oxford University Press is a department of the University of Oxford.

It furthers the University's objective of excellence in research, scholarship,
and education by publishing worldwide in

Oxford   New York

Auckland   Cape Town   Dar es Salaam   Hong Kong   Karachi
Kuala Lumpur   Madrid   Melbourne   Mexico City   Nairobi
New Delhi   Shanghai   Taipei   Toronto

With offices in

Argentina   Austria   Brazil   Chile   Czech Republic   France   Greece
Guatemala   Hungary   Italy   Japan   Poland   Portugal   Singapore
South Korea   Switzerland   Thailand   Turkey   Ukraine   Vietnam

Oxford is a trade mark of Oxford University Press in the UK and
in certain other countries

Published in Canada
by Oxford University Press

Copyright © Oxford University Press Canada 2010

The moral rights of the author have been asserted

Database right Oxford University Press (maker)

First Published 2010

Originally published by Oxford University Press, 198 Madison Avenue,
New York, NY 10016, USA. Copyright © Oxford University Press 2008

Oxford Picture Dictionary Low Intermediate Workbook was originally published
in 2008. This edition is published by arrangement with Oxford University Press.

CD 1 audio tracks 5, 6, 7, 9, 14, 15, 18, 23, 31, 32 and CD 2 audio tracks 2, 4, 7, 8, 9,
13, 14 copyright © Oxford University Press Canada 2010.

All other tracks originally published in Oxford Picture Dictionary Lesson Plans in 2009.
This edition is published by arrangement with Oxford University Press.

**Library and Archives Canada Cataloguing in Publication**

Fuchs, Marjorie, 1949–
        The Oxford picture dictionary, second Canadian edition.
        Low intermediate workbook / Marjorie Fuchs, Margaret Bonner.

ISBN 978-0-19-543353-1

        1. Picture dictionaries, English–Problems, exercises, etc.
        2. English language—Textbooks for second language learners.
        I. Bonner, Margaret  II. Title.

PE1629.S49 2009 Suppl. 3        423'.17        C2009-901413-0

Oxford University Press is committed to our environment. This book is
printed on Forest Stewardship Council certified paper, harvested from
a responsibly managed forest.

Printed and bound in Canada.

1  2  3  4 – 13  12  11  10

Chapter icons designed by Von Glitschka/Scott Hull Associates

**Art Credits:**

Gary Antonetti: 201; Argosy: 194, 286; Barb Bastian: 15, 156; Kenneth Batelman:
13, 46; John Batten: 3, 88-89; Kathy Baxendale: 32, 108, 119, 195, 241; Annie
Bisset: 12, 26, 123, 143, 159, 177; Arlene Boehm: 70, 71; Kevin Brown/Top Dog
Studio: 7, 238, 302, 315; Dominic Bugatto/Three-in-a-Box: 100, 114; Carlos
Castellanos: 58, 62, 245; Andrea Champlin: 25, 91, 241, 284; Dominik D'Andrea:
97; Mona Daly/Mendola Art: 90, 106; Jim Delapine: 235; Bill Dickson/Contact
Jupiter: 10, 42, 269, 294; Jody Emery: 67, 131, 178, 246, 290; Jim Fanning/Ravenhill
Represents: 66, 81; Mike Gardner: 142, 175; Glenn Gustafson: 76, 124, 296; Ben
Hasler/NB Illustration: 148; Betsy Hayes: 139; Kevin Hopgood: 2, 43, 179, 299;
Infomen/Debut Art: 51, 54, 74, 115, 150, 172, 207, 244; Emma Jacob/Lemonade:
33, 94; Janos Jantner/Beehive Illustration: 79, 171, 181, 217, 256; Ken Joudrey/
Munro Campagna: 68; Mike Kasun/Munro Campagna: 74, 102, 158, 189, 291;
Keithley Associates: 153, 248; Denis Luzuriaga: 34, 47; Scott MacNeill: 19, 66, 75,
112, 236, 292; Adrian Mateescu/The Studio: 28, 55, 242; Karen Minot: 116, 155,
184, 225; Paul Mirocha/The Wiley Group: 211, 216; Terry Pazcko: 47, 53, 83, 215;
Pronk&Associates: 4, 5, 6, 8, 9, 11, 14, 16, 17, 18, 19, 20, 21, 27, 28, 29, 33, 35, 36,
37, 38. 40-41, 49, 50, 52, 57, 59, 65, 68, 71, 72-73, 77, 78, 82, 83, 84, 85, 92, 94, 95,
97, 101, 105, 106, 110, 113, 117, 128, 132, 142, 144-145, 152, 154, 157. 160. 161,
165, 173, 175, 179, 185, 192, 193, 198, 203, 210, 215, 219, 223, 227, 235, 239; Mark
Reidy/Munro Campagna: 134 (stamp); Robert Roper/Wilkinson Design Studio: 23,
60, 267; Marcos Schaaf/NB Illustration: 76, 93; Phil Scheuer: 167, 218, 251; Robert
Schuster: 24, 34, 48, 69, 151, 227 (icons), 229; Ben Shannon/Magnet Reps: 143;
Geoffrey Paul Smith: 180, 233; Sam Tomasello: 63, 176, 208, 209; Anna Veltfort:
129, 259; Ralph Voltz/Deborah Wolfe: 154, 237, 249; William Waitzman: 18,
163, 174; Mark Watkinson/Illustrationweb.com: 169, 228, 234; Simon Williams/
Illustrationweb.com: 45; Graeme Wilson/Graham-Cameron Illustration: 56, 62,
107 ; Tracey Wood/Reactor Art: 105.

**Photo Credits:**

Agefotostock: Creatas, 49 (Smithfield home); Mike Kemp, 140 (woman reading
newspaper); Alamy: ACE STOCK LIMITED, 204 (Angel Falls); The Print Collector,
199 (Alessandro Volta); Photos 12, 199 (Rosa Parks); Mary Evans Picture Library,
199 (J.S. Bach); Classic Image, 199 (Vasco da Gama); Directphoto.org, 199 (I.M. Pei);
Big Stock Photo: Zdenka Micka, 32; Nikolay Mamluke, 48; Gautier Wallaume, 98
(wool); Lisa Turay, 177; Dreamstime: Anne Kitzman, 49 (Lincoln home); Volodymyr
Kyrylyuk, 50; Pablo Caridad, 98 (leather); 99 (nylon); Kevin Fletcher, 127 (Olympic
stadium); Richard Gunion, 140 (demonstration); Yu Liang Wong, 140 (speaker
with microphone); 140 (woman at mosque); Jan De Wild, 185; 186; Lisa F. Young,
250 (construction worker); Getty Images: Hulton Archive, 40; Photographer's
Choice, 51 (police woman); Time and Life Pictures, 243 (kiss); Inmagine: Corbis,
80, 115 (optometrist); Brand X Pictures, 49 (Greenville home); Blendimages,
171; Digitalvision, 250 (factory worker); fstop, 250 (farmer); GoGo Images, 108;
Image100, 72; iStockphoto: James Tutor, 84; Tarek El Sombati, 98 (linen); Michael
Krinke, 120 (female surgeon); Norman Pogson, 126 (Biosphere); Jim Jurica, 140
(picketers); Shelly Perry, 207 (Asian male); Ilda Masa, 221 (skier); John Pitcher,
221 (polar bears); Sebastian Santa, 221 (Niagara Escarpment); Photodisc, 133;
Polkadot, 207 (Hispanic male); Jupiterimages: 99 (corduroy), 184; Magnum Photos:
Bruno Barbey, 243 (elderly Chinese men); Leonard Freed, 243 (father and son);
Michael Goldman, 250 (office worker); Moodboard, 119; PhotoAlto, 115 (depressed
man); Rubberball, 136; Stockbyte, 140 (witness stand), 152; Shutterstock.com: 39,
95, 118, 141, 204 (globe); 205, 214 (peacock), 224, 226, 231(volleyball)

# Acknowledgements

The publisher and authors would like to acknowledge the following individuals for their invaluable feedback during the development of this workbook:

**Patricia S. Bell,** Lake Technical County ESOL, Eustis, FL

**Patricia Castro,** Harvest English Institute, Newark, NJ

**Druci Diaz,** CARIBE Program and TBT, Tampa, FL

**Jill Gluck,** Hollywood Community Adult School, Los Angeles, CA.

**Frances Hardenbergh,** Southside Programs for Adult and Continuing Ed, Prince George, VA

**Mercedes Hern,** Tampa, FL

**(Katie) Mary C. Hurter,** North Harris College, Language and Communication, Houston, TX

**Karen Kipke,** Antioch Freshman Academy, Antioch, TN

**Ivanna Mann-Thrower,** Charlotte Mecklenburg Schools, Charlotte, NC

**Holley Mayville,** Charlotte Mecklenburg Schools, Charlotte, NC

**Jonetta Myles,** Salem High School, Conyers, GA

**Kathleen Reynolds,** Albany Park Community Center, Chicago, IL

**Jan Salerno,** Kennedy-San Fernando CAS, Grenada Hills, CA

**Jenni Santamaria,** ABC Adult School, Cerritos, CA

**Geraldyne Scott,** Truman College/ Lakeview Learning Center, Chicago, IL

**Sharada Sekar,** Antioch Freshman Academy, Antioch, TN

**Terry Shearer,** Region IV ESC, Houston, TX

**Melissa Singler,** Cape Fear Community College, Wilmington, NC

**Cynthia Wiseman,** Wiseman Language Consultants, New York, NY

Special thanks to:

Stephanie Karras and Sharon Sargent for their dedication and hard work in managing a very complex project; and Justine Eun, Maj-Britt Hagsted, and Stacy Merlin for making sure that the many graphic elements illustrated and enhanced the text; and Pronk&Associates for their commitment and skill;

Bruce Myint, who contributed to the early stages of the Workbook and made excellent suggestions for bringing this new edition into a new century;

Katie La Storia, who applied her sharp mind and eyes to the manuscript, always offering excellent advice. With her steadfast energy, enthusiasm, and encouragement, she was a pleasure to work with;

Kathryn O'Dell for her fine, creative contributions to the listening exercises and story pages;

Melinda Beck, who made insightful comments and queries;

Sarah Dentry, who made things flow smoothly, assuring that we always had what we needed when we needed it;

Jayme Adelson-Goldstein, who provided support and who, along with Norma Shapiro, created a rich trove of materials on which to base the exercises in the Workbook;

Luke Frances for always being himself. His honesty, spontaneity, and humor make creativity happen;

Rick Smith, as always, for his unswerving support and for his insightful comments on all aspects of the project. Once again, he proved himself to be equally at home in the world of numbers and the world of words.

The publisher would like to thank the following for their permission to reproduce copyrighted material:

**pp. 51:** © **Copyright 2009,** Her Majesty the Queen in Right of Canada as represented by the Royal Canadian Mounted Police

# To the Teacher

The *Low Beginning*, *High Beginning*, and *Low Intermediate Workbooks* that accompany the *Oxford Picture Dictionary* have been designed to provide meaningful and enjoyable practice of the vocabulary that students are learning. These workbooks supply high-interest contexts and real information for enrichment and self-expression.

Writing a second edition has given us the wonderful opportunity not only to update material, but also to respond to the requests of our first-edition users. As a result, this new edition of the *Low Intermediate Workbook* contains more graphs and charts, more writing and speaking activities, more occasions for critical thinking, opportunities to use the Internet, and a brand-new listening component. It still, of course, has the features that made the first edition so popular.

The Workbooks conveniently correspond page-for-page to the 163 topics of the Picture Dictionary. For example, if you are working on page 50 in the Dictionary, the activities for this topic, Apartments, will be found on page 50 in all three Picture Dictionary Workbooks.

All topics in the *Low Intermediate Workbook* follow the same easy-to-use format. Exercise 1 is always a "look in your dictionary" activity where students are asked to complete a task while looking in their Picture Dictionaries. The tasks include judging statements true or false, correcting false statements, completing charts and forms, categorizing, finding the odd one out, and pronoun reference activities where students replace pronouns with the vocabulary items they refer to.

Following this activity is at least one content-rich contextualized exercise, such as multiple choice, quizzes, tests, describing picture differences, or the completion of forms, reports, letters, articles, or stories. These exercises often feature graphs and charts with real data for students to work with as they practise the new vocabulary. Many topics include a personalization exercise that asks "What about you?" where students can use the new vocabulary to give information about their own lives or to express their opinions.

Many topics also include a Challenge which can be assigned to students for additional work in class or as homework. Challenge activities provide higher-level

speaking and writing practice, and for some topics will require students to interview classmates, conduct surveys, or find information outside of class by looking in the newspaper, for example, or online.

At the end of the 12 units is a section called Another Look, a review which allows students to practise vocabulary from all the topics of a unit in a game or puzzle-like activity, such as picture comparisons, "What's wrong with this picture?" activities, photo essays, word maps, word searches, or crossword puzzles. These activities are at the back of the *Low Intermediate Workbook* on pages 242–253.

A variety of listening activities are recorded on CDs which come with the Workbook. The CDs give students the opportunity to hear the language of each topic in natural, real-life contexts. The listening exercises are in the back of the Workbook beginning on page 261. In some cases, the target language is in the listening itself and students need to recognize it. In other cases, the target language is in the exercise text and students need to interpret the listening to choose the correct answer.

Throughout the Workbook, vocabulary is carefully controlled and recycled. Students should, however, be encouraged to use their Picture Dictionaries to look up words they do not recall, or, if they are doing topics out of sequence, may not yet have learned.

The *Oxford Picture Dictionary Workbooks* can be used in the classroom or at home for self-study.

We hope you and your students enjoy using this Workbook as much as we have enjoyed writing it.

*Marjorie Fuchs    Margo Bonner*

Marjorie Fuchs and Margaret Bonner

# To the Student

The *Oxford Picture Dictionary* has over 4,000 words. This Workbook will help you use them in your everyday life.

It's easy to use! The Workbook pages match the pages in your Picture Dictionary. For example, to practise the words on page 23 in your Picture Dictionary, turn to page 23 in your Workbook.

This book has exercises you will enjoy. Some exercises show real information. A chart showing men's and women's favourite fast foods is on page 79 and a bar graph comparing how long different animals live is on page 216. Other exercises, which ask "What about you?" give you a chance to use your own information. You will find stories, puzzles, and conversations, too.

At the end of many topics there is a Challenge: a chance to use your new vocabulary more independently. There are also listening exercises in which you will hear conversations, news and weather reports, and interviews. And finally, every unit has a puzzle activity or picture comparison called Another Look. This can be found at the back of the book.

Learning new words is both challenging and fun. We had a lot of fun writing this Workbook. We hope you enjoy using it!

*Marjorie Fuchs Margo Bonner*

Marjorie Fuchs and Margaret Bonner

# Table of Contents

## 1. Everyday Language

## 2. People

## 3. Housing

## 4. Food

## 5. Clothing

## 6. Health

# Contents

## 7. Community

## 8. Transportation

## 9. Work

## 10. Areas of Study

## 11. Plants and Animals

## 12. Recreation

1. **Look in your dictionary. How many people are doing the following things? Write the number.**

   _4_ **a.** saying "Hello"

   ___ **b.** hugging

   ___ **c.** smiling

   ___ **d.** waving

   ___ **e.** asking "How are you?"

   ___ **f.** introducing themselves

   ___ **g.** introducing a friend

   ___ **h.** kissing

   ___ **i.** bowing

   ___ **j.** shaking hands

   ___ **k.** saying "Goodbye"

   ___ **l.** greeting people

2. **Look at the pictures.** *True* **or** *False*?

   **a. Picture 1:** Eric says "Hello" to Ana.   _false_

   **b. Picture 1:** Soo Jin and Ana smile.   _____

   **c. Picture 1:** Soo Jin and Ana kiss.   _____

   **d. Picture 2:** Eric introduces himself.   _____

   **e. Picture 2:** Eric smiles.   _____

   **f. Picture 3:** Ana and Eric bow.   _____

   **g. Picture 4:** Eric says "Goodbye."   _____

   **h. Picture 4:** Ana waves goodbye.   _____

3. **Match. Then write what they are doing. You can use your dictionary for help.**

| | | |
|---|---|---|
| _4_ a. Hi, I'm Mario. | 1. Fine, thanks. | _____ |
| ____ b. Bye. | 2. Goodbye. | _____ |
| ____ c. How are you? | 3. Hi. | _____ |
| ____ d. Carlo, this is Beata. | 4. Hi, I'm Olga. | _introducing themselves_ |
| ____ e. Hello. | 5. Nice to meet you. | _____ |

4. **Circle the words to complete the sentences.**

# DIFFERENT GREETINGS
People from different countries (greet)/ meet in different ways.
a.

In some countries, people <u>bow / kiss</u>.
b.

In some countries people

<u>wave / shake</u> hands.
c.

In other countries people <u>hug / wave</u>,
d.
and sometimes good friends <u>hug / kiss</u>.
e.

Sometimes people just

<u>smile / wave</u> and say,
f.
"Goodbye" / "Hello."
g.

Hello.

b.

c.

d.

e.

f.

5. **What about you? How do you greet people? Check (✓) the columns.**

| | Bow | Shake Hands | Kiss | Hug | Say, "Hello." |
|---|---|---|---|---|---|
| a good friend (woman) | | | | | |
| a family member (man) | | | | | |
| a classmate (man) | | | | | |

**Challenge** Look at Exercise 2. Write the story. Begin: *Eric and Soo Jin are in school. Soo Jin sees Ana . . .*

3

1. **Look in your dictionary. Match the information with its number on the School Registration Form. Write the number.**

   a. January 15, 1980   <u>13</u>

   b. John Zakarovsky   ___

   c. (403) 429-0665   ___

   d. Zakarovsky   ___

   e. 210 Parker Road   ___

   f. T4R 0K8   ___

2. **Circle four more mistakes on Ann Brown's registration form.**

   **CALGARY ADULT CENTRE**     **REGISTRATION FORM**

   1. Name (please print): ___(Ann)___    ___(Brown)___    M.
      last name     first name     middle initial

   2. Sex: ☐ male ☑ female    3. social insurance number: 077 - 228 - 765

   4. Address (please print): ___92 Adams Street___    3
      street     apt. #

   ___Calgary___    AB ___
   city     province     postal code

   5. Phone number: (403) 555-3253    6. Cellular phone: 555-6434
      (area code)     (area code)

   7. Date of birth: March 1, 1981    8. Place of birth: ___ Germany
      city     country

   9. Signature: Ann M. Brown

3. **What about you? Fill out the form with your own information.**

   **CALGARY ADULT CENTRE**     **REGISTRATION FORM**

   1. Name (please print): ___
      last name     first name     middle initial

   2. Sex: ☐ male ☐ female    3. social insurance number: ___ ___ ___

   4. Address (please print): ___
      street     apt. #

   ___
   city     province     postal code

   5. Phone number: ___    6. Cellular phone: ___
      (area code)     (area code)

   7. Date of birth: ___    8. Place of birth: ___
      city     country

   9. Signature: ___

**Challenge** Describe the mistakes in Exercise 2. **Example:** *In number 1, she wrote her first name first.*

   See page 263 for listening practice.

1. **Look in your dictionary. Complete the notes with the job titles.**

**Sunnydale School NEWSLETTER**

September / October 2010

**Sunnydale STAFF NOTES**

a. Welcome, all. It's going to be a great year! *Leyla Kashani,* _____Principal_____

b. Seniors—Let's talk about college soon. *Rita Cheng,* _____

c. If you're late, come to the office to sign in. *Miki Kato,* _____

d. Our class will visit historic places near school. *Doug Tran,* _____

e. Meet me at the track for running practice. *Sam Powell,* _____

2. **Look at the list of events. Write the names of the places. Use the words in the box.**

| computer lab | ~~library~~ | gym | main office | cafeteria | auditorium |

| DATE | TIME | EVENT | PLACE |
|---|---|---|---|
| a. Sept. 24 | 2:00 | Reading Club | library |
| b. Oct. 1 | 12:00–1:00 | Pizza Lunch | |
| c. Oct. 15 | 7:00 p.m. | Concert: Sunnydale Chorus | |
| d. Oct. 23 | 2:30 | Learn Internet Safety | |
| e. Oct. 25 | all day | Registration for Senior Class Trip | |
| f. Oct. 30 | 4:30 | Girls' Basketball Practice | |

3. **Make words with the scrambled letters.**

**SCHOOL SCRAMBLE**

a. rcakt    t   r   a   (c)   k

b. lacsmoors  ___ ___ ___ ___ ___ ___ ___ ___ ___

c. hwsamoros  ___ ___ ___ ___ ___ ___ ___ ___ ___

d. lalhyaw  ___ ___ ___ ___ ___ ___ ___

Make a new word with the circled letters: ___ ___ ___ ___ ___ ___

**Challenge** Draw a map of your school. Label the places.

1.  **Look in your dictionary. *True* or *False*? Correct the underlined words in the false sentences.**

    a.  Picture A:  ~~The teacher~~ is raising his hand.    *A student*    ___false___

    b.  Picture B:  The teacher is listening to the student.    _____

    c.  Picture C:  The student is using headphones.    _____

    d.  Picture G:  The student is opening his dictionary.    _____

    e.  Picture I:  The student is picking up a CD.    _____

    f.  Picture J:  The student is picking up a pencil.    _____

2.  **Circle the words to complete the instructions.**

    ### Test Instructions

    Tomorrow is our first test. Please bring a pen / (pencil) with an eraser.
    **a.**

    When you come into the classroom, please sit down / stand up at your
    **b.**

    desks / LCD projectors. Close / Open your test books, pick up / put down
    **c.**                    **d.**                          **e.**

    your pencils, and begin the test. If you have a question for me,

    listen to a CD / raise your hand and ask. Please do not talk to other
    **f.**

    students / teachers during the test. When you are finished,
    **g.**

    pick up / put down your pencils, and bring your tests to me. Good luck!
    **h.**

3.  **Cross out the word that doesn't belong.**

    | | | | |
    |---|---|---|---|
    | a.  chalk | ~~headphones~~ | pen | pencil |
    | b.  bookcase | chair | clock | desk |
    | c.  dry-erase marker | 3-ring binder | workbook | spiral notebook |
    | d.  dictionary | picture dictionary | notebook paper | textbook |
    | e.  chalkboard | marker | screen | whiteboard |

6

**4.** **Complete the classroom inventory.**

### Classroom Inventory — Room 304

| | NUMBER | ITEMS | | NUMBER | ITEMS |
|---|---|---|---|---|---|
| a. | 2 | bookcases | h. | | computers |
| b. | 0 | bulletin boards | i. | 19 | |
| c. | | LCD projector | j. | | markers |
| d. | 20 | | k. | | overhead projectors |
| e. | 1 | | l. | 3 | |
| f. | | chalkboard erasers | m. | | screens |
| g. | | clocks | | | |

**5.** **What about you? Write about items that are in your classroom. Use your own paper.**

Example: *There are four bookcases. There aren't any bulletin boards.*

**Challenge** Describe the ideal classroom. What does it have? How many of each item?

**See page 264 for listening practice.**

**1. Look in your dictionary. What are the students using to do the following things? Check (✓) the correct box or boxes.**

|  | Textbook | Dictionary | Notebook |
|---|:---:|:---:|:---:|
| a. check pronunciation | ☐ | ✓ | ☐ |
| b. copy a word | ☐ | ☐ | ☐ |
| c. draw a picture | ☐ | ☐ | ☐ |
| d. look up a word | ☐ | ☐ | ☐ |
| e. share a book | ☐ | ☐ | ☐ |

**2. Fill in the blanks to complete the instructions for the test. Then take the test.**

# Review Test

1. ___Circle___ the words to complete the questions.

   a. (What)/ Who is your name?          b. When / Where do you live?

2. _____ the word that does not belong.

   a. coach          principal          ~~marker~~          teacher

   b. pen          chalk          computer          pencil

3. _____ the words.

   __3__ a. Check                    1. a sentence.

   ____ b. Help                      2. a classmate.

   ____ c. Dictate                   3. the pronunciation.

4. _____ the blanks.

   Put ___away___ your books and _____ a piece of paper.
         a.                                b.

5. _____ the words.

   a. n a t r s t a l e ___translate___          b. s c u d s i s _____

6. _____ the pictures.

   a. ___pencil___                    b. _____

**3. Circle the words to complete the article.**

## There are many different ways to learn. Here are just a few.

| | |
|---|---|
| * "Word-smart" | students like to dictate / (read) books and copy / cross out information <br>         a.                b. <br> into their notebooks. |
| * "Picture-smart" | students like to check / draw pictures. They also find it helpful to <br>             c. <br> ask / copy new words. <br>   d. |
| * "People-smart" | students love to ask / work with a partner or in a group. They like to <br>          e. <br> brainstorm / translate solutions. They often help / share their classmates. <br>      f.                  g. |
| * "Feelings-smart" | students like to discuss / translate problems and put away / share their <br>           h.               i. <br> feelings with their classmates. |

### In which ways are you smart? Find your style, and make learning fun!

**4. What about you? What helps you learn? For each activity, check (✓) the column that describes your learning style.**

| Activity | Helps me a lot | Helps me some | Helps me a little | Doesn't help me |
|---|---|---|---|---|
| Looking up words | | | | |
| Copying words | | | | |
| Translating words | | | | |
| Helping classmates | | | | |
| Asking questions | | | | |
| Reading definitions | | | | |
| Discussing problems | | | | |
| Dictating sentences | | | | |
| Working in groups | | | | |
| Drawing pictures | | | | |
| Other: _____ | | | | |

**Challenge** Interview someone about his or her learning style. Use the ideas from the questionnaire. Write a paragraph about what you learn.

## Succeeding in School

1. **Look in your dictionary. *True* or *False*? Correct the underlined words in the false sentences.**

   a. **Picture D:** The student is studying ~~in school~~. *at home*          ____false____

   b. **Picture E and Number 4:** The student's test grade (78%) is <u>B</u>.          _____

   c. **Picture G and Number 4:** The student's test grade (96%) is <u>B</u>.          _____

   d. **Picture J:** The student is working <u>in a group</u>.          _____

2. **Match.**

   _3_ **a.** set a goal          **1.** "Oh. That's not right. The answer is 4c."

   ___ **b.** hand in a test          **2.** "Last time I got a C. This time I got a B!"

   ___ **c.** make progress          **3.** "I want to read the newspaper in English."

   ___ **d.** correct a mistake          **4.** "Here you are, Mr. Smith."

3. **Complete the paragraph. Use the words in the box.**

   | asked | filled in | checked | corrected | got | handed in |
   |---|---|---|---|---|---|
   | participated | ~~passed~~ | set | studied | took | |

   Antonello is a student. He ____passed____ his first test, but his
   a.

   grade was only a D. Antonello _____ a goal: He wanted
   b.

   to get better grades. Before his next test, he _____
   c.

   at home for several days, and he _____ for help in
   d.

   class when he didn't understand something. He also

   _____ better notes and _____ more
   e.                              f.

   in class discussions. During the test, Antonello carefully _____ the answers with his
   g.

   pencil. Then, before he _____ his answer sheet to the teacher,
   h.

   he _____ his answers and _____ one or two mistakes. Yesterday
   i.                              j.

   Antonello got his test back. He _____ a good grade—a B! Antonello was happy.
   k.

   **Challenge** Make a list of ways to succeed in school. Compare your list with a classmate's list.

10

1. **Look in your dictionary. Answer the questions.**

   a. What time do the students enter the classroom?  <u>6:55</u>

   b. Who turns on the light?  _____

   c. How many students are taking a break?  _____

   d. Which room number does the student deliver the books to?  _____

   e. What time do the students leave class?  _____

2. **Complete the student's composition. Use the correct form of the words in the box.**

| buy | carry | drink | have | go back |
|-----|-------|-------|------|---------|
| leave | ~~run~~ | take | turn off | walk |

# My Day at School

I go to school every Tuesday and Thursday after work. Sometimes I

_____<u>run</u>_____ to class. I don't want to be late! When I have more time,
    **a.**

I _____. I like it better that way because I always _____
  **b.**                                        **c.**

a lot of things—my textbook, a dictionary, and a 3-ring binder. Class

meets for two hours, and we always _____ a fifteen-minute
                                          **d.**

break. I usually _____ a snack in the cafeteria. I also
                 **e.**

_____ a cup of coffee while I _____ a conversation with
  **f.**                      **g.**

some of my classmates. After the break, we _____ to class. At
                                   **h.**

8:00 p.m., the teacher _____ the lights and we all _____
               **i.**                      **j.**

the classroom and go home.

**Challenge** Write about a day at your school.

**1. Look in your dictionary. Match.**

_4_ **a.** start a conversation

____ **b.** explain something

____ **c.** disagree

____ **d** decline an invitation

____ **e.** check your understanding

**1.** "Sorry. I'm busy Friday night."

**2.** "You're wrong! It's not bad. It's good!"

**3.** "Then, sign your name here."

**4.** "Tell me about your class."

**5.** "Now?"

**2. Read part of a story. Match each numbered sentence with its description below.**

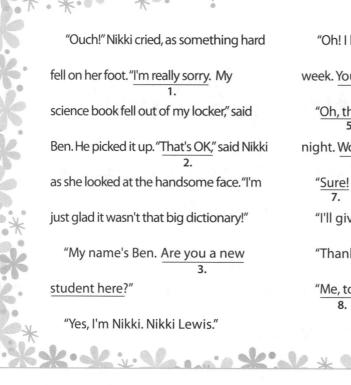

"Ouch!" Nikki cried, as something hard fell on her foot. "I'm really sorry. My
<u>1.</u>
science book fell out of my locker," said Ben. He picked it up. "That's OK," said Nikki
<u>2.</u>
as she looked at the handsome face. "I'm just glad it wasn't that big dictionary!"

"My name's Ben. Are you a new
<u>3.</u>
student here?"

"Yes, I'm Nikki. Nikki Lewis."

"Oh! I heard your piano concert last week. You were great!"
<u>4.</u>
"Oh, thanks! I'm playing again Friday
<u>5.</u>
night. Would you like to come?"
<u>6.</u>
"Sure! Where is it?" Ben asked.
<u>7.</u>
"I'll give you the address," said Nikki.

"Thanks. I'm glad we met, Nikki."

"Me, too. See you soon, Ben!"
<u>8.</u>

**a.** ____ Ben started a conversation.

**b.** ____ Ben accepted an invitation.

**c.** _1_ Ben apologized.

**d.** ____ Nikki agreed with Ben.

**e.** ____ Nikki invited Ben.

**f.** ____ Nikki accepted an apology.

**g.** ____ Ben complimented Nikki.

**h.** ____ Nikki thanked Ben.

**Challenge** Choose an item in your dictionary (for example, *make small talk*). Make a list of ways to do this. Compare your list with a classmate's. **Example:** *What do you think of this weather?*

1. **Look in your dictionary. Label the weather symbols.**

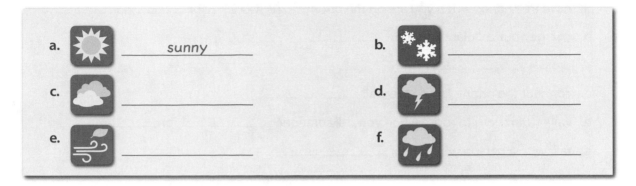

a. _____sunny_____

b. _____

c. _____

d. _____

e. _____

f. _____

2. **Look at the weather map. Write reports for six cities. Use your own paper.**

**Example:** *It's warm and rainy in Vancouver, with temperatures in the 20s.*

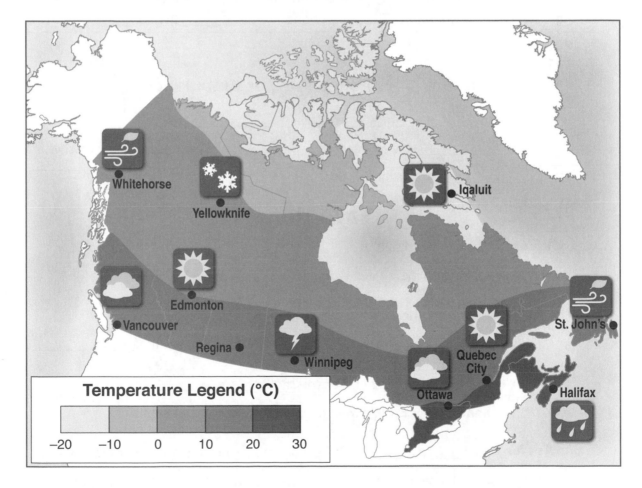

3. **What about you? Write today's weather report for your city. Use Exercise 2 as an example.**

**Challenge** Look at page 254 in this book. Follow the instructions.

**1. Look in your dictionary. What do you need to do the following things?**

   **a.** have free hands when you are on the phone \_\_\_\_*headset*\_\_\_\_ or _____

   **b.** charge your cellular phone _____

   **c.** press * _____

   **d.** connect the phone line to the wall _____

   **e.** walk from room to room when you call someone _____ or _____

   **f.** talk with a person who is deaf _____

**2. Complete this information from a phone book. Use the words and numbers in the box.**

| country | dial | directory assistance | ~~emergency~~ | state |
|---|---|---|---|---|
| give | hang up | international | local | stay |
| long distance | operator | pay phone | 911 | 0 |

## For Fire, Police, or Ambulance

To make an \_\_\_\_*emergency*\_\_\_\_ call, dial: _____ .
            a.                        b.

_____ the emergency, _____ your name, and, if possible,
    c.                           d.

_____ on the line. Don't _____!
    e.                           f.

## Save Money!

**Look it up!** You can avoid calls to _____ by using the phone book or
                        g.

looking online.

**Dial direct and save.** Calling another city or province? It costs less when you make a

_____ call yourself. If possible, try not to use the _____ .
  h.                                i.

**Ask for credit.** If you call a wrong number, you should _____ "0"
                        j.

immediately. Explain what happened so you can get credit.

**Ask for a refund.** If a _____ takes your money but you don't speak to anyone,
        k.

report it by dialing _____ (operator) from another phone.
            l.

We'll see that the phone gets repaired and mail you a refund. To make an

_____ call, you will need: the _____ code, the
  m.                            n.

area code, and the _____ number.
            o.

**3. Look at Jenny Lee's phone bill. Answer the questions.**

**rtr**

Your Phone Company Statement
October 8-November 8, 2010

Customer ID 250-555-6090

Jenny Lee
1212 Marble Lane
Victoria, BC V8N 1A1

LOCAL CALLS

| DATE | NUMBER CALLED | TIME | RATE |
|---|---|---|---|
| OCT 12 | 250-555-2346 | 2:15 p.m. | day |
| OCT 17 | 250-555-7890 | 7:30 p.m. | night |
| NOV 1 | 250-555-6176 | 7:00 a.m. | day |
| NOV 8 | 250-555-7890 | 6:30 p.m. | night |

**rtr**

Customer ID 250-555-6090
Jenny Lee

LONG DISTANCE CALLS

| DATE | NUMBER CALLED | WHERE | TIME | RATE |
|---|---|---|---|---|
| OCT 10 | 902-555-1234 | Halifax, NS | 3:00 p.m. | day |
| OCT 31 | 306-555-6874 | Regina, SK | 9:45 p.m. | eve |

INTERNATIONAL CALLS

| OCT 30 | 56-2-555-1394 | Chile | | |
|---|---|---|---|---|
| OCT 30 | 81-3-555-2086 | Japan | | |

a. What is Jenny's area code?          *250*

b. How many local calls did she make in November?          _____

c. How many long distance calls did she make within Canada?          _____

d. What is the area code for Halifax, NS?          _____

e. How many international calls did Jenny make?          _____

f. What is the country code for Japan?          _____

**4. What about you? How often did you use the telephone last week? Answer the questions. How many times did you do the following things?**

a. make or receive an international call   ____

b. call from a pay phone   ____

c. make an Internet phone call   ____

d. use a calling card   ____

e. leave a voice message   ____

f. use an automated phone system   ____

g. have a weak cellular phone signal   ____

h. receive a text message   ____

**Challenge** Look at page 254 in this book. Follow the instructions.

**1. Look at the Table of Contents in the beginning of your dictionary. Write the numbers.**

a. On what page does the Table of Contents begin?  <u>v</u>

b. On what page does it end?  <u>    </u>

c. How many pages are in the Table of Contents?  <u>    </u>

d. The first unit of your dictionary is called Everyday Language. What is the name of the eleventh unit?  <u>    </u>

e. How many pages are in the eighth unit?  <u>    </u>

**2. Look at the math test. Circle all the mistakes. Then give the test a percentage grade (each question = five points).**

| | |
|---|---|
| **Baker High School** | Grade: _____ % <br> Student's Name: <u>Ryan Jones</u> |

**1. What's next?**

a. eleven, twelve, thirteen,  <u>fourteen</u>

b. one, three, five,  <u>seven</u>

c. two, four, six,  <u>(ten)</u>

d. ten, twenty, thirty,  <u>forty</u>

e. ten, one hundred, one thousand,  <u>ten thousand</u>

**2. Write the numbers.**

a. XX  <u>twenty</u>

b. IX  <u>nine</u>

c. LI  <u>fifty-one</u>

d. IV  <u>six</u>

e. C  <u>one hundred</u>

**3. Match the numbers with the words.**

<u>1</u>  a. 12          1. ordinal number

<u>3</u>  b. DL          2. cardinal number

<u>2</u>  c. 2nd         3. Roman numeral

**4. Write the numbers.**

a. zero  <u>0</u>

b. one hundred  <u>100</u>

c. one million  <u>1,000,000,000</u>

d. ten thousand  <u>10,000</u>

e. one hundred thousand  <u>100,000</u>

f. one billion  <u>1,000,000</u>

g. one thousand  <u>1,000</u>

**Challenge**  Explain the mistakes on the test in Exercise 2. **Example:** *Question 1c—the next number is eight, not ten.*

See page 266 for listening practice.

1. **Look in your dictionary. Cross out the number or word that doesn't belong. Write the category.**

   a. _____Percentages_____   20%      70%      ~~80%~~      100%

   b. _____   1/3      .5      2/4      1/2

   c. _____   .10      .333      .75      25

   d. _____   inch      height      width      depth

2. **Forty-two percent of the students at Baker High School are female. Which pie chart is correct? Circle the correct letter.**

   a. 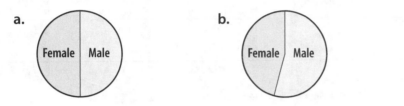   b.   c.

3. **Look at the pie chart. Answer the questions.**

   All of the graduating students at Baker High School took the same math test. The maximum score was 100.

   What percent of students scored between 50 and 74?

   **a.** forty      **b.** fifty      **c.** sixty

   **Math SAT Scores**

   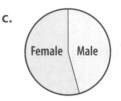

   Below 50 **15%**

   50–74 _____%

   75–100 **25%**

4. **Look at these test scores. Rank the students. (first = the student with the highest score)**

   | Name | Rank |
   |------|------|
   | a. Raz | _____ |
   | b. Eva | _____ |
   | c. Ito | _____ |
   | d. Dan | _____ |
   | e. Mai | _____ |
   | f. Ali | _first_ |
   | g. Luz | _____ |
   | h. Ivy | _____ |

   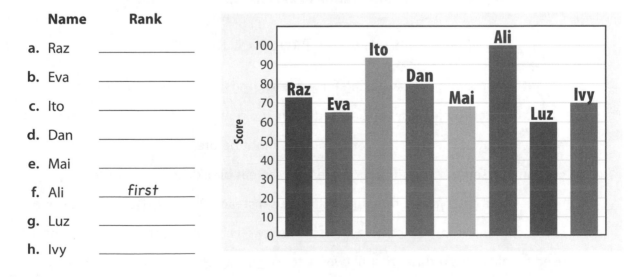

**Challenge** How many students are in your class? What percentage is male? What percentage is female? Draw a pie chart like the ones in Exercise 2.

1. **Look at pages 38 and 39 in your dictionary. Write the time of each activity in numbers and words. Use your own paper.**

   **a.** get dressed          **b.** eat breakfast          **c.** clean the house          **d.** go to bed

   **Example:** *get dressed: 6:30, six-thirty*

2. **Look at Ed's time management worksheet. The clocks show the time that he begins each activity. Complete his worksheet.**

**CLOCKER** Inc.          TIME MANAGEMENT WORKSHEET          *Ed Tresante*

|  | ACTIVITY | TIME BEGAN | TIME ENDED | TOTAL TIME |
|---|---|---|---|---|
| **a.** | get dressed | 7:15 a.m. | 8:00 a.m. | 45 minutes |
| **b.** | brush teeth | | 8:01 a.m. | |
| **c.** | drive to work | | 9:00 a.m. | |
| **d.** | have lunch | | 1:15 p.m. | |
| **e.** | attend class | | 9:15 p.m. | |
| **f.** | talk to Ana | | 11:40 p.m. | |

3. **Complete the report. Use the information in Exercise 2.**

**CLOCKER** Inc.          TIME MANAGEMENT PROGRAM REPORT

Before our program, Ed was taking forty-five <u>seconds / (minutes)</u> to get dressed,
                                                                    **a.**

from a quarter <u>to / after</u> seven until eight <u>p.m. / o'clock</u>. Now it takes him fifteen
               **b.**                             **c.**

<u>hours / minutes</u>. (He puts his clothes out the night before.) Because he finishes
   **d.**

getting dressed by seven-<u>thirty / fifteen</u>, Ed can eat breakfast, brush for three
                         **e.**

minutes, and catch an eight <u>hour / o'clock</u> bus instead of driving. He studies during
                            **f.**

his lunch hour, from <u>half past / a quarter after</u> twelve until a quarter <u>to / after</u> one. Ed
                     **g.**                                                **h.**

used to talk to his girlfriend until twenty to <u>eleven / twelve</u>. Now he calls her forty
                                               **i.**

minutes earlier, at <u>twenty to / half past</u> ten, and he gets more sleep.
                    **j.**

4. **Look at the time zone map in your dictionary. Ed is planning several business trips. Complete the online flight information.**

```
○ ○ ○                          PICK YOUR FLIGHT
◁    ▷    ✚    ⊘    ⌂        http://www.flightpicker_reservation_schedule.ca          C
Back Forward Stop Refresh Home
```

| | FLIGHT NUMBER | FLIGHT | DEPARTURE TIME | ARRIVAL TIME | TOTAL TRAVEL TIME |
|---|---|---|---|---|---|
| a. | Select 20 Q | Montreal, QC Victoria, BC | 10:30 a.m. (Eastern) | *1:30 p.m.* (Pacific) | 6 hours |
| b. | Select 453 Q | Edmonton, AB Anchorage, AK | 8:00 p.m. (Mountain) | _____ (Alaska) | 4 hours |
| c. | Select 34 Q | Regina, SK Halifax, NS | 12:00 p.m. (Central) | _____ (Atlantic) | 3 hours 30 minutes |
| d. | Select 733 Q | Ottawa, ON Dallas, TX | 8:00 a.m. (Eastern) | _____ (Central) | 5 hours |

Options

5. **Complete the article. Use the words in the box. (You will use two words more than once.) Use your dictionary for help.**

| Atlantic | daylight saving | earlier | later | Pacific | standard | Alaska | time zones |

# It's A Question of Time

In 1884, people in different countries agreed to have ___*standard*___ time. They divided the
a.

world into 24 _____ . Some large countries have more than one. Canada, for
b.

example, has six. They are Newfoundland, Atlantic, Eastern, Central, Mountain, and _____ .
c.

In the United States, _____ and Hawaii have their own time zones. The time difference
d.

between one zone and the next is one hour (except for Newfoundland time). For example, when it's

noon Eastern time, it's 1:00 p.m. _____ time. (That's one hour _____ .)
e.                                f.

At the same time, it's 11:00 a.m. Central time. (That's one hour _____ .) Many countries
g.

change the clock in order to have more hours of light in the summer. This is called _____
h.

time. In Canada, it begins the second Sunday in March and ends the first Sunday in November. The

country then returns to _____ time.
i.

**Challenge** Look at page 255 in this book. Follow the instructions.

1. **Look at page 21 in your dictionary. Which month begins on the following days?**

   a. a Sunday ___August___

   b. a Tuesday and has 30 days _____

   c. a Thursday and has four 7-day weeks _____

   d. a weekday and ends on a weekend _____, _____, _____,
      and _____

2. **Read Eva's email. *True* or *False*?**

   | MY EMAIL | ⎯ ☐ ✕ |
   |---|---|
   | Subject: | your visit |
   | Date: | 3-19-11 11:51:11 PM EST |
   | From: | EvaL@uol.ca |
   | To: | DaniaX@uol.us |

   Hi Dania!

   It's Saturday night. I just returned to Hamilton yesterday. There were no classes for a week, so I flew to Winnipeg last Saturday to visit my parents. Classes begin again on Monday. It's a busy semester. I have English three times a week (Mondays, Wednesdays, and Fridays). I usually go to the language lab every Thursday, too. Next week, however, there's no language lab—I go to the computer lab instead. In addition to English, I'm studying science. I have science class twice a week, on the days that I don't have English. And I go to the science lab on Tuesdays.

   Last Sunday, daylight saving time began. Do you have that in the US? I like it a lot. The days seem much longer.

   I'm glad it's the weekend. Tomorrow I'm seeing Tom. (I told you about him in my last email.) I've got to go now. On Saturdays I go to the gym to work out. We can go together when you come! I'm really looking forward to your visit. Just two weeks from today!

   Oh, and bring your appetite! On Sunday there's a cake sale at the school cafeteria. See you soon.

   Eva

   a. It's March. ___true___

   b. It's summer. _____

   c. It's the weekend. _____

   d. Eva is in Winnipeg this week. _____

   e. Science class meets three days every week. _____

   f. Eva goes to the gym every day. _____

**3. Complete Eva's calendar. Use the information in Exercise 2.**

## March

| Sunday | Monday | Tuesday | Wednesday | Thursday | Friday | Saturday |
|--------|--------|---------|-----------|----------|--------|----------|
|        |        | 1       | 2         | 3        | 4      | 5        |
| 6      | 7      | 8       | 9         | 10       | 11     | 12       |
| 13     | 14     | 15      | 16        | 17       | 18 return to Hamilton | 19 |
| 20     | 21     | 22      | 23        | 24       | 25     | 26       |
| 27     | 28     | 29      | 30        | 31       |        |          |

**4. What about you? Complete your calendar for this month. Write the month, the year, and the dates. Then write your schedule in the calendar.**

_____

| Sunday | Monday | Tuesday | Wednesday | Thursday | Friday | Saturday |
|--------|--------|---------|-----------|----------|--------|----------|
|        |        |         |           |          |        |          |
|        |        |         |           |          |        |          |
|        |        |         |           |          |        |          |
|        |        |         |           |          |        |          |
|        |        |         |           |          |        |          |

**Challenge** Write a letter or email to a friend. Describe your schedule for this month.

1. **Look in your dictionary. Complete the chart.**

| Statutory Holidays—Canada 2011 | |
|---|---|
| **a.** Christmas | Dec. 25 |
| **b.** *Victoria Day* | May 23    (Monday before May 25) |
| **c.** Thanksgiving | |
| **d.** | Sept. 5    (1st Mon. of the month) |
| **e.** | Dec. 26 |
| **f.** | Nov. 11 |
| **g.** New Year's Day | |
| **h.** | July 1 |
| **i.** | Apr. 22 (Friday before Easter Sunday) |

2. **Read the sentences. Write the events. Use the words in the box.**

| | | | |
|---|---|---|---|
| anniversary | appointment | ~~birthday~~ | religious holiday |
| legal holiday | parent-teacher conference | vacation | wedding |

   **a.** "I'm twenty-one today!"                                    _____birthday_____

   **b.** "Your son is an excellent student, Mrs. Gupta."        _____

   **c.** "Let's light candles and celebrate together!"           _____

   **d.** "The doctor will see you in a minute, Mr. Chen."       _____

   **e.** "The post office is closed today."                        _____

   **f.** "I really needed this! Two weeks and no work!"        _____

   **g.** "We were married ten years ago today!"                _____

   **h.** "Jennifer looks beautiful in her white dress."          _____

3. **What about you? Check (✓) the events and holidays you celebrate.
   How do you celebrate?**

   ☐  birthdays        _____

   ☐  anniversaries    _____

   ☐  New Year's Day   _____

   ☐  Other:           _____

**Challenge** Look at the chart on page 255. Follow the instructions.

See page 267 for listening practice.

1. **Look in your dictionary. Write all the words that end in *-y*. Then write their opposites.**

   a. ___empty___  ___full___          d. _____  _____

   b. _____  _____          e. _____  _____

   c. _____  _____          or _____

2. **Look at the classrooms. Find and describe six more differences. Use your own paper.**

   **Example:** *Classroom A has a little clock, but the clock in Classroom B is big.*

3. **What about you? How does your classroom compare to the classrooms in Exercise 2? Write about the differences. Use your own paper.**

**Challenge** Write six sentences that describe this workbook. Use words from page 23 in your dictionary.

1. **Look at page 156 in your dictionary. What colour is the following vehicle?**

   a. 4-door car ___blue___

   b. SUV _____

   c. limousine _____

   d. sports car _____

   e. hybrid _____

   f. convertible _____

   g. cargo van _____

   h. school bus _____

2. **Complete the article. Use the information in the bar graph.**

   What is the most popular car colour in Canada? At about 20% of sales, _____

   a.

   is the number one choice of Canadians. Why? Many people believe this is because dirt is

   not as visible on light colours. However, _____ , which is the darkest colour,

   b.

   is the second-most popular colour, tied with silver at 17%. In fourth place with 13% is

   _____. This is followed closely by _____ , which can be very bold

   c.                                              d.

   and bright, and _____ , which is usually a softer, duller colour. Less popular

   e.

   colours — at less than 5% each — include gold, _____ , and _____ .

   f.                                g.

   Now that's a colourful list!

**Challenge** What are the three favourite car colours of your classmates? Take a survey. Are they the same as the top three colours in Exercise 2?

1. **Look at page 24 in your dictionary. Complete the sentences. Write the locations.**

    a. The white sweaters are ____under____ the black ones, on the ____right____.

    b. The violet sweaters are _____ the turquoise ones, in the _____.

    c. The light blue sweaters are _____ the green and the brown ones.

    d. The green sweaters are _____ the orange ones, on the _____.

2. **Look at the checklist and the picture of the school supply room. Check (✓) the items that are in the correct place.**

| Supply Room | |
|---|---|
| ☐ alphabet chart | in front of the number chart |
| ✓ chalk | next to the erasers, on the right |
| ☐ clock | on the bookshelf |
| ☐ erasers | between the chalk and the rulers |
| ☐ headphones | on the wall |
| ☐ LCD projector | next to the overhead projector, on the left |
| ☐ map | behind the bookshelves |
| ☐ notebook paper | under the headphones |
| ☐ overhead projector | on the bottom shelf, below the pens |
| ☐ pencils | next to the workbooks, on the left |
| ☐ rulers | in the blue box |
| ☐ workbooks | above the LCD projector |

3. **Look at Exercise 2. Write about the items that are in the wrong place. Use your own paper.**

    **Example:** *The alphabet chart is behind the number chart. It isn't in front of it.*

**Challenge** Write ten sentences about items in your classroom.

1. **Look in your dictionary. On your own paper, write the fewest coins and bills you can use to make the following amounts.**

   **a.** $7.05       **b.** $.64       **c.** $1.37       **d.** $380

   Example: *$7.05: a five-dollar bill, one toonie, and . . . .*

2. **Look at the chart. Complete the sentences.**

   **Average Weekly Spending Money of Canadian Teens**

   | All Teens | Ages 12-13 | Ages 14-15 | Ages 16-17 |

   **a.** The average teen spends ____$16.30____ a week.

   **b.** A 13-year-old spends _____.

   **c.** A 15-year-old spends _____.

   **d.** A 17-year-old spends _____. That's _____ more than a 13-year-old.

3. **Circle the words to complete the sentences.**

   ## How do today's teens feel about money?

    At the end of each day, I put all my bills /(coins) in a glass bottle. It's how I save money, and I never need to get change / pay back when I go to the vending machine!

    I get a weekly allowance from my parents, but sometimes I don't have enough for a new CD or video game. I hate to borrow / lend money from my friends, but...

    My best friend wanted to buy a new sweater, but she didn't have the money. I was happy to borrow / lend it to her. I know she'll borrow / pay back the money as soon as she can.

   **Challenge** Write at least ten combinations of bills and coins that equal $10.10.

See page 268 for listening practice.

1. **Look in your dictionary. *True* or *False*? Correct the <u>underlined</u> words in the false sentences.**

   One shopper . . .

   a. used a National First Bank ~~credit card~~. *debit card*     ___false___

   b. used a $15 <u>gift card</u>.     _____

   c. wrote a <u>traveller's cheque</u> to pay for a lamp. _____

   d. paid $27.06 <u>cash</u>.     _____

2. **Circle the words to complete the shopper's advice column.**

# Ask Sam the Smart Shopper!

**Q**: Recently I bought a lamp at the (regular) / sale price. A week later I saw it at the
a.
same store for 20% less. Is there anything I can do?

**A**: When that happens, some stores will give you the cheaper price if you show your
sales tax / receipt. That's why you should always keep it.
b.

**Q**: I gave my nephew a sweater for his birthday. He wants to buy / return it and use the
c.
money for some CDs. When I cashed / bought the sweater, it was $29.99, but now
d.
it's on sale for only $19.99. How much will they give him?

**A**: Give him the receipt / gift card and SKU number / price tag to bring to the store.
e.                        f.
He should get $29.99.

**Q**: I bought three pairs of jeans. The sales tax / price tag showed $14.99 each, but the
g.
cash register showed only $26.97. The clerk said the jeans just went on sale. How
did the cash register know?

**A**: The new price / total was in the store computer. When the computer "read" the
h.
receipt / bar code (those black lines), the cash register showed the correct tax / total.
i.                                                                        j.
What a nice surprise!

**Challenge** Write a question for the shopper's advice column. Give it to a classmate. Try to answer your classmate's question.

Go to page 242 for Another Look (Unit 1). | See page 269 for listening practice.

1.  **Look in your dictionary. *True* or *False*? Correct the <u>underlined</u> words in the false sentences.**

    a.  There was a ~~shoe~~ *sweater* sale on October 22nd.      <u>   *false*   </u>

    b.  Manda and Anya have <u>the same</u> birthday.      _____

    c.  Mrs. Kumar bought two matching <u>red</u> sweaters.      _____

    d.  She paid <u>$19.99</u> for each sweater before tax.      _____

    e.  She bought the sweaters on <u>October 20th</u>.      _____

    f.  Manda <u>kept</u> her sweater.      _____

    g.  Anya was <u>happy</u> with hers.      _____

    h.  Anya exchanged her green sweater for a <u>white</u> sweater.      _____

2.  **Look at the pictures. Complete the email with the words in the box.**

| | | | | | |
|---|---|---|---|---|---|
| sweaters | twins | ~~matching~~ | return | disappointed | the same |
| matching | happy | shop | different | matching | keep |

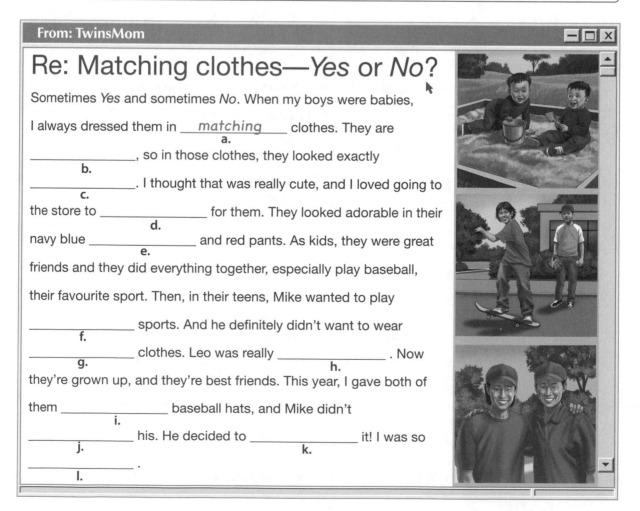

**From: TwinsMom**      _ □ X

# Re: Matching clothes—*Yes* or *No*?

Sometimes *Yes* and sometimes *No*. When my boys were babies,

I always dressed them in ____*matching*____ clothes. They are
                 **a.**

_____, so in those clothes, they looked exactly
     **b.**

_____. I thought that was really cute, and I loved going to
     **c.**

the store to _____ for them. They looked adorable in their
                 **d.**

navy blue _____ and red pants. As kids, they were great
             **e.**

friends and they did everything together, especially play baseball,

their favourite sport. Then, in their teens, Mike wanted to play

_____ sports. And he definitely didn't want to wear
     **f.**

_____ clothes. Leo was really _____ . Now
     **g.**                               **h.**

they're grown up, and they're best friends. This year, I gave both of

them _____ baseball hats, and Mike didn't
            **i.**

_____ his. He decided to _____ it! I was so
     **j.**                            **k.**

_____ .
     **l.**

3. **Look in your dictionary. Match.**

_5_ **a.** Mrs. Kumar likes to shop because

____ **b.** The store had a sale, so

____ **c.** Mrs. Kumar got matching sweaters because

____ **d.** Anya didn't want a matching sweater because

____ **e.** Manda kept her green sweater, but

____ **f.** Navy blue is Anya's favourite colour, so

____ **g.** Now both twins have sweaters they like, and

1. she bought sweaters.

2. she exchanged it for a navy blue one.

3. she didn't want to look the same.

4. they're warm and happy.

5. she loves to buy things for her twins.

6. it was hard to choose two colours.

7. Anya returned hers.

4. **Circle the words to complete the sentences.**

My cousins Bena and Myra are twins. They (have)/ don't have the same birthday,
                                                      **a.**

but they don't look or act the same / different. Bena was a noisy / quiet
                              **b.**                        **c.**

child, and you always knew when she was in the room. She was a good / bad
                                                      **d.**

student because she just wasn't happy at school. Today, Bena is a big / small
                                                        **e.**

woman, more than six feet tall. She's never in a hurry about anything—

especially shopping. She only buys things on sale, and she doesn't pay the

regular price / sale price for anything. She's never happy / disappointed
                       **f.**                                                       **g.**

with her purchases. I love to shop with her.

5. **Now complete the sentences about Myra. Use words from Exercise 4.**

Myra ___was a quiet child___, and you never knew she was in the room. She
                  **a.**

_____ because she liked school. Today, Myra _____,
                **b.**                                              **c.**

less than five feet tall. She's always in a hurry—especially in stores. She buys the first thing

she sees, and I don't think she _____ for anything. She's often
                                                    **d.**

_____ her purchases. When Myra says, "Let's go shopping," I usually say,
                **e.**

"Sorry, I'm busy today."

6. **What about you? Should parents dress twins the same? Why or why not? Discuss your answers with a classmate.**

**Challenge** Write a paragraph. Compare two people you know. Use Exercises 4 and 5 as a model.

## Adults and Children

1. Look in your dictionary. *True* or *False*? Correct the underlined words in the false sentences.

   *seven*
   a. There are ~~six~~ men and women at the round table. _____false_____

   b. A <u>man</u> is holding an infant. _____

   c. The <u>toddler</u> wants to sit in a chair. _____

   d. The <u>six-year-old boy</u> is having a bad time. _____

   e. The <u>senior citizen</u> is talking to a man. _____

   f. The <u>baby</u> is sleeping. _____

2. Put the words in the box in the correct category.

   | | | | | |
   |---|---|---|---|---|
   | ~~baby~~ | boy | girl | infant | man |
   | senior citizen | teen | toddler | woman | |

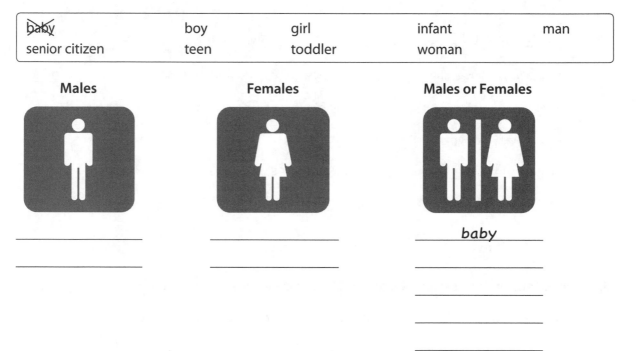

   **Males**

   _____

   _____

   **Females**

   _____

   _____

   **Males or Females**

   _____baby_____

   _____

   _____

   _____

   _____

   _____

3. Look in your dictionary. *Male* or *Female*? Check (✓) the answers.

   |  | Male | Female |  |  | Male | Female |
   |---|---|---|---|---|---|---|
   | a. baby | ✓ | ☐ | | c. senior citizen | ☐ | ☐ |
   | b. teenager | ☐ | ☐ | | d. toddler | ☐ | ☐ |

4. What about you? Look in your dictionary. Imagine you are at the dinner. Who would you like to sit next to? Why?

   **Example:** *I'd like to sit next to the baby. I love babies.*

**5. Look in your dictionary. Guess their ages. Then match.**

_5_ **a.** man     **1.** one year old

____ **b.** senior citizen  **2.** fourteen years old

____ **c.** toddler    **3.** ten years old

____ **d.** teen     **4.** six years old

____ **e.** boy     **5.** forty years old

____ **f.** infant    **6.** sixty-eight years old

____ **g.** baby     **7.** thirty-eight years old

____ **h.** woman    **8.** two months old

____ **i.** girl     **9.** three years old

**6. Look at the pie chart. Circle the words to complete the sentences.**

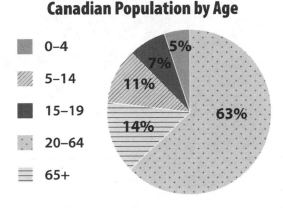

**Canadian Population by Age**

- 0–4
- 5–14
- 15–19
- 20–64
- 65+

5%, 7%, 11%, 14%, 63%

**a.** Seven percent of the Canadian population are <u>senior citizens</u> / <u>(teenagers.)</u>

**b.** <u>Men and women</u> / <u>Boys and girls</u> are 63% of the population.

**c.** Babies, infants, and <u>teens</u> / <u>toddlers</u> are in the 5% group.

**d.** A <u>ten-year-old girl</u> / <u>fifty-year-old woman</u> is in the 63% group.

**e.** There are more senior citizens than <u>boys and girls</u> / <u>teens</u>.

**f.** The biggest percent of the population are <u>babies, infants, and toddlers</u> / <u>men and women</u>.

**7. What about you? Look at the chart in Exercise 6. Which group are you in?**

**Challenge** What's a good gift for a baby girl? A baby boy?
A teenage girl? A teenage boy? Discuss your answers with a partner.

1. **Look in your dictionary. Cross out the word that doesn't belong. Write the category.**

   a.  ___Weight___   heavy   thin   ~~physically challenged~~   average weight

   b.  _____   tattoo   mole   pierced ear   elderly

   c.  _____   elderly   pregnant   middle-aged   young

   d.  _____   visually impaired   hearing impaired   middle-aged   physically challenged

   e.  _____   short   cute   average height   tall

2. **Circle the words to complete the article.**

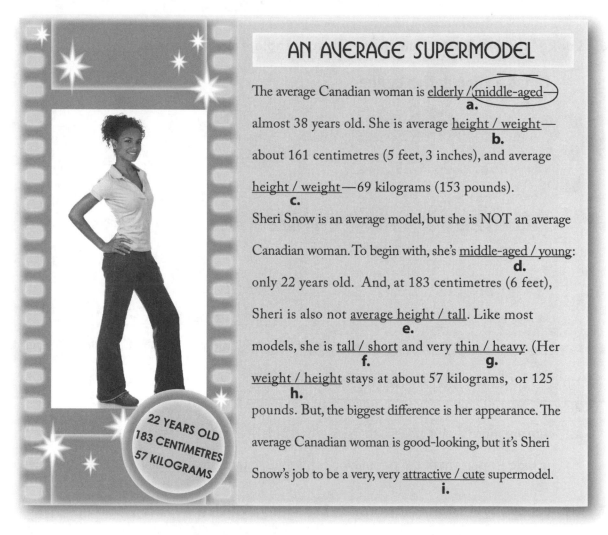

### AN AVERAGE SUPERMODEL

The average Canadian woman is elderly /(middle-aged)—
**a.**
almost 38 years old. She is average height / weight—
**b.**
about 161 centimetres (5 feet, 3 inches), and average

height / weight—69 kilograms (153 pounds).
**c.**
Sheri Snow is an average model, but she is NOT an average

Canadian woman. To begin with, she's middle-aged / young:
**d.**
only 22 years old.  And, at 183 centimetres (6 feet),

Sheri is also not average height / tall. Like most
**e.**
models, she is tall / short and very thin / heavy. (Her
**f.**              **g.**
weight / height stays at about 57 kilograms,  or 125
**h.**
pounds. But, the biggest difference is her appearance. The

average Canadian woman is good-looking, but it's Sheri

Snow's job to be a very, very attractive / cute supermodel.
**i.**

22 YEARS OLD
183 CENTIMETRES
57 KILOGRAMS

3. **What about you? Write a paragraph about a person you know. Describe the person's age, height, weight, and appearance.**

   Example: *My Uncle Tony is middle-aged. He is tall and . . .*

**Challenge** Compare yourself or someone you know to the average Canadian man or woman.

See page 270 for listening practice.

1. **Look in your dictionary. *True* or *False*? Correct the underlined words in the false sentences.**

   a. The bald hair stylist has a ~~brush~~ in his hand.
      *blow dryer*                                    _____*false*_____

   b. The woman in his chair has <u>brown</u> hair.        _____

   c. The hair stylist with red hair is using <u>scissors</u>.   _____

   d. The hair stylist with blond hair is <u>setting</u> hair.   _____

2. **Complete the advice column with the words in the box.**

   | | | | |
   |---|---|---|---|
   | beard | blond | blow dryer | colour |
   | dye | ~~grey~~ | moustache | perm | wavy |

   ### Ask Harry

   **Q:** I'm only twenty, but I've got a lot of
   _____*grey*_____ hair.
       **a.**

   **A:** Why not _____ it? You can
       **b.**
   _____ it black, brown, red, or
       **c.**
   _____ . Ask your hairdresser
       **d.**
   about the shade.

   **Q:** I want _____ hair, but I hate rollers.
       **e.**

   **A:** _____ it. You'll have the style
       **f.**
   you want with no work.

   **Q:** I always use a _____ after I
       **g.**
   wash my hair. Is hot air bad for my hair?

   **A:** Yes. Use a towel some of the time.

   **Q:** My husband says he spends too much time
   shaving.

   **A:** Tell him to grow a _____ and a
       **h.**
   _____ . He'll have to shave
       **i.**
   less!

3. **Find and correct four more mistakes in this ad.**

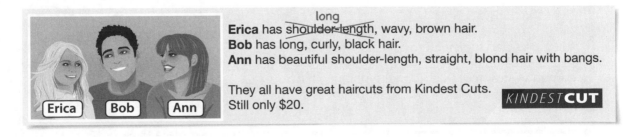

   *long*
   **Erica** has ~~shoulder-length~~, wavy, brown hair.
   **Bob** has long, curly, black hair.
   **Ann** has beautiful shoulder-length, straight, blond hair with bangs.

   They all have great haircuts from Kindest Cuts.
   Still only $20.                      *KINDEST* **CUT**

   Erica   Bob   Ann

   **Challenge** Look in a magazine, newspaper, or your dictionary. Find a hairstyle you like.
   Describe what a stylist did to create the style.

1. **Look at the children on page 34 in your dictionary. Who said the following things?**

   a. "I play softball with my two brothers."  _____Lily_____

   b. "My baby brother just started to walk."  _____

   c. "I don't have any brothers or sisters."  _____

   d. "Aunt Ana made a pretty dress for me."  _____

2. **Complete the family tree. Show each person's relationship to Danica.**

May — a. *mother-in-law*

Charles — b. _____

Danica — Kevin — c. _____

Nate — d. _____

Tia — e. _____

Damon — f. _____

Cala — g. _____

Ali — h. _____

Jena — i. _____

3. **Look at Danica's niece Jena in Exercise 2. Use information from the family tree to complete Jena's blog post.**

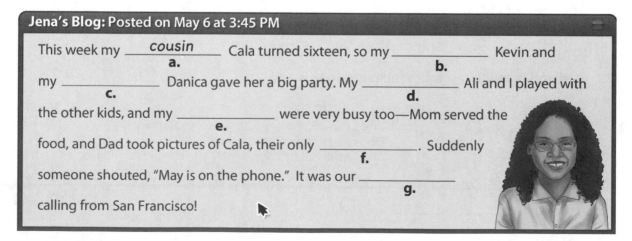

**Jena's Blog:** Posted on May 6 at 3:45 PM

This week my _____cousin_____ Cala turned sixteen, so my _____ Kevin and
   a.                                                       b.

my _____ Danica gave her a big party. My _____ Ali and I played with
   c.                                             d.

the other kids, and my _____ were very busy too—Mom served the
                              e.

food, and Dad took pictures of Cala, their only _____. Suddenly
                                                        f.

someone shouted, "May is on the phone." It was our _____
                                                          g.

calling from San Francisco!

4. **What about you? Draw your family tree. Use your own paper.**

5. **Look at page 35 in your dictionary.** *True* or *False*?

   a. David's father is Lisa's stepfather.          _____true_____

   b. Kim's mother is married to Lisa's father.     _____

   c. Mary is Kim's stepsister.                     _____

   d. Carol is divorced from Bill's stepfather.     _____

6. **Complete the entries from Lisa's diary. Use the words in the box.**

   | ~~divorced~~ | half sister | married | remarried | single father |
   |---|---|---|---|---|
   | stepfather | stepsister | stepmother | wife | |

   3/15/08—Dad moved away this week. He and Mom got ___divorced___. That means
   a.
   they're not _____ anymore. I feel bad, but Mom says I didn't do anything wrong.
   b.

   4/1/08—Dad's new apartment is cool. He says he'll always be my father, but now

   he's a _____, not a married one.
   c.

   10/4/10—Mom says she wants to get _____ someday. That man Rick
   d.
   seems nice. Maybe she'll be his _____ someday.
   e.

   12/10/10—Mom and Rick got married! Rick's my _____ now.
   f.
   I wonder—can I still visit Dad?

   12/12/10—I had a great time at Dad's this weekend. Bill and Kim were there. When

   Dad and Sue get married, I'll be Bill and Kim's _____. Dad will be their
   g.
   stepfather, and Sue will be my _____.
   h.

   11/14/11—We have a new baby! Her name is Mary. I'm her _____. Mom says I
   i.
   can help take care of her.

**Challenge** Look at page 256 in this book. Follow the instructions.

1. **Look in your dictionary. Read the sentences. Write the activities.**

   a. "Mmm. This looks good. Now open your mouth!"  <u>feed the baby</u>

   b. "Next you're going to have a nice bath." _____

   c. "Don't cry, sweetie. You're going to be fine." _____

   d. "Great! That's right. The spoon goes there. Next to the plate." _____

   e. "Good. Now we can drive to Grandma's!" _____

   f. "Once upon a time, there was a little boy who had a big dog." _____

   g. "Goodnight, honey. Sleep well and sweet dreams." _____

   h. "Don't touch it! It's hot!" _____

2. **Circle the words to complete the instructions to the babysitter.**

If Tommy cries, try (comforting) / disciplining him by
                        a.
dressing / rocking him or give him baby lotion / a pacifier. When
        b.                                    c.
you change / bathe his diapers, please use the cloth / disposable
        d.                                              e.
ones. You can put the dirty ones in the baby bag / diaper pail in
                                                f.
his room. We'll wash them tonight. Please don't hold / feed him
                                                    g.
or give him a bottle / rattle after 2:30. I'll bathe / nurse him
                h.                                i.
when I get home at 5:00.

   If Sara has trouble sleeping, you can read / sing a lullaby
                                            j.
to her from her new book of nursery rhymes.

Thanks. Call me at 555-3234 with any problems!

Monica

3. **Cross out the word that doesn't belong. Give a reason.**

a. high chair  ~~baby bag~~  car safety seat

   Babies don't sit in a baby bag.

b. nipple  training pants  diaper

c. formula  baby food  teething ring

d. safety pins  rattle  teddy bear

e. carriage  stroller  night light

4. **Complete these thank-you notes. Use the words in the box.**

| bib | car safety seat | carriage | ~~high chair~~ | nursery rhymes | teddy bear |

a.
> THANK YOU
>
> Dear Elisa,
>
>    Thanks for the ___high chair___ !
> Now Johnny can sit and eat with us
> at the table. The _____
> is great, too. It's cute.
>
> Melissa

b.
> THANK YOU
>
> Dear Aunt Alice,
>
>    Thank you for the
> _____ . Now when we
> drive to visit Grandma, Julie will be
> happy and safe!
>
> Love, Angela and Scott

c.
> THANK YOU
>
> Dear Lili and Quon,
>
>    We all love the _____ !
> We read them to Louisa every day. The
> _____ is great, too.
> Louisa loves playing with him and
> can't sleep without him!
> Love, Jason

d.
> THANK YOU
>
> Dear Bill,
>
>    The _____ is great!
> I put Tommy in it yesterday when
> I went to the market. He slept
> happily and I didn't have to carry
> him. Thanks so much!
>
> Love, Amanda

**Challenge** Look in your dictionary. Imagine someone gave you a baby gift.
Choose an item and write a thank-you note for it.

1. **Look in your dictionary. Who does what in the Lim family? Check (✓) the correct box or boxes.**

| TO DO | Mom | Dad | Tess | Marc |
|---|---|---|---|---|
| a. make lunch | ✓ | ☐ | ☐ | ☐ |
| b. take the children to school | ☐ | ☐ | ☐ | ☐ |
| c. drive to work | ☐ | ☐ | ☐ | ☐ |
| d. go to class | ☐ | ☐ | ☐ | ☐ |
| e. go to the grocery store | ☐ | ☐ | ☐ | ☐ |
| f. pick up the kids | ☐ | ☐ | ☐ | ☐ |
| g. clean the house | ☐ | ☐ | ☐ | ☐ |
| h. exercise | ☐ | ☐ | ☐ | ☐ |
| i. do homework | ☐ | ☐ | ☐ | ☐ |
| j. read the paper | ☐ | ☐ | ☐ | ☐ |
| k. check email | ☐ | ☐ | ☐ | ☐ |

2. **Read this article about the Lim family. <u>Underline</u> six more mistakes.**

## The Fast Track Family

David and Mai Lim want a lot from life, and their daily routine shows it. They both get up early in the morning. At 6:30 David <u>takes a shower</u>. Then Mai makes breakfast while David eats with the kids. At 7:30 David takes the kids to school. Then David goes to work, and Mai drives to school. At 4:30 Mai picks up the children. Then she cleans the house with the kids and cooks dinner. At 5:00 David leaves work and goes home. The family has dinner together. After dinner the children always do homework. At 8:00 Mai reads the paper and David checks email. Then David watches TV. They go to sleep at 10:30. It's a busy schedule, but the Lims enjoy it.

3. **Correct the mistakes in Exercise 2. Write the correct activity.**

a.  At 6:30 David doesn't take a shower. He gets dressed.

b. _____

c. _____

d. _____

e. _____

f. _____

g. _____

**4. Make questions from the scrambled words.**

**a.** time What you up do get     <u>What time do you get up?</u>

**b.** eat breakfast When you do     _____

**c.** you leave When the house do     _____

**d.** home come you do time What     _____

**e.** to bed go do When you     _____

**5. What about you? On the first PDA, write information about your daily routine. Then interview another person. Use questions like the ones in Exercise 4.**

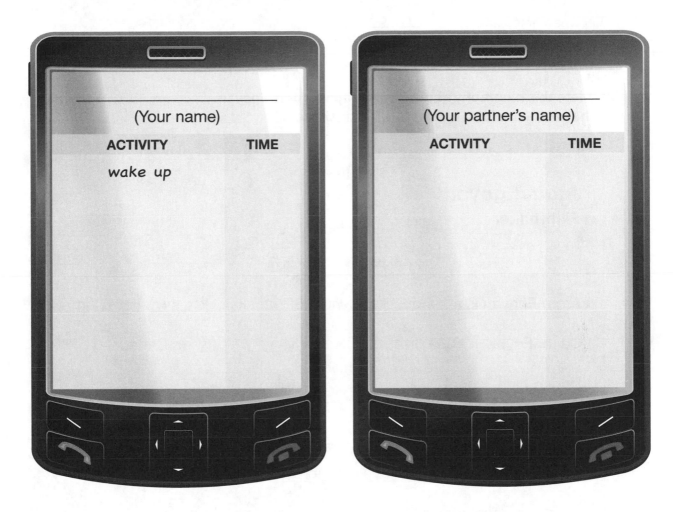

| (Your name) | |
|---|---|
| **ACTIVITY** | **TIME** |
| wake up | |

| (Your partner's name) | |
|---|---|
| **ACTIVITY** | **TIME** |

**Challenge** Compare the routines in Exercise 5. Write six sentences. **Example:** *I get up at 6:00, but Kyung gets up at 7:00. We both leave for class at 8:00.*

**See page 273 for listening practice.**

1. **Look in your dictionary. How old was Martin Perez when he did the following?**

   a. learned to drive     <u>18 years old</u>

   b. graduated     _____

   c. became a citizen     _____

   d. got married     _____

   e. had a baby     _____

   f. bought his first home     _____

   g. became a grandparent     _____

   h. died     _____

2. **Complete this biography about photographer Atom Egoyan. Use the past tense form of the words in the boxes.**

---

### BIOGRAPHY

## Atom Egoyan
**Filmmaker**

| start | immigrate | ~~be born~~ |

Atom Egoyan is a famous independent filmmaker. He <u>was born</u> in
            **a.**

Cairo, Egypt, in 1960. In 1963, his family _____ to Canada.
      **b.**

During high school, he _____ reading and writing plays.
      **c.**

| fall in love | study | meet | marry | graduate | start |

Atom _____ at the University of Toronto, and he _____ with a
   **d.**          **e.**

degree in International Relations in 1982. After university, he _____
      **f.**

producing full-length films and directing television shows. While working

on one of these films, he _____ and became friends with an actress
      **g.**

named Arsinee Khanjian. They _____ and later _____.
      **h.**        **i.**

| buy | have a baby | name | continue | volunteer |

The couple _____ a house and settled in Toronto. They both

**j.**

_____ to work in the film industry and Arsinee _____ her

**k.**                                                                                          **l.**

time to help local artists. In 1993, the couple _____, Arshile. He

**m.**

was _____ after the artist Arshile Gorky, who was the subject of

**n.**

*Ararat*, one of Atom's most famous films.

3. **Read the sentences about Atom Egoyan. *True* or *False*? Put a question mark (?) if the information isn't in the reading in Exercise 2.**

   a. Atom Egoyan was born in Canada.                    _____*false*_____

   b. He went to university in Toronto.                    _____

   c. He became a citizen of Canada.                    _____

   d. Egoyan got married before he immigrated to Canada.    _____

   e. He and his wife had a baby in 1993.                    _____

   f. He has lived in Canada since 1971.                    _____

4. **Check (✓) the documents Atom Egoyan probably has. Use the information in Exercise 2.**

   ✓ high school diploma          ☐ deed          ☐ university degree

   ☐ marriage licence             ☐ passport       ☐ birth certificate

5. **What about you? Write a short autobiography that includes the most important events of your life. Use your own paper.**

**Challenge** Think of a famous person and look up biographical information about him or her in an encyclopedia or online. Write a paragraph about the person's life.

**See page 274 for listening practice.**

**1. Look in your dictionary. Find and write the opposite of these words.**

a. worried    _relieved_

b. hot    _____

c. nervous    _____

d. sick    _____

e. happy    _____

f. full    _____

**2. Complete the sentences. Use the words in the box.**

| disgusted | full | ~~homesick~~ | in pain | relieved |

a.

What's wrong?

I'm really _homesick_.

b. Ow!

What's wrong? Are you _____?

c. Yuck! What IS that!?

You look _____!

d. You're home! I am SO _____!

Sorry. The train was late.

e. More turkey?

No, thanks. I'm _____.

**3. Circle the words to complete the story.**

Minh Ho had so many feelings his first day of school. When he left home, he felt (scared) / excited.
a.

His mother looked nervous / calm, but his little brother just looked sad / sleepy. When he got to
b.                                                        c.

school, he walked into the wrong class. The teacher looked bored / surprised, and Minh Ho was
d.

very embarrassed / thirsty. He felt much better in math class. He was proud / frustrated when he
e.                                                                            f.

did a problem correctly. His teacher looked upset / happy. At lunchtime, he looked at his food
g.

and was confused / relieved. "What is this?" He wasn't angry / hungry at all. As he sat in the
h.                                                        i.

cafeteria, Minh Ho was feeling very full / sad and tired / lonely. Then someone said, "Can I sit here?"
j.                        k.

Suddenly his feelings changed. He felt happy / homesick. Was he in love / in pain?
l.                                    m.

**4. What about you? How did you feel on your first day of school? Write sentences on your own paper.**

┤**Challenge**  Look at the picture on page 256. Follow the instructions.

Go to page 243 for Another Look (Unit 2).  |  See page 275 for listening practice.

1. **Look in your dictionary.** *True* or *False*? **Rewrite the false sentences. Make them true.**

   a. Ben has a <u>small</u> family.               _____*false*_____
      *Ben has a big family.* _____

   b. <u>Every year</u>, his family has a reunion.      _____
      _____

   c. The reunion is at <u>his aunt's</u> house.        _____
      _____

   d. This year he decorated with <u>balloons and a banner</u>.   _____
      _____

   e. His grandfather and his aunt are talking about <u>the baseball game</u>.   _____
      _____

   f. Some <u>adults</u> are misbehaving.          _____
      _____

   g. Ben's relatives are laughing and Ben is having a <u>good</u> time.   _____
      _____

   h. There are <u>two</u> new babies at the reunion this year.   _____
      _____

   i. By the next reunion, Ben's <u>son</u> will have a new brother or sister.   _____
      _____

   j. Ben is <u>sorry</u> the reunion is only once a year.   _____
      _____

2. **Look in your dictionary. Who is saying the following things? Match.**

   _6_ a. "The Mets are terrible this year!"             **1.** Ben's grandmother

   ___ b. "Let's stop talking and watch the game."      **2.** Ben's aunt

   ___ c. "In my opinion, you should have two more children."   **3.** Ben's sister

   ___ d. "The babies are laughing. I guess they're having a good time!"   **4.** Ben

   ___ e. "May, stop misbehaving! Take your hand off the cake."   **5.** Ben's mother-in-law

   ___ f. "Aunt Terry! I'm so glad you came."         **6.** Ben's grandfather

3. **What about you? Imagine you are at the family reunion. What are you doing? Write three sentences.**

   **Example:** *I'm drinking pop.*

   a. _____

   b. _____

   c. _____

   **What aren't you doing? Write three sentences.**

   **Example:** *I'm not eating cake.*

   d. _____

   e. _____

   f. _____

4. **Complete Ben's aunt's email. Use the words in the box.**

   | baby | baseball game | father | glad | nephew |
   |------|---------------|--------|------|--------|
   | good time | big | opinions | relatives | ~~reunion~~ |

   **My Email** ⎯ ☐ ☒

   Every year I go to a family _____*reunion*_____ at my _____'s
                 **a.**                        **b.**

   house. All of my _____ are there. I'm always
                   **c.**

   _____ to see them. We have a _____ family,
         **d.**                      **e.**

   and next year it will be even larger. Ben and his wife are going to have a new

   _____ ! This year,
        **f.**

   my _____ and I watched
          **g.**

   a _____ . We had very different
       **h.**

   _____ about it, but we also
     **i.**

   had a _____ !
         **j.**

**Challenge** Imagine you are one of the people at the Lu Family Reunion. Write about the reunion. Use the email in Exercise 4 as an example.

1. **Look in your dictionary.** *True* or *False*? **Correct the** <u>underlined</u> **words in the false statements.**

         *bedrooms*
   a. This home has two ~~bathrooms~~ and a baby's room.   ___*false*___

   b. The <u>bedroom</u> door is open.      _____

   c. The <u>kitchen</u> has three windows.    _____

   d. Mr. Marino is in the <u>attic</u>.      _____

   e. Mrs. Marino is in the <u>dining area</u>.   _____

   f. One daughter is in the <u>basement</u>.   _____

2. **Look in your dictionary. Label the floor plans.**

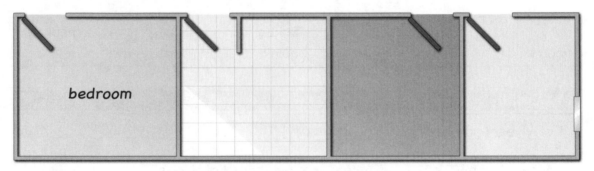

bedroom

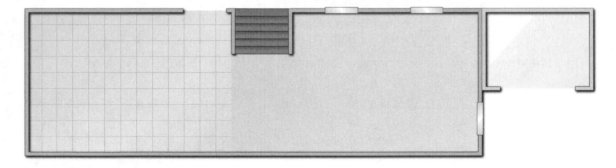

3. **What about you? Draw a floor plan of your home. Label the rooms.**

[ My Home ]

4. **Look in your dictionary. Where are these items?**

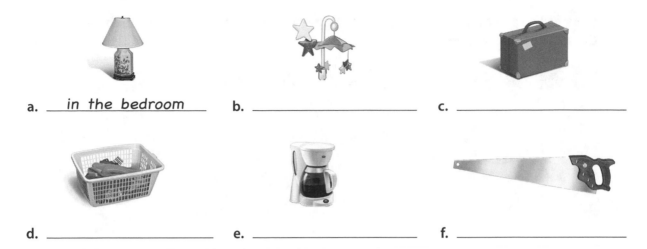

a. __in the bedroom__    b. _____    c. _____

d. _____    e. _____    f. _____

5. **Look in your dictionary. Circle the words to complete the ad.**

# Great for a Family!

Two-bathroom /(bedroom) house with baby's room. One <u>bathroom / bedroom</u>. Large
      a.                                                       b.

<u>attic / kitchen</u> with dining <u>area / window</u>. <u>Basement / Living room</u> with a lot of light
    c.                         d.                      e.

(three <u>doors / windows</u>). <u>Floor / Basement</u> and attic. One-car <u>attic /garage</u>.
          f.               g.                               h.

**Call 555-2468 for more information**

6. **What about you? Describe your "dream" home.**

a. How many bedrooms does it have? _____

b. How many bathrooms? _____

c. Does it have a dining area or a separate
dining room? _____

d. Does it have a garage? _____
If *yes*, how many cars can fit in the garage? _____

e. Does it have a basement? _____
If *yes*, what is in the basement? _____

f. How many windows are there? _____
Which rooms have windows? _____

g. What colour is the living room? _____

**Challenge** Write an ad for your "dream" house. Use the ad in Exercise 5 as an example.

1. Look at the ads on page 48 in your dictionary. Which apartment fits each description? Check (✓) the correct column.

|  | Internet Listing | Classified Ad |
|---|---|---|
| **a.** is in the city |  | ✓ |
| **b.** has one bedroom |  |  |
| **c.** has two bathrooms |  |  |
| **d.** is more expensive |  |  |
| **e.** includes utilities |  |  |

2. Circle the words to complete the article.

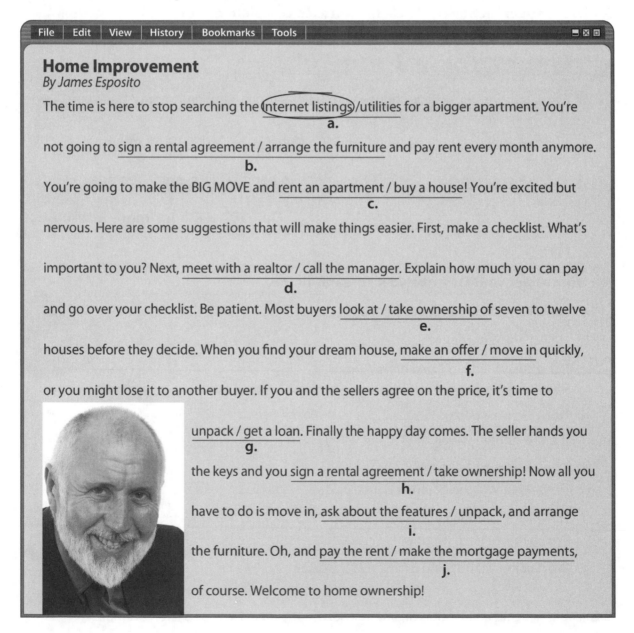

| File | Edit | View | History | Bookmarks | Tools |

## Home Improvement
*By James Esposito*

The time is here to stop searching the (Internet listings)/utilities for a bigger apartment. You're
 **a.**

not going to <u>sign a rental agreement / arrange the furniture</u> and pay rent every month anymore.
 **b.**

You're going to make the BIG MOVE and <u>rent an apartment / buy a house</u>! You're excited but
 **c.**

nervous. Here are some suggestions that will make things easier. First, make a checklist. What's

important to you? Next, <u>meet with a realtor / call the manager</u>. Explain how much you can pay
 **d.**

and go over your checklist. Be patient. Most buyers <u>look at / take ownership</u> of seven to twelve
 **e.**

houses before they decide. When you find your dream house, <u>make an offer / move in</u> quickly,
 **f.**

or you might lose it to another buyer. If you and the sellers agree on the price, it's time to

<u>unpack / get a loan</u>. Finally the happy day comes. The seller hands you
 **g.**

the keys and you <u>sign a rental agreement / take ownership</u>! Now all you
 **h.**

have to do is move in, <u>ask about the features / unpack</u>, and arrange
 **i.**

the furniture. Oh, and <u>pay the rent / make the mortgage payments</u>,
 **j.**

of course. Welcome to home ownership!

## 3. Look in your dictionary. What are they doing?

a. "I think we need some more boxes!" _____packing_____

b. "How about $125,000?" _____

c. "Let's put the table there, in front of the window." _____

d. "The keys to our new house! Thank you." _____

e. "Thank you. Now we have the money for the house!" _____

## 4. Look at the classified ads. Answer the questions.

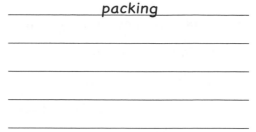

**Smithfield** New 2bdrm 2ba house large front yd near schools and shopping $300,000

**Greenville** 3bdrm 2ba house large sunny kit close to transportation. Move-in condition! $258,000

**Lincoln** Small 2bdrm, 1ba for sale or rent. Just painted! $185,000

a. Which house is the biggest?     _____the house in Greenville_____
   How many bedrooms does it have?   _____

b. What is the price?     _____

c. Which house is the smallest?     _____
   How many bathrooms does it have?   _____

d. Which house is the least expensive?   _____
   What is the price?     _____

e. Which house is best for a family with   _____
   one child? Why?

f. Which house has a large kitchen?     _____

## 5. What about you? Check (✓) all the items that are important to you.

| | | | |
|---|---|---|---|
| **Type** | ☐ Apartment | ☐ House | ☐ Other: _____ |
| **Location** | ☐ City | ☐ Suburbs | ☐ Country |
| **Near** | ☐ School | ☐ Shopping | ☐ Work |
| **Space** | ☐ Number of rooms | ☐ Size of rooms | |
| **Cost** | ☐ Rent | ☐ Mortgage | *CITY* **REALTY** |

**Challenge** Write a paragraph about looking for and finding a new home.

See page 276 for listening practice.

**1. Look in your dictionary. Where can you hear the following things?**

a. "Bye. I'm going up now."  _____the elevator_____

b. "The water looks great! I'll go in after this chapter."  _____

c. "All I ever get are bills and ads."  _____

d. "I watch this program every Monday night."  _____

e. "Just sign here, and the apartment is yours!"  _____

f. "Oh, good. My clothes are all dry."  _____

**2. Circle the words to complete the ad.**

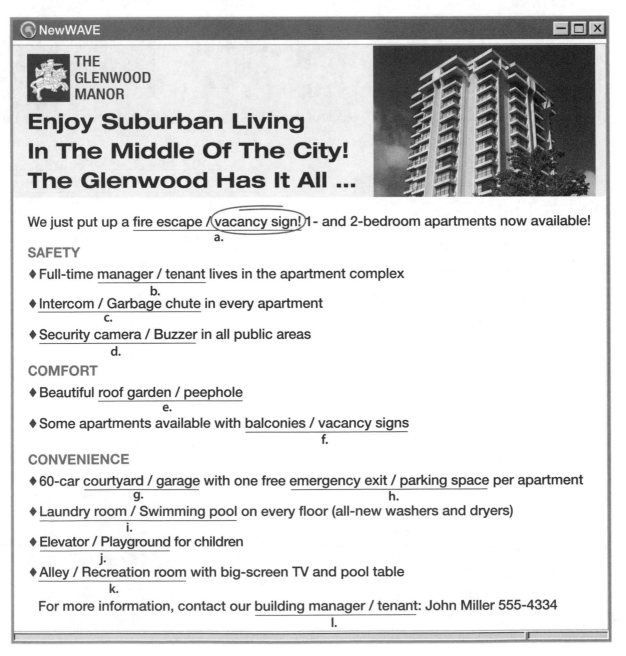

NewWAVE

**THE GLENWOOD MANOR**

**Enjoy Suburban Living In The Middle Of The City! The Glenwood Has It All ...**

We just put up a fire escape / (vacancy sign!) 1- and 2-bedroom apartments now available!
a.

**SAFETY**

◆ Full-time manager / tenant lives in the apartment complex
        b.
◆ Intercom / Garbage chute in every apartment
        c.
◆ Security camera / Buzzer in all public areas
        d.

**COMFORT**

◆ Beautiful roof garden / peephole
        e.
◆ Some apartments available with balconies / vacancy signs
        f.

**CONVENIENCE**

◆ 60-car courtyard / garage with one free emergency exit / parking space per apartment
        g.                              h.
◆ Laundry room / Swimming pool on every floor (all-new washers and dryers)
        i.
◆ Elevator / Playground for children
        j.
◆ Alley / Recreation room with big-screen TV and pool table
        k.
        For more information, contact our building manager / tenant: John Miller 555-4334
        l.

3. **Complete the safety pamphlet. Use the words in the box.**

| | | | | |
|---|---|---|---|---|
| buzzer | dead bolt lock | door chain | elevator | fire escape |
| ~~intercom~~ | smoke detector | peephole | key | stairs |

**Better Safe Than Sorry**

▶ Don't allow strangers into the building. Always use your _____*intercom*_____ to ask
**a.**
"Who's there?" <u>before</u> you use your

_____.
**b.**

▶ Look out your _____ before
**c.**
you open your apartment door. When you're
at home, keep your _____ on.
**d.**

▶ Install a _____. It's the
**e.**
strongest lock.

▶ Give a copy of your _____
**f.**
to the building manager. In case of an
emergency, it will be easier to enter your
apartment.

▶ Keep a _____ on the wall or
**g.**
ceiling between your bedroom and your
apartment door. Check it every month!

▶ In case of fire, do not use the

_____ (The heat can cause it
**h.**
to stop between floors.) Use the

_____ instead.
**i.**

▶ Feel the door of your apartment. If it's hot,
the fire may be out in the hall. Use the

_____ to leave your apartment.
**j.**

*For serious emergencies dial 911. All
other times, call your local police or fire
department.*

4. **What about you? How safe is your home? Check (✓) the things your home has.**

☐ dead bolt lock      ☐ door chain      ☐ emergency exit      ☐ fire escape

☐ intercom      ☐ peephole      ☐ security camera      ☐ security gate

☐ smoke detector      ☐ Other: _____

**Challenge** Describe your ideal apartment building.

See page 277 for listening practice.

Different Places to Live

1. **Look in your dictionary. Where can you hear the following things?**

    a. "My roommate is studying chemistry."    <u>a university residence</u>

    b. "I became homeless after I lost my job."    _____

    c. "We raise horses."    _____

    d. "All four houses look the same."    _____

2. **Complete the letter. Use the words in the box.**

| city | condo | country | ~~farm~~ | mobile home |
|------|-------|---------|----------|-------------|
| nursing home | senior housing | suburbs | townhouse | |

> Dear Fran,
>
>     You asked me to tell you about the places I've lived. I grew up on a potato
>
> ____<u>farm</u>____ . After your grandfather and I got married, we bought a small
>    **a.**
>
> _____ in a very large building. I didn't like living in a big
>    **b.**
>
> _____ like Vancouver. I really prefer living in the _____ ,
>    **c.**                                                   **d.**
>
> where I grew up. I was happy when we bought a _____ in the
>                                                           **e.**
>
> _____ , only fifteen miles from the city. When your grandfather retired,
>    **f.**
>
> we wanted to travel. We bought a _____ and for a while, we moved our
>                                                        **g.**
>
> little home every few years! After your grandfather died, I wanted to be around more
>
> people my age, so I moved to _____ . Then I got sick and needed more
>                                                             **h.**
>
> help, so I moved here to this _____ . When you were younger, you used
>                                                  **i.**
>
> to think all the elderly people here were your grandparents, too! We're all looking
>
> forward to your next visit.
>
> Love,
> Grandma

3. **What about you? Where have you lived? Make a chart like the one below.**

| Name of Place | City, Suburbs, or Country | Type of Home | Year You Moved There | How Long You Lived There |
|---------------|---------------------------|--------------|----------------------|--------------------------|
| Fredericton | city | apartment | 2004 | 6 years |

**Challenge** Write a paragraph about the places you've lived. Use information from Exercise 3.

**1. Look in your dictionary. What can you use to do the following things?**

a. eat outside      <u>patio furniture</u>

b. cook outside      _____

c. take a nap      _____

d. water the lawn      _____ and _____

e. grow your own tomatoes      _____

**2. Look at the houses. Find and describe 8 more differences. Use your own paper.**

**Example:** *House A's mailbox is big, but House B's is small.*

**3. What about you? Plan your ideal yard. Check (✓) the items you would like.**

☐ a patio      ☐ flower beds      ☐ a hammock      ☐ Other: _____

**Challenge** Draw your ideal yard and write a paragraph describing it.

53

**1. Look in your dictionary. Complete the sentences.**

a. The _____kettle_____ is on the back right burner of the stove next to the pot.

b. The _____ is on the counter, to the right of the sink.

c. The _____ are on the wall, under the cabinet and above the dish rack.

d. The _____ is below the oven.

**2. Look at the chart. *True* or *False*? Correct the underlined words in the false statements.**

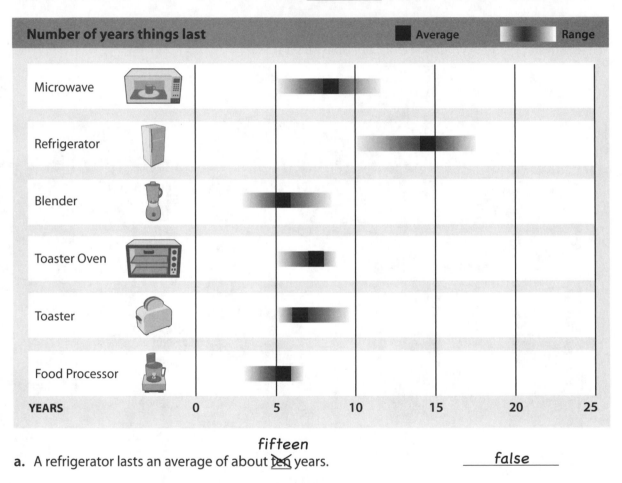

| Number of years things last | ■ Average | ▨ Range |

Microwave
Refrigerator
Blender
Toaster Oven
Toaster
Food Processor

YEARS    0    5    10    15    20    25

                                 *fifteen*
a. A refrigerator lasts an average of about ~~ten~~ years.        ___false___

b. A microwave lasts an average of about <u>nine</u> years.        _____

c. On average, a food processor lasts as long as a <u>blender</u>.        _____

d. The average life of a toaster oven is <u>shorter</u> than the life of a toaster.        _____

e. A toaster lasts from about <u>five to ten</u> years.        _____

**Challenge** Which five items in the kitchen do you think are the most important. Why?

1. **Look in your dictionary. List the items on the dining room table and on the tray. Use your own paper.**

   Example:  *4 placemats*

2. **Complete the conversations. Use the words in the box.**

| fan | hutch | platter | serving bowl | ~~tablecloth~~ | tray | vase |
|-----|-------|---------|--------------|----------------|------|------|

   **a. Alek:** I'm setting the table. Are we going to use placemats?

   **Ella:** No. Put on the white _____*tablecloth*_____ instead.

   **b. Alek:** Are we going to serve each guest a piece of fish?

   **Ella:** No. I'll put the fish on a big _____ in the middle of the table.

   **c. Alek:** Where are the good plates?

   **Ella:** They're in the _____. The _____ for the vegetables is there, too.

   **d. Alek:** Where should I put the coffee mugs?

   **Ella:** I'll carry them out on a _____ after we finish eating.

   **e. Alek:** Is it hot in here?

   **Ella:** Yes. Why don't you turn on the _____?

   **f. Alek:** The flowers are beautiful!

   **Ella:** I'll get a _____ for them.

3. **What about you? Draw a picture of the table from a meal you had recently. Label the items.**

**Challenge** Find a picture of a dining area in a newspaper or magazine. Describe it to a classmate. Your classmate will draw a picture of it.

1.  **Look in your dictionary. *True* or *False*? Correct the underlined words in the false sentences.**

    entertainment centre

    a.  There's a painting on the wall over the ~~mantle~~.    _____false_____

    b.  The DVD player is to the left of the stereo system.    _____

    c.  The magazine holder is next to the fire screen.    _____

    d.  There are throw pillows on the armchair.    _____

    e.  There's a candle holder and candle on the coffee table.    _____

2.  **Look at the pictures. Circle the words to complete the sentences.**

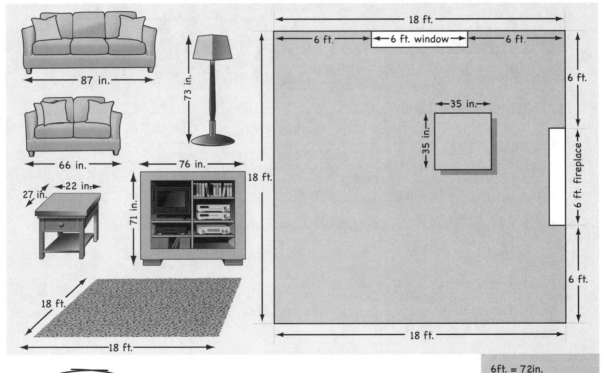

    a.  The (coffee table) / end table is already in the living room.

    b.  The entertainment centre / loveseat can go to the left of the window.

    c.  The loveseat / sofa won't fit to the right of the fireplace.

    d.  The carpet is bigger than / the same size as the living room.

    e.  The floor lamp is shorter / taller than the entertainment centre.

3.  **What about you? Draw a floor plan of your living room. Label the items.**

**Challenge** How would you decorate the living room in Exercise 2? Write sentences. **Example:** *I'd put the sofa in the middle of the living room, across from the window . . . .*

See page 278 for listening practice.

1. **Look in your dictionary. What do the <u>underlined</u> words refer to?**

   a. "<u>It</u>'s in the toothbrush holder."                          <u>toothbrush</u>

   b. "Can I put my dirty jeans in <u>here</u>?"                       _____

   c. "I'm going to hang your bath towel and washcloth <u>here</u>."   _____

   d. "There's hair in <u>it</u>. The water isn't going down."          _____

2. **Complete the article. Use the words in the box.**

   | medicine cabinet | hot water | grab bar | soap dish | sink | shower head |
   |---|---|---|---|---|---|
   | shower curtain | wastebasket | faucets | bath mat | ~~bathtub~~ | rubber mat | toilet |

   # Keep bath time safe and happy by following these safety rules:

   1  Never leave a young child alone in the _____<u>bathtub</u>_____.
      **a.**
      Even small amounts of water can be dangerous.

   2  Avoid burns from _____. Turn the temperature on your water heater down to
                        **b.**
      32°C. Fix all dripping _____ and don't forget the _____
                             **c.**                                  **d.**
      —hot drops from above can hurt, too.

   3  Prevent falls. Keep a _____ in the bathtub and a non-slip _____
                            **e.**                                           **f.**
      on the floor. And don't forget to put that slippery soap back in the _____ after
                                                                           **g.**
      you wash. Never hold onto the _____ when you get out of the bathtub. Install a
                                    **h.**
      _____ on the bathtub wall. Provide a stool so that children can reach the
      **i.**
      _____ safely to wash their hands and brush their teeth.
      **j.**

   4  Keep medicines locked in the _____. Never throw old medicines away in a
                                   **k.**
      _____ where children can get them. Do not flush them down the _____
      **l.**                                                                    **m.**
      either.  Ask your pharmacist what to do with your unused medicine.

3. **What about you? What do you do to prevent injuries and accidents in the bathroom? Write sentences on your own paper.**

   **Example:** *We put a rubber mat in the bathtub.*

   **Challenge** Draw a picture of your bathroom. Label the items.

**1.** **Look in your dictionary.** *True* or *False*? **Correct the <u>underlined</u> words in the false sentences.**

               *on the wood floor*

**a.** The cat is <s><u>under the bed</u></s>.               ___*false*___

**b.** There is a <u>full-length mirror</u> in the closet.     _____

**c.** The alarm clock is on the <u>dresser</u>.            _____

**d.** The <u>light switch</u> and the outlet are on the same wall.   _____

**e.** The woman is lifting the <u>mattress</u> and the dust ruffle.   _____

**2.** **Read the letter and look at the picture. Complete Tran's list. Use your own paper.**

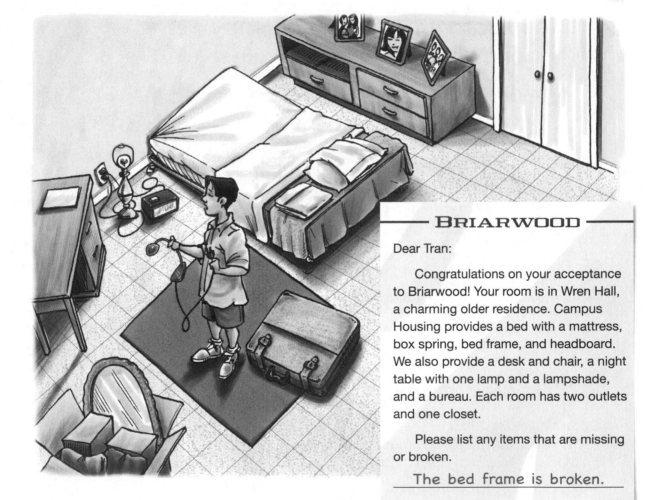

BRIARWOOD

Dear Tran:

    Congratulations on your acceptance to Briarwood! Your room is in Wren Hall, a charming older residence. Campus Housing provides a bed with a mattress, box spring, bed frame, and headboard. We also provide a desk and chair, a night table with one lamp and a lampshade, and a bureau. Each room has two outlets and one closet.

    Please list any items that are missing or broken.

    *The bed frame is broken.*

**3.** **Look at Exercise 2. What did Tran bring? Make a list.**

**Example:** *sheets*

**Challenge** Write a paragraph about your ideal bedroom.

1. **Look in your dictionary. Cross out the word that doesn't belong.**

   a. **For sleeping**     crib          ~~puzzle~~          bunk bed          cradle

   b. **For safety**       baby monitor   safety rail        bumper pad        blocks

   c. **For playing**      ball           changing pad       doll              crayons

   d. **Furniture**        changing table  chest of drawers  toy chest         colouring book

2. **Complete the article. Use the words in the box.**

   | | | | |
   |---|---|---|---|
   | mobile | changing table | wallpaper | stuffed animals |
   | ~~crib~~ | bedspread | chest of drawers | |

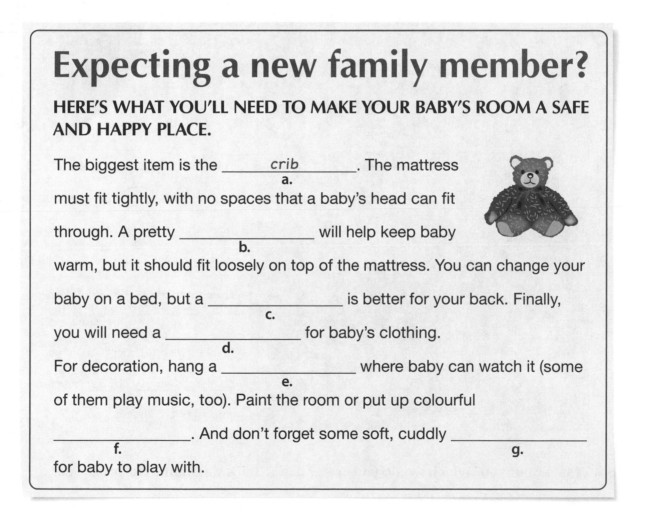

# Expecting a new family member?

**HERE'S WHAT YOU'LL NEED TO MAKE YOUR BABY'S ROOM A SAFE AND HAPPY PLACE.**

The biggest item is the _____crib_____. The mattress
　　　　　　　　　　　　　　**a.**
must fit tightly, with no spaces that a baby's head can fit

through. A pretty _____ will help keep baby
　　　　　　　　　　　　**b.**
warm, but it should fit loosely on top of the mattress. You can change your

baby on a bed, but a _____ is better for your back. Finally,
　　　　　　　　　　**c.**
you will need a _____ for baby's clothing.
　　　　　　　　**d.**
For decoration, hang a _____ where baby can watch it (some
　　　　　　　　　　　　　**e.**
of them play music, too). Paint the room or put up colourful

_____. And don't forget some soft, cuddly _____
　　　**f.**　　　　　　　　　　　　　　　　　　　　　　　　　　　**g.**
for baby to play with.

3. **What about you? Describe your favourite toy or game as a child.**

   **Example:** *I loved my teddy bear. It was ...*

   **Challenge**  Look at page 257 in this book. Follow the instructions.

**1.  Look in your dictionary. Correct the underlined words.**

                        *recycling*

  **a.**  The man in B is ~~putting away~~ newspapers.    **c.**  The girl in N is <u>washing</u> the dishes.

  **b.**  The man in D is <u>sweeping</u> the floor.    **d.**  The woman in O is <u>dusting</u> the counter.

**2.  Look at the room. Circle the words to complete the note.**

Hi! I wasn't quite able to do everything.

I polished the (desk) / dresser, but I didn't
                 **a.**

dust the <u>desk / dresser</u>. I <u>swept /</u>
          **b.**            **c.**

<u>vacuumed</u> the floor, and I washed the

<u>dishes / windows</u>. I also washed the
        **d.**

<u>sheets / glasses</u>, but didn't make
        **e.**

<u>lunch / the bed</u>. Sorry! Could you
      **f.**

<u>take out / empty</u> the garbage and
      **g.**

put away the <u>dishes / books</u>? *Viktor*
              **h.**

**3.  What about you? Which would you prefer to do? Tell a classmate. Do you agree?**

  **Example:**  *I'd prefer to dry the dishes.*

  **a.**  wash the dishes / dry the dishes    **c.**  sweep the floor / vacuum the carpet

  **b.**  dust the furniture / polish the furniture    **d.**  make the bed / change the sheets

**Challenge**  Conduct a survey. Ask five people about their favourite and least favourite kinds of
              housework. Write their answers.

**1. Look in your dictionary. Add a word to complete the list of cleaning supplies.**

a. glass ___*cleaner*___   d. rubber _____   g. garbage _____

b. oven _____   e. recycling _____   h. scrub _____

c. vacuum _____   f. furniture _____   i. sponge _____

**2. Complete the conversations. Use the words in Exercise 1.**

a. **Paulo:** Do you have any ___*garbage bags*___?
I want to empty the wastebasket.

   **Sara:** Sorry. I used the last one.

b. **Ben:** The mirror is very dirty.

   **Ann:** Use some _____.

c. **Basanti:** The _____ doesn't seem to
be working well.

   **Mario:** Maybe the bag is full. Have you checked it?

d. **Taro:** What should we do with the empty bottles?

   **Rika:** Don't throw them away. Put them in the _____ in the alley.

e. **Amber:** I dusted the desk, but it still doesn't look clean.

   **Chet:** Try some _____ on it.

f. **Nikhil:** You're doing a great job on that stove, but that _____
isn't good for your hands.

   **Vera:** You're right. Do we have any _____?

g. **Layla:** The kitchen floor is really dirty. The _____ isn't getting it clean.

   **Zaki:** I know. You have to get down and use the _____ on it.

**3. Cross out the word that doesn't belong. Give a reason.**

a. dust pan          broom          ~~disinfectant wipes~~          sponge mop

   ___*You don't use them to clean the floor.*___

b. steel-wool soap pads    dishwashing liquid    dish towel          bucket

   _____

c. scrub brush          sponge          feather duster          sponge mop

   _____

**Challenge** Imagine you have just moved into a new home. You need to dust the furniture, clean the
oven, wash the windows, and mop the kitchen floor. Make a shopping list.

**1. Look in your dictionary. Who could fix each problem?**

a.

> There's a water stain on the ceiling. I think the roof is leaking.

roofer

b.

> A toy is stuck in the toilet!

_____

c.

> The front door key isn't working!

_____

d.

> Sorry, Mom. I kicked my soccer ball through the front window.

_____

**2. Look at Tracy and Kung's cabin. Complete the telephone conversations. Describe the problem or problems for each repair service.**

a. **Repair person:** Bob Derby Carpentry. Can I help you?

   **Tracy:** _The door on our kitchen cabinet is broken._

b. **Repair person:** Plumbing Specialists, Ron here.

   **Kyung:** _____,

   _____, and _____

c. **Repair person:** Chestertown Electricians. This is Pat.

   **Kyung:** _____

d. **Repair person:** Nature's Way Exterminators. What's the problem?

   **Tracy:** _____

3. **Look at the chart. *True* or *False*? Write a question mark (?) if the information isn't in the chart.**

| Pests | Where They Live | How to Prevent Them | How to Get Rid of Them |
|---|---|---|---|
| | on pets, carpets, and furniture | Keep pets either inside or outside all the time. | Vacuum often. Comb pets daily. Wash them with water and lemon juice. |
| | behind walls, under roofs and floors | Repair cracks and holes in roofs and walls. Keep garbage in tightly closed garbage cans. | Poison is dangerous to humans. Put traps along walls. Put a piece of cheese in each trap. |
| | in wood, especially wet or damaged places | Repair cracks and holes. Repair leaks in pipes. Check repairs every 1–2 years. | Call the exterminator. You need a professional to get rid of these pests, which destroy your house by eating the wood. |
| | gardens and lawns | Repair wall cracks. Clean floors and shelves often. Wipe spilled honey or jam immediately. | Find where they enter the house and repair that hole. Put mint leaves in food cupboards. |
| | behind walls, in electric appliances | Clean carefully. Keep food in closed containers. Repair all cracks and holes. | Make a trap by putting a piece of banana in a wide-mouthed jar. Put petroleum jelly around the inside of the jar to keep trapped bugs inside. Place in corners or under sinks. Call an exterminator. |
| | in sheets, blankets, mattresses, and cracks in the bed; in cracks on the wall | Don't buy used sheets, blankets, or mattresses. Clean up around the outside of the house. Don't allow birds or squirrels to build nests on or in the house. | Wash sheets and blankets in hot water; vacuum the bed and mattress. A professional exterminator is often necessary. |

a. To prevent most pests, you must repair household problems.   _____true_____

b. You have to use poison to get rid of mice.   _____

c. Sometimes cockroaches get into the toaster oven.   _____

d. Fleas like sweet food.   _____

e. You have to buy cockroach traps.   _____

f. Ants carry diseases.   _____

g. Mint leaves help get rid of termites.   _____

h. Mice eat people's food.   _____

i. You should put a piece of fruit in a mouse trap.   _____

j. Bedbugs live only in beds.   _____

**Challenge**  Write some other ways of dealing with household pests.

**See page 280 for listening practice.**

1. **Look in your dictionary. *True* or *False*? Rewrite the false sentences. Make them true.**

   a. Tina and Sally are <u>sisters</u>.                                    <u>false</u>
      *Tina and Sally are roommates.*

   b. They had a <u>DJ</u> for their party.                               _____
      _____

   c. The neighbours were <u>irritated</u> about the music at the first party.  _____
      _____

   d. There was a big mess in the <u>rec room</u> after the first party.    _____
      _____

   e. The tenants made two <u>rules</u> at the tenant meeting.            _____
      _____

   f. Sally and Tina were <u>happy</u> at the tenant meeting.            _____
      _____

   g. Now it's against the rules to have loud music on <u>weekends</u>.   _____
      _____

   h. Their neighbours got invitations to the <u>second</u> party.        _____
      _____

2. **Circle the words to complete the conversations.**

   **Ms. Sanders:** Look at this (mess)/ noise! What happened?
                                        a.
   **Mr. Clarke:** There was a big <u>meeting / party</u> in 2B last night. All the <u>tenants / roommates</u> are
                                        b.                                                    c.
                   <u>irritated / happy</u>.
                        d.

   **Mr. Dean:** We need to make some <u>rules / invitations</u> about parties. Any suggestions?
                                            e.
   **Mr. Clarke:** No loud <u>mess / music</u>!
                              f.

   **Tina:** Ms. Sanders, we're very <u>sorry / irritated</u> about our party.
                                          g.
   **Ms. Sanders:** Thanks, girls. I know it won't happen again.

   **Sally:** Did you get our invitation to the <u>rec room / hallway</u> party?
                                                        h.
   **Mr. Clarke:** Yes, I did! Thanks. I'll be there.

3. **What about you? Are there any rules for the residents where you are living now? Are they good rules? Why or why not? What are some good rules for people in an apartment or a university residence?**

4. **Look in your dictionary. When did Tina and Sally do the following things? Put the sentences in order (1–8).**

___ a. clean the mess in the hallway

___ b. dance with their neighbours in the rec room

_1_ c. clean the apartment for the first party

___ d. make Mr. Clark in 2A very irritated

___ e. make some rules at the tenant meeting

___ f. give out the invitations to the neighbours

___ g. have a party in 2B

___ h. get an invitation to the tenant meeting

5. **Complete Sally and Tina's sign with the words in the box.**

| | | | | |
|---|---|---|---|---|
| mess | noise | dance | rec room | rules |
| sorry | ~~neighbours~~ | irritated | apartment | tenants |

# To Our ___Neighbours___
a.

We made a lot of _____ at our party last night, and we
b.

_____ our neighbours. We're very _____ about
c.                                                     d.

the loud music and the _____ in the hallway. We agree with
e.

the new _____ , and it won't happen again. We've given all
f.

the _____ in the building invitations to our party on
g.

Saturday, December 13th. We'll have great food and music, so please

come and _____ with your neighbours in the _____.
h.                                                                i.

Tina and Sally, _____ 2B
j.

**Challenge** Plan a party. Work with a group. When will your party take place? What do you have to do and when? Use the ideas in the word box or your own.

| | | |
|---|---|---|
| choose the place | choose the music | send out invitations |
| plan the food | clean up after the party | |

**1.** Look in your dictionary. Which foods come from these animals?

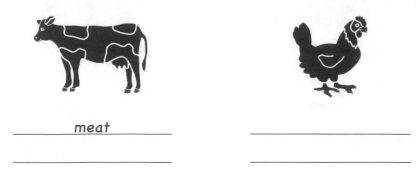

<u>   meat   </u>

_____

_____

_____

**2.** Marisol is going to make these meals. Write the foods she needs.

eggs

**3.** Look at Marisol's shopping list in Exercise 2. Check (✓) the coupons she can use.

Save $1.00 on every package of Paulo's

SAVE 50¢ on all brands!

Freshly Baked Buy 12, get the 13th one FREE!

Farm Fresh! SAVE $1.00 on 12

4. **Complete the conversations. Use the words in the box.**

| coupons | fruit | grocery bag | meat | ~~milk~~ | shopping list | vegetables |

**Ling:** What would you like to drink?

**Kong:** _____ Milk _____, please.
              **a.**

**Liza:** Would you like a hamburger?

**Elek:** No, thanks. I don't eat _____.
                                    **b.**

**Hoa:** Do you like bananas?

**Lan:** I love bananas. They're my favourite _____.
                                                **c.**

**Dan:** I'm going to the market. Do we need more milk?

**Eva:** Yes, I wrote it on the _____.
                                  **d.**

**Dan:** What about carrots or peas?

**Eva:** No. We have enough _____.
                              **e.**

**Eva:** Oh. Don't forget to take these _____.
                                          **f.**

**Dan:** Great. We'll save a lot of money with them!

**Mike:** Can I have another _____?
                              **g.**

**Cashier:** Sure. Paper or plastic?

5. **What about you? Do you eat the foods listed below? If *yes*, what types? Use pages 68–71 and page 76 in your dictionary for help.**

|  | Yes | No | Examples |
|---|---|---|---|
| vegetables | ☐ | ☐ | _____ |
| fruit | ☐ | ☐ | _____ |
| cheese | ☐ | ☐ | _____ |
| meat | ☐ | ☐ | _____ |
| fish | ☐ | ☐ | _____ |
| eggs | ☐ | ☐ | _____ |
| bread | ☐ | ☐ | _____ |

**Challenge** Work with a classmate. Plan a meal together. Use the food on pages 66 and 67 in your dictionary.

1. **Look in your dictionary. Complete the sentences.**

   a. A _bunch of bananas_ costs 50¢.

   b. The _____ are between the prunes and dates.

   c. The _____ are tall and have green leaves on top.

   d. The _____ are above the blueberries.

2. **Look at the pictures. Complete the chart.**

| Fruit | Best during | Buy ones that are |
|---|---|---|
| a. _watermelons_ | June, July, August | dark red inside when cut open |
| b. _____ | June and July | big and dark red |
| c. _____ | July and August | bright orange with soft skins |
| d. _____ | December to June | heavy |
| e. _____ | April to July | dry and dark red, size not important |
| f. _____ | July and August | dark green |

3. **Look at Exercise 2. Circle the words to complete the sentences.**

   a. The best grapefruits / mangoes are heavy.

   b. Don't buy a watermelon / kiwi unless it is dark red inside.

   c. Plums / Strawberries are good in April.

   d. Grapefruits / Peaches are good in the winter.

   e. When you buy cherries / strawberries, size is important.

   f. Summer is a good time to buy lemons / limes.

   g. Apples / Peaches should have soft skins.

4. **What about you? List your favourite types of fruit. When do you buy them?**

**Challenge** Make a chart like the one in Exercise 2 for your favourite fruit.

1. **Look in your dictionary. Put these vegetables in the correct category.**

| | | | | |
|---|---|---|---|---|
| ~~artichokes~~ | ~~beets~~ | ~~bell peppers~~ | bok choy | cabbage |
| chili peppers | corn | cucumbers | eggplants | carrots |
| peas | radishes | spinach | string beans | lettuce |
| sweet potatoes | tomatoes | turnips | zucchini | squash |

| **Root Vegetables** | **Leaf Vegetables** | **Vegetables with Seeds** | |
|---|---|---|---|
| beets | artichokes | bell peppers | |
| | | | |
| | | | |
| | | | |
| | | | |

2. **Complete the recipe with the amounts and names of the vegetables in the picture.**

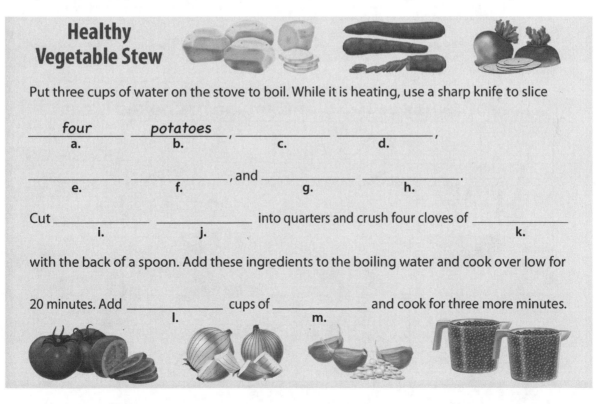

**Healthy Vegetable Stew**

Put three cups of water on the stove to boil. While it is heating, use a sharp knife to slice

_____four_____ _____potatoes_____ , _____ _____ ,
    a.         b.            c.           d.

_____ _____ , and _____ _____ .
    e.         f.            g.           h.

Cut _____ _____ into quarters and crush four cloves of _____
    i.         j.                             k.

with the back of a spoon. Add these ingredients to the boiling water and cook over low for

20 minutes. Add _____ cups of _____ and cook for three more minutes.
               l.                     m.

3. **What about you? Which vegetables do you like in a stew? Make a list.**

**Challenge** Write the recipe for a vegetable dish. Look online or in a cookbook, or ask a friend.

**See page 281 for listening practice.** 💿     **69**

1. **Look in your dictionary. Cross out the word that doesn't belong. Write the category.**

   a. ___Poultry___    chicken    duck    ~~lamb~~    turkey

   b. _____    chops    ham    sausage    tripe

   c. _____    chops    leg    shank    wing

   d. _____    drumsticks    ribs    steak    veal cutlets

2. **Complete the article with information from the charts.**

# FAT FACTS

A 100-gram serving of _____sausage_____ has 31 grams of fat.
 <br>a.

A serving of _____ and a serving of _____ have the same
 <br>b. c.

amount of fat.

_____ has the highest amount of fat.
 <br>d.

_____ has the lowest amount of fat.
 <br>e.

A chicken _____ with skin on it has two times as much fat as a skinless one.
 <br>f.

With 18 grams of fat, _____ has 13 more grams than _____
 <br>g. h.

from the same animal.

## Fat Grams per 100-gram Serving of Cooked Meat

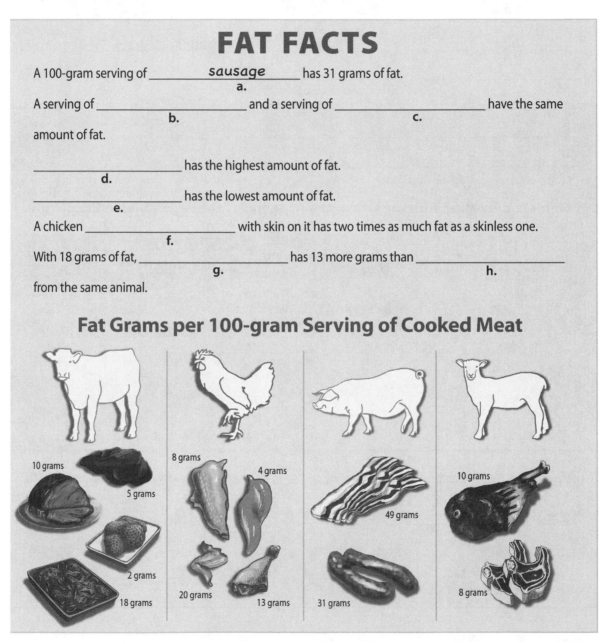

**Challenge** Write a list of the meat you (or another person) ate last week. Figure out the fat content.
Use the information in Exercise 2.

1. **Look in your dictionary. *True* or *False*? Correct the underlined words in the false sentences.**

   a. The swordfish is ~~frozen~~ *fresh*.                                          ___*false*___

   b. The cod is next to the <u>tuna</u>.                                          _____

   c. The <u>scallops</u> are to the right of the mussels.                         _____

   d. Salami and pastrami are in the <u>deli</u> section.                          _____

   e. The <u>wheat bread</u> is between the white bread and the rye bread.         _____

   f. The woman is reaching for the <u>mozzarella</u> cheese.                      _____

   g. The Swiss cheese is between the cheddar and the <u>processed</u> cheese.     _____

   h. There's a special price for the <u>whole salmon</u>.                         _____

2. **Look at the seafood prices and the recipe cards. How much will the seafood for each recipe cost? (You can use page 75 in your dictionary for information about weights and measures.)**

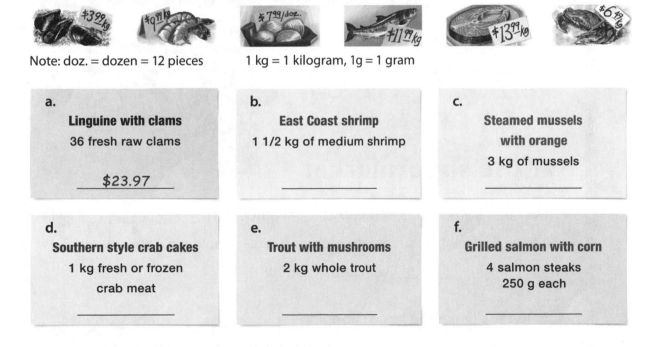

   Note: doz. = dozen = 12 pieces       1 kg = 1 kilogram, 1g = 1 gram

   | a. **Linguine with clams** 36 fresh raw clams ___$23.97___ | b. **East Coast shrimp** 1 1/2 kg of medium shrimp _____ | c. **Steamed mussels with orange** 3 kg of mussels _____ |
   |---|---|---|
   | d. **Southern style crab cakes** 1 kg fresh or frozen crab meat _____ | e. **Trout with mushrooms** 2 kg whole trout _____ | f. **Grilled salmon with corn** 4 salmon steaks 250 g each _____ |

3. **What about you? Work with a classmate. Order lunch from the deli.**

   **Example:** *I'll have a smoked turkey sandwich on wheat bread with mozzarella cheese. What about you?*

**Challenge** What other seafood and deli foods can you name? Make a list.

**1. Look in your dictionary. Cross out the item that doesn't belong. Write the section of the store.**

a. <u>Canned foods</u>    beans     ~~frozen dinner~~   soup     tuna

b. _____    bagels     bananas     oranges     tomatoes

c. _____    ice cream     margarine     sour cream     yogourt

d. _____    apple juice     coffee     pop     oil

e. _____    bagels     cake     cookies     nuts

f. _____    chocolate bars     nuts     pop     potato chips

g. _____    flour     oil     pet food     sugar

**2. Complete this article. Use the words in the box.**

| | | | | | |
|---|---|---|---|---|---|
| aisles | basket | beans | bottle return | cart | cashier |
| cash register | checkouts | coffee | ~~cookies~~ | customer | line |
| manager | margarine | broccoli | scale | self-checkout | vegetables |

# SAVE TIME and MONEY
## at the supermarket

- Never shop when you're hungry. Those chocolate <u>cookies</u> will
  a.
  be hard to resist on an empty stomach. You should also stay away
  from _____ with snack foods!
  b.

- Do you really need a large shopping _____ or is a smaller
  c.
  shopping _____ enough? Having too much room may
  d.
  encourage you to buy more than you need.

- Be a smart _____. Shop with a list. That makes it easier to
  e.
  buy only what you need.

- Keep a price book of items that you buy frequently. *Example*: If you drink a lot of _____, compare prices at different stores.
  f.

- Always check the unit price. *Example*: It may be cheaper to buy a large can of black _____ than a small can. Check: How much does it cost per kilogram?
  g.

- Do you need a kilogram of potatoes? Don't guess. Use the _____ and buy the exact amount.
  h.

- Watch for sales. Buy a lot of the items you need.

- Buy the store brand. *Example*: The supermarket brand of butter or _____ will probably cost less than the popular brands.
  i.

- If the carrots and _____ don't look fresh, buy frozen _____. They'll look and taste better.
  j.
  k.

- Avoid standing in _____. Try to shop when the store is less crowded. If all of the _____ aren't open, speak to the store _____. Remember: Sometimes the _____ is faster.
  l.
  m.
  n.
  o.

- Always watch the _____ when the _____ is ringing up your order. Is the price right? Mistakes can happen!
  p.
  q.

- Don't throw away those empty bottles! At some stores, you can recycle your glass or plastic bottles. Take them to the _____.
  r.

3. **What about you? Which of the shopping tips in Exercise 2 do you use? What other ways do you save money when you go food shopping? Write about them.**

**Challenge** Look at page 257 in this book. Follow the instructions.

See page 282 for listening practice.

1.  **Look in your dictionary. Complete the flyer.**

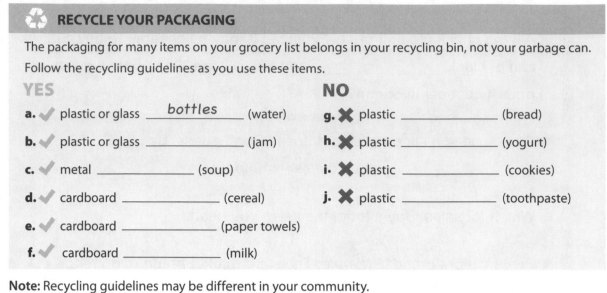

### ♻ RECYCLE YOUR PACKAGING

The packaging for many items on your grocery list belongs in your recycling bin, not your garbage can. Follow the recycling guidelines as you use these items.

**YES**

a. ✓ plastic or glass ___bottles___ (water)

b. ✓ plastic or glass _____ (jam)

c. ✓ metal _____ (soup)

d. ✓ cardboard _____ (cereal)

e. ✓ cardboard _____ (paper towels)

f. ✓ cardboard _____ (milk)

**NO**

g. ✖ plastic _____ (bread)

h. ✖ plastic _____ (yogurt)

i. ✖ plastic _____ (cookies)

j. ✖ plastic _____ (toothpaste)

**Note:** Recycling guidelines may be different in your community.

2.  **Look at the groceries that Mee-Yon bought this week. Which items have packaging that she can recycle? Which items don't? Use information from Exercise 1. Make two lists. Use you own paper.**

    **Example:** *She can recycle the packaging for the bottle of oil. She can't recycle the bags from the two loaves of bread.*

3.  **What about you? What can and can't you recycle in your community? Make two lists.**

**Challenge** Look in your dictionary. Write six sentences about other items that come in the same containers and packaging. **Example:** *Juice and vegetable oil also come in bottles.*

1. **Look at the charts in your dictionary. Circle the larger amount.**

   a. 3 teaspoons / ~~3 tablespoons~~ (circled)

   b. 100 millilitres / 2 fluid ounces

   c. 3 pounds / 2 kilograms

   d. 6 cups / 1 litre

   e. 1 litre / 1 gallon

   f. 50 millilitres / 4 tablespoons

2. **Look at the nutrition facts. Answer the questions. Use your dictionary for help.**

**Nutrition Facts**
Kidney Beans — Per serving (120 g)

| Amount | % Daily Value |
|---|---|
| Calories 110 | |
| Fat 0 g | 0% |
| Carbohydrate 22 g | 7% |
| Calcium | 6% |
| Iron | 10% |

**Nutrition Facts**
Skim Milk — Per glass (500 mL)

| Amount | % Daily Value |
|---|---|
| Calories 90 | |
| Fat 0g | 0% |
| Protein 8 g | 16% |
| Calcium | 30% |
| Vitamin D | 25% |

**Nutrition Facts**
Rice — Per serving (50 g uncooked, 200 g cooked)

| Amount | % Daily Value |
|---|---|
| Calories 170 | 0% |
| Fat 0 g | 13% |
| Carbohydrate 38 g | 8% |
| Protein 4 g | 2% |
| Calcium | 8% |
| Iron | |

**Nutrition Facts**
Chocolate Candy — Per piece (15 g)

| Amount | % Daily Value |
|---|---|
| Calories 90 | |
| Fat 4g | 6% |
| Protein 1 g | 2% |

**Note:** % Daily Value = % of the total amount you should have in one day

a. Which has more protein, a cup of beans or a cup of milk? ___a cup of beans___

b. How many pieces of chocolate candy are there in one kilogram? _____

c. How many millilitres of milk are needed to get 100% of the daily value of Vitamin D? _____

d. How much fat is there in 75 grams of chocolate candy? _____

e. How much milk do you need to drink to get 90% of the daily value of calcium? _____

f. What percentage of the daily value of calcium do you get from 500 millilitres of milk and two servings of rice? _____

g. A serving of rice and beans contains 60 grams of beans and 100 grams of cooked rice. How much carbohydrate is there in a serving? _____

h. What percentage of the daily value of iron is there in a serving of rice and beans? _____

**Challenge** Look at page 257 in this book. Follow the instructions.

1. **Look at page 76 in your dictionary. Then look at the pictures here. What does Laura do right? What does she do wrong? Check (✓) the correct box. Write sentences.**

|  | Right | Wrong |  |
|---|:---:|:---:|---|
| a. | ✓ | ☐ | She cleans the counters. |
| b. | ☐ | ✓ | She doesn't |
| c. | ☐ | ☐ | |
| d. | ☐ | ☐ | |
| e. | ☐ | ☐ | |

2. **Look at the chart. Complete the sentences.**

**Calories in 85 gram Chicken Breast**

| 150 | 161 | 222 |
|:---:|:---:|:---:|
| **172** | **168** | **175** |

a. __Roasted__ chicken has 172 calories.

b. _____ chicken has 11 more calories than boiled chicken.

c. _____ chicken has the most calories.

d. _____ chicken has the lowest number of calories.

e. With 168 calories, _____ chicken has 7 more calories than grilled chicken.

f. _____ chicken has 175 calories, but fewer calories than fried chicken.

3. **Look in your dictionary. Circle the words to complete the cookbook definitions.**

a. **beat** / stir: Make mixture smooth by quick motion with a spoon, fork, or whisk.

b. **boil** / sauté: Cook in very hot liquid (100°C for water).

c. peel / **chop**: Cut into pieces with a knife.

d. slice / **dice**: Cut into very small pieces with a knife (smaller than chopping).

e. **grate** / grease: Cut into small pieces using small holes of a grater.

f. **mix** / bake: Combine ingredients, usually with a spoon.

g. grate / **peel**: Take off the outer skin.

h. **sauté** / steam: Cook in a small amount of hot butter or oil.

i. boil / **simmer**: Cook slowly in liquid just below the boiling point.

j. preheat / **steam**: Cook over boiling water, not in it.

4. **Look at Paulo's recipe. It got wet, and now he can't read parts of it. Complete the recipe. Use the words in the box.**

| add | bake | grease | microwave | mix | ~~preheat~~ | slice | spoon |
|-----|------|--------|-----------|-----|------------|-------|-------|

**FISH**

## Baked cod in sour cream

250 g cod                1/4 c. mayonnaise

1 tbsp. butter          1 c. sour cream

salt and pepper        300 g mushrooms

Preheat ___ the oven to 175°C. ___ a baking dish with a
     a.                                        b.

little butter. Place the fish in the dish, top with the rest of the butter.

___ salt and pepper. ___ the mayonnaise and
     c.                          d.

sour cream together and ___ it over the fish. ___
                              e.                          f.

the mushrooms, and add them to the dish. ___ in the oven for
                                              g.

45 minutes or ___ on high for about 7 minutes.
                  h.

**Servings:** 2

**Challenge** Write one of your favourite recipes.

See page 284 for listening practice.   77

1. **Look in your dictionary.** *True* or *False*? **Change the** underlined **words to correct the false sentences.**

   *cake*
   a. There are two ~~pie~~ pans above the cookie sheets.      *false*

   b. There's a lid on the <u>casserole dish</u>.      _____

   c. There's a roasting rack in the <u>mixing bowl</u>.      _____

   d. There's butter in the <u>saucepan</u>.      _____

   e. There's a <u>garlic press</u> between the wooden spoon and the casserole dish.      _____

   f. One of the cooks is using the <u>can opener</u>.      _____

   g. One of the cooks is using the <u>vegetable peeler</u>.      _____

2. **Circle the words to complete the cookbook information.**

   # Some utensils you need in your kitchen

   a. <u>Grater / **Whisk**</u>: to beat eggs, cream, etc.

   b. <u>**Steamer / Colander**</u>: to remove water from cooked pasta, vegetables, etc.

   c. <u>**Ladle / Spatula**</u>: to spoon soup, sauces, etc. out of a pot

   d. <u>**Paring / Carving** knife</u>: to cut up small fruits and vegetables

   e. <u>**Lid / Tongs**</u>: to cover pots and pans

   f. <u>**Plastic storage container / Strainer**</u>: to keep food fresh

   g. <u>**Pot / Pot holders**</u>: to handle hot utensils

   h. <u>**Egg beater / Wooden spoon**</u>: to stir soups, sauces, etc.

   i. <u>**Double boiler / Roasting rack**</u>: to cook food slowly on top of the stove

   j. <u>**Cake and pie pans / pots**</u>: to bake desserts

**Challenge** Think of a recipe. Make a list of all the utensils you need for the recipe. What do you need each one for? **Example:** *I need a whisk to beat the eggs.*

**1. Look in your dictionary. Cross out the word that doesn't belong.**

a. cheeseburger ~~chicken sandwich~~ hamburger hot dog

b. burrito ice cream cone nachos taco

c. iced tea milkshake pop mustard

d. muffin onion rings ice cream cone doughnut

**2. Look at the chart. *True* or *False*? Put a question mark (?) if the information isn't in the chart.**

**Based on information from:** Horovitz, B, "Restaurant sales climb with bad-for-you food," *USA Today*, May 12, 2005, http://www.usatoday.com/money/industries/food/2005-05-12-bad-food-cover_x.htm.

a. Women order chicken sandwiches more than men do. ___true___

b. French fries are more popular among women than among men. _____

c. Pizza is the third most popular food for both men and women. _____

d. Tacos are the fifth most popular food for men. _____

e. Women probably go to the salad bar more often than men do. _____

f. Men eat more doughnuts than women do. _____

g. Hot dogs are the most popular fast food for men and women. _____

h. Pop is more popular than iced tea for men and women. _____

**Challenge** Take a survey of your classmates' five favourite fast foods.

# A Coffee Shop Menu

1. **Look in your dictionary. What could you order to get the following extra items?**

    a. sour cream and butter _____*baked potato*_____

    b. mashed potatoes _____

    c. rice _____

    d. raisins, milk, and brown sugar _____

    e. honey _____

    f. two slices of tomato _____

    g. a baked potato _____

    h. a pickle _____

    i. butter and syrup _____ and/or _____

    j. garlic bread _____ and _____

    k. lemon _____ and _____

    l. milk or cream _____ and _____

2. **Complete the conversation.**

    **Anton:** I'll have the steak and _____*potatoes*_____.
    <br>a.

    **Server:** Baked or mashed? Or maybe potato salad?

    **Anton:** Baked potato, please. And the steamed

    _____.
    <br>b.

    **Server:** Ok. Anything to start?

    **Anton:** I think I'd like a cup of

    _____ to begin with.
    <br>c.

    **Server:** We only have chicken noodle today. OK?

    **Anton:** Er, no. I'll have a small dinner _____ instead.
    <br>d.

    Oh, and bring me some garlic bread, please.

    **Server:** Very good. Would you like something for dessert?

    **Anton:** Do you have apple _____?
    <br>e.

    **Server:** Sorry, we don't.

    **Anton:** Well, then, I'll have the layer _____ and a cup of decaf
    <br>f.

    _____. Thank you.
    <br>g.

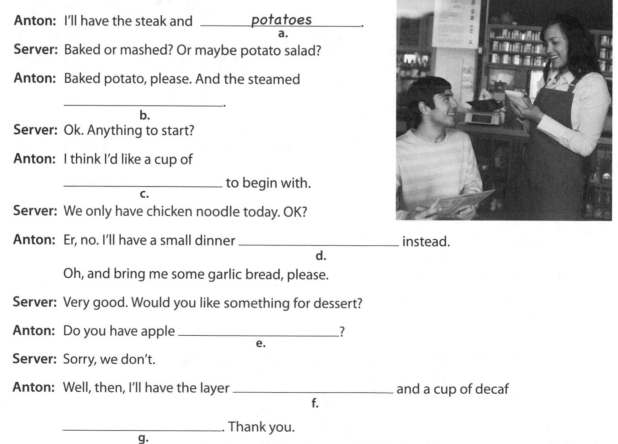

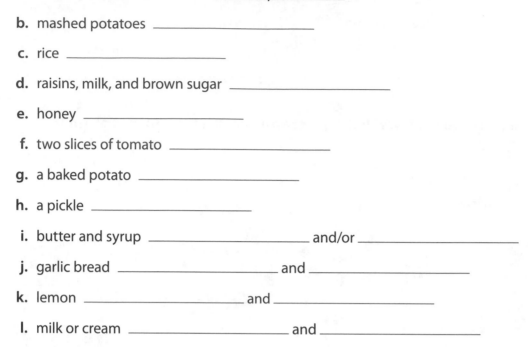

3.  **Look at Exercise 2. Write the order.**

CARL'S Coffee Shop
——— ORDER FORM ———

steak
_____    _____
_____    _____
_____    _____

4.  **Read the order in Exercise 3. Look at the food the server brought Anton. The server made six mistakes. Describe the mistakes.**

a.  ___The server gave him rolls, but he asked for garlic bread.___

b.  _____

c.  _____

d.  _____

e.  _____

f.  _____

5.  **What about you? Look at the menu in your dictionary. What would you like? Write your order.**

CARL'S Coffee Shop
——— ORDER FORM ———

_____    _____
_____    _____
_____    _____

**Challenge**  Imagine you own a coffee shop. Write your own dinner menu.

**See page 285 for listening practice.**

1. **Look at the top picture on pages 82 and 83 in your dictionary.**
   **Who says the following things?**

   a. "Your table is ready, Mr. and Mrs. Smith."    _____hostess_____

   b. "Would you like asparagus or zucchini with that?"    _____

   c. "Here. Have some bread."    _____

   d. "We also have chocolate, coconut, and mango ice cream."    _____

   e. "The dishes are clean now."    _____

   f. "I'm coming through with some more dirty dishes!"    _____

   g. "I need to beat this a little more."    _____

2. **Circle the words to complete this restaurant review.**

---

**A.J. Clarke's** 290 Macdonald Ave. 555-3454

At Clarke's, you'll relax in the comfortable green (dining room)/ kitchen that can serve about
**a.**

50 chefs / diners. The hostess seated / served my guest and me in a quiet booth / high chair, and we got a
**b.**              **c.**                                **d.**

bread basket / soup bowl filled with fresh rolls. The service was great. The patron / server continued to
**e.**                                                              **f.**

pour / clear water throughout the meal.
**g.**

And what a meal it was! The bill / menu had something for everyone. Our busser / server, Todd,
**h.**                                          **i.**

recommended the fish of the day, tuna. My friend ordered / served the chicken à l'orange. After Todd
**j.**

carried / took our orders, he brought us two salad plates / saucers with the freshest lettuce I've ever eaten. This
**k.**                                **l.**

was followed by two large bowls / plates of onion soup. Our main dishes did not disappoint us. The tuna was so
**m.**

tender that you could cut it without a steak knife / teaspoon. The chicken, too, was wonderful.
**n.**

When we were finished, the busser cleared the dishes / set the table. Time for dessert! Todd
**o.**

carried / left out the dessert fork / tray filled with cakes and pies—all baked in the restaurant's
**p.**              **q.**

kitchen / dish room. Raspberry pie and a cup / saucer of delicious hot coffee ended our perfect meal. We
**r.**                                        **s.**

happily paid / poured the bill and left / took Todd a nice tip. My tip to you: Eat at A.J. Clarke's.
**t.**                        **u.**

And don't forget to ask for a napkin / to-go box to take home the food you can't finish!
**v.**

Reservations recommended.

---

**3. Look at the picture. Complete the article.**

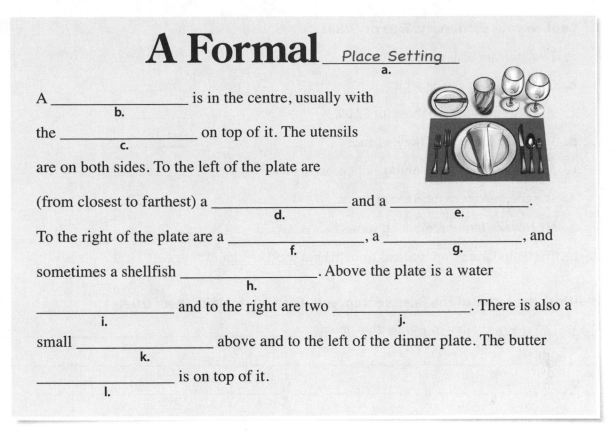

# A Formal _Place Setting_
a.

A _____ is in the centre, usually with
b.

the _____ on top of it. The utensils
c.

are on both sides. To the left of the plate are

(from closest to farthest) a _____ and a _____.
d.                                              e.

To the right of the plate are a _____, a _____, and
f.                                    g.

sometimes a shellfish _____. Above the plate is a water
h.

_____ and to the right are two _____. There is also a
i.                                              j.

small _____ above and to the left of the dinner plate. The butter
k.

_____ is on top of it.
l.

**4. What about you? Most people's table settings do not look like the formal one in Exercise 3. Draw your table setting. How is it the same as the table setting in Exercise 3? How is it different? Write sentences.**

Example: *We put the napkin under the fork.*

_____

_____

_____

_____

_____

_____

**Challenge** Write a description of a meal you had at a restaurant or at someone's home.

Go to page 245 for Another Look (Unit 4).

**1. Look in your dictionary. *True* or *False*?**

    **a.** Two men are playing <u>football</u>.                  *false*

    **b.** Cara's sells <u>organic vegetables</u>.             _____

    **c.** The <u>watermelons</u> are three for $3.00.        _____

    **d.** The herb vendor sells <u>flowers</u>, too.          _____

    **e.** A market worker is <u>weighing</u> eight avocados.   _____

    **f.** The children are tasting the <u>samples</u>.         _____

    **g.** Mr. Novak's father is drinking some <u>tea</u>.      _____

    **h.** The lemonade stand is across from the <u>hot-food vendor</u>.  _____

**2. Write the letter of the false sentences in Exercise 1. Make them true.**

    *a.*     *Two men are playing live music.* _____

    \_\_\_  _____

    \_\_\_  _____

    \_\_\_  _____

    \_\_\_  _____

**3. Circle the words to complete the blog post.**

http//www.farmersmarket.ca            ⊟ ☐ ☒

Saturday, August 2

Today I went to the Tenth Street (Farmers' Market) / Grocery Store.
                                              **a.**

I saw the free <u>avocados / samples</u> first, so I tried some
                       **b.**

<u>lemonade / fruit</u>—peaches and strawberries. Then I bought some
      **c.**

cookies from the <u>bakery / herb vendor</u>. I drank some lemonade
                  **d.**

next—it was really <u>hot / sour</u> after those <u>sweets / herbs</u>. I wasn't
               **e.**                  **f.**

planning to buy groceries, but the <u>organic / canned</u> vegetables were beautiful so I got
                                 **g.**

some corn and some <u>peaches / avocados</u>. Before I left, I stopped at the <u>hot-food / flower</u>
                       **h.**                                     **i.**

vendor for a taco, and I ate it while I listened to a local band called Sounds of Mexico.

You can't hear <u>live / radio</u> music at the grocery store!
           **j.**

**4. Look in your dictionary. What's at the farmers' market? Check (✓) the items.**

- [✓] live music
- [ ] frozen foods
- [ ] baked goods
- [ ] flowers
- [ ] vendors

- [ ] fruit
- [ ] pet food
- [ ] herbs
- [ ] bottle return
- [ ] samples

- [ ] organic vegetables
- [ ] soup
- [ ] beverages
- [ ] canned foods
- [ ] hot food

**5. Complete the flyer. Use words from the box.**

| dill | samples | cucumbers | hot food | ~~farmers' market~~ | fruit |
|------|---------|-----------|----------|--------------------|-------|
| basil | lemonade | organic | live music | vegetables | sweets |

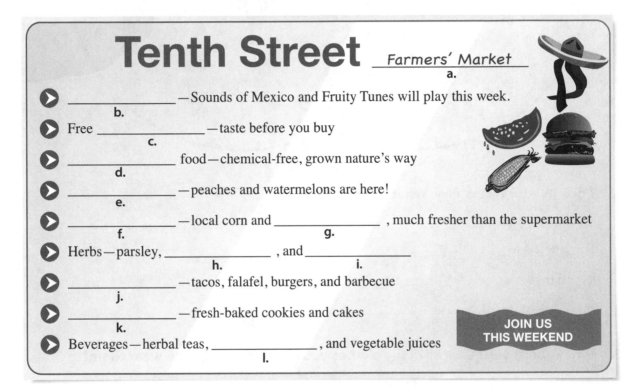

# Tenth Street  <u>Farmers' Market</u>
**a.**

> _____—Sounds of Mexico and Fruity Tunes will play this week.
> **b.**
> Free _____—taste before you buy
> **c.**
> _____ food—chemical-free, grown nature's way
> **d.**
> _____—peaches and watermelons are here!
> **e.**
> _____—local corn and _____ , much fresher than the supermarket
> **f.**                          **g.**
> Herbs—parsley, _____ , and _____
> **h.**                **i.**
> _____—tacos, falafel, burgers, and barbecue
> **j.**
> _____—fresh-baked cookies and cakes
> **k.**
> Beverages—herbal teas, _____ , and vegetable juices
> **l.**

**JOIN US THIS WEEKEND**

**6. What about you? Look in your dictionary. What do you like about the farmers' market? What do you like about a grocery store? Make a list for each.**

Farmers' market

___fresh vegetables___

_____

_____

_____

Grocery store

___open all week and all year___

_____

_____

_____

**Challenge** Work with a classmate. Make a flyer for a farmers' market. Use Exercise 5 as a model.

85

**1. Look in your dictionary. What are the people wearing? Complete the diagram.**

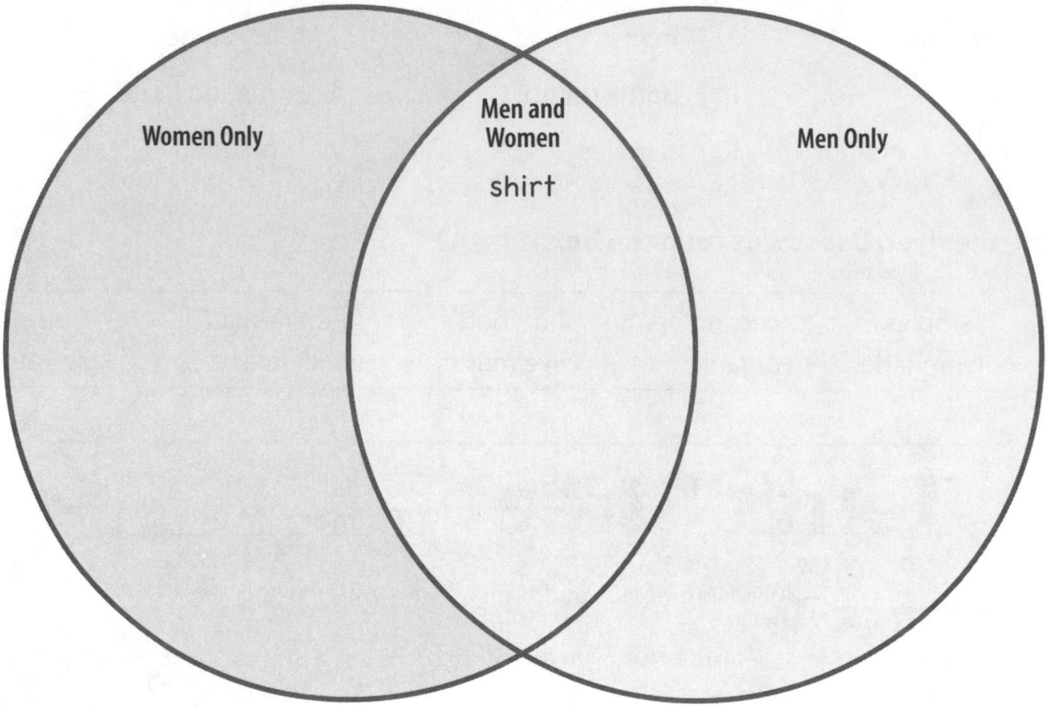

Women Only

Men and Women

shirt

Men Only

**2. Look in your dictionary. What can people wear . . .**

a. under a sweater?   _shirt_   _____   _____   _____

b. with a skirt?   _____   _____   _____   _____

c. on their feet?   _____   _____   _____

d. on their heads?   _____

**3. What about you? Check (✓) the clothes you have. Where do you wear them?**

**Where?**

☐ jeans   _at home,_ _____

☐ athletic shoes   _____

☐ T-shirt   _____

☐ suit   _____

☐ sweater   _____

☐ baseball cap   _____

**4.** **Look in your dictionary. Circle the words to complete the sentences.**

a. The man in the blue shirt is wearing (jeans)/ slacks.

b. The woman in the blue blouse has a handbag / sweater.

c. The man at the ticket window is wearing a blue shirt / T-shirt.

d. The woman in the yellow dress / white skirt is putting on a sweater.

e. The girl with the handbag / baseball cap is tying her shoe.

f. The girl in the athletic shoes / shoes is wearing socks.

g. The man in jeans / the suit is looking at his watch.

**5.** **Look in your dictionary. Complete the phrase** *a pair of . . .*

a. _____jeans_____

b. _____

c. _____

d. _____

e. _____

**6.** **What about you? What will you wear? Imagine you are going to the following places or events. You can use your dictionary for help.**

a. a jazz concert _____

b. a job interview _____

c. the park _____

d. school _____

e. a Friday night party with your classmates _____

f. a family reunion _____

g. the grocery store _____

**Challenge** Look at Exercise 1. Name two more pieces of clothing for each of the following. You can use pages 86–91 in your dictionary for help.

Only Women _____     _____

Women and Men _____     _____

Only Men _____     _____

1. **Look in your dictionary. Who is doing the following?**

   a. wearing sandals                                    _the woman in capris_

   b. carrying a briefcase                               _____

   c. wearing a bow tie                                  _____

   d. walking with the man in the tank top              _____

   e. wearing a pullover sweater                         _____

   f. wearing high heels                                 _____

   g. talking on the phone                               _____

   h. helping a woman with her luggage                  _____

   i. sitting on the couch                               _____

   j. sitting on the floor                               _____

2. **Circle the words to complete the advice column.**

# Clothes Encounters

Q  I'm looking for a job as an office manager.

   What should I wear on interviews?

A  You can't go wrong with a dark blue
   business suit / tuxedo. Wear it with
        a.
   a white shirt and bow tie / tie. Then
            b.
   just grab your briefcase / clutch bag
            c.
   and you're good to go! After you get

   the job, you can change to a

   sports jacket / vest. Wear it with
       d.
   shorts / a sports shirt or a
       e.
   cardigan / pullover sweater for a neat look.
       f.

**Q** I'm going on a business trip to Calgary this summer. Can you suggest something casual to wear between meetings? I don't want to wear jeans, but I want to feel comfortable.

**A** After work, relax in a pair of
<u>capris /sweatpants</u>, a T-shirt, and
     g.
<u>high heels / sandals</u>. You'll feel very
     h.
comfortable and look great. If it gets

cool, put on a <u>knit top / tank top</u>.
           i.

**Q** My husband and I got invited to a wedding. The invitation says "black tie."

What does that mean?

**A** For men, black tie means a <u>tuxedo / uniform</u>, and usually a <u>bow tie / tank top</u>.
                       j.                        k.
Many men don't own these items, but they can rent them! For women, black tie

can mean either a <u>cocktail dress / sweatpants</u> or <u>an evening gown / overalls</u>.
                     l.                     m.
Complete the outfit with <u>high heels / sandals</u> and have fun!
                          n.

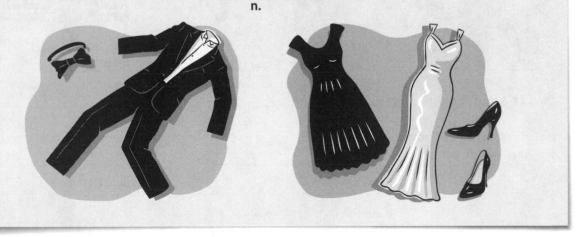

3. **What about you? What do you think are the most important items of clothing to have? Where do you wear these clothes?**

   Example: *a sports shirt—I wear it at work, at school, and at home.*

   **Challenge** Choose five people from your dictionary. Describe their clothes.

   Example: *On page 73 the woman near the snacks is wearing a black skirt, a purple pullover sweater, and black high heels.*

**See page 286 for listening practice.**

**1.** **Look in your dictionary. Cross out the word that doesn't belong. Write the weather condition.**

a. _____Windy_____   overcoat   ~~cover-up~~   winter scarf   jacket

b. _____   poncho   rain boots   umbrella   ski hat

c. _____   straw hat   swimsuit   parka   sunglasses

d. _____   down jacket   leggings   ski mask   windbreaker

**2.** **Correct the ad.**

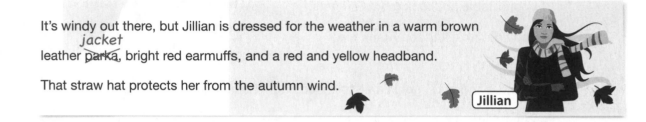

It's windy out there, but Jillian is dressed for the weather in a warm brown
*jacket*
leather ~~parka~~, bright red earmuffs, and a red and yellow headband.

That straw hat protects her from the autumn wind.

Jillian

**3.** **Write ads for Abdulla, Polly, and Jean-Marc's clothing. Use Exercise 2 as an example.**

Abdulla        Polly        Jean-Marc

a. *It's sunny out there, but Abdulla* _____

_____

_____

b. _____

_____

_____

c. _____

_____

_____

**Challenge** What do you like to wear in different weather conditions? Write short paragraphs like the ones in Exercise 3.

Underwear and Sleepwear

**1. Look in your dictionary. Find the words that complete *a pair of* . . .**

long underwear

**2. Put the items in the correct list.**

| Mom | Dad | Amy | Brian |
|---|---|---|---|
| bikini panties | | | |

**Challenge** You're going on a trip next weekend. List the underwear and sleepwear you'll take.

91

1. **Look in your dictionary. What is it?**

   **a.** It protects his clothes when he cooks.        _chef's jacket_

   **b.** It has her name on it.                         _____

   **c.** He keeps his hammer in it.                     _____

   **d.** He wears it with his blazer.                   _____

   **e.** It's blue and he wears his badge on it.        _____

   **f.** It helps him breathe.                          _____

2. **Circle the words to complete the article.**

---

# Dressing for Safety

Part of a job is wearing the right clothes. A manager wants to look good in

a (blazer) / work shirt and smock / tie. But many workers need to dress for safety, too.
   a.               b.
Here are some examples—from head to toe.

★ **Protect your head.** Construction workers need hairnets / hard hats to protect
                                               c.
  themselves from falling objects.

★ **Protect your face.** A medical technician needs a surgical gown / face mask to
                                                d.
  avoid breathing in dangerous substances.

★ **Protect your eyes.** You only have two. That's the reason why many jobs
  require special safety glasses / ventilation masks.
                        e.

★ **Protect your body.** Working on the road? Cars need to see you. That's why
  road workers need to wear brightly coloured waist aprons / safety vests.
                                                        f.

★ **Protect your feet.** Things can fall on your feet, too. That's why road workers,
  construction workers, and other workers wear coveralls / steel toe boots.
                                                                g.

Many workers need to protect *other* people, too. A surgeon, for example, needs a

helmet / scrub cap and a surgical mask / smock to protect patients from germs.
        h.                                   i.

*Wearing the right clothes at the right time can help make the workplace a*
*safe place.*

**3.** **Look in your dictionary. Cross out the word that doesn't belong. Give a reason.**

a. cowboy hat      bump cap      bandana      ~~badge~~

     *You don't wear a badge on your head.*

b. safety glasses      ventilation mask      blazer      surgical mask

     _____

c. work pants      jeans      lab coat      security pants

     _____

d. polo shirt      smock      apron      waist apron

     _____

**4.** **Look at the pictures. What are the problems? Write sentences.**

a.

     *He isn't wearing a hard hat.*

     *He isn't wearing steel toe boots.*

b.

     _____

     _____

c.

     _____

     _____

d.

     _____

     _____

**5.** **What about you? Look in your dictionary. What workplace clothing do you have? When do you wear this clothing?**

     **Example:** *I wear an apron when I cook.*

**Challenge** Look at pages 166–169 in your dictionary. Find three job titles. What workplace clothing do these people wear? **Example:** *A dental assistant wears a face mask and latex gloves.*

### Shoes and Accessories

**1. Look in your dictionary. Read the sentences. What are the people talking about?**

a. "I always keep my coins in <u>one</u>—separate from my bills."  <u>change purse</u>

b. "According to this <u>one</u>, it's 3:00."  _____

c. "Wow! <u>This</u> has even more room than the backpack!"  _____

d. "Ow, my finger! <u>This</u> is pretty, but it's sharp!"  _____

e. "John gave <u>one</u> to me. I put his photo in it."  _____

f. "Oh, no. I forgot to put my credit card back in <u>it</u>."  _____

g. "<u>It</u>'s a little too big for my finger."  _____

**2. Look at the ad. Complete the sentences.**

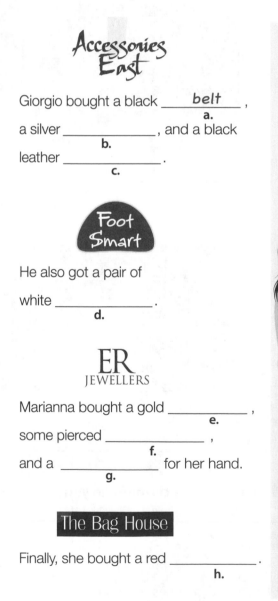

### Accessories East

Giorgio bought a black __<u>belt</u>__ ,
**a.**
a silver _____ , and a black
**b.**
leather _____ .
**c.**

### Foot Smart

He also got a pair of

white _____ .
**d.**

### ER JEWELLERS

Marianna bought a gold _____ ,
**e.**
some pierced _____ ,
**f.**
and a _____ for her hand.
**g.**

### The Bag House

Finally, she bought a red _____ .
**h.**

YOUR ONE STOP FOR
FALL FASHIONS

Maple City Mall

FOOT SMART

E.R.

94

**3. Look at the shopping list. Where can you buy these items?
Use the stores from Exercise 2.**

**YOUR ONE STOP FOR**
FALL FASHIONS

brown purse          _The Bag House_

gold bracelet        _____

backpack             _____

string of pearls     _____

black flats          _____

**4. Circle the words to complete the information from a shoe store.**

**YOUR ONE STOP FOR**
FALL FASHIONS

# If the Shoe Fits

Be a smart (customer) / salesclerk. When you purchase / wait in
  a.                                         b.
line for shoes, always try them on at the end of the day—your

feet are bigger then! Ask yourself: is there enough room at the

sole / toe? There should be a bit more than one centimetre
  c.

between the end of your foot and the beginning of the shoe.

And remember: you need different kinds of shoes for different

kinds of activities. Women may want to wear high heels / oxfords
                                                          d.
to an evening party, but tennis shoes / pumps are a better
                                               e.
choice for the office. Shoes with lower heels / pins, are more
                                              f.
comfortable. Both women and men can relax at home in a

pair of  hiking boots / loafers, but you'll want shoes with
                        g.

scarves / shoelaces for walking.
         h.

**Challenge** Which accessories make good gifts? Explain who you would buy them for and why.
  **Example:** *I'd buy a backpack for my girlfriend because she loves to hike.*

**See page 287 for listening practice.**

1. **Look in your dictionary. Cross out the word that doesn't belong. Write the category.**

   a. ___Sweater styles___  V-neck  crewneck  ~~wide~~  turtleneck

   b. _____  light  print  paisley  floral

   c. _____  large  medium  small  too small

   d. _____  ripped  sleeveless  unravelling  too big

2. **Look at the pictures. Complete the sentences.**

Lisa                Amira

   a. Lisa's skirt looks like a ___mini___ skirt. It's also too _____ .

   b. Amira's skirt is _____ length. It's too _____ .

   c. The zipper on Amira's skirt is _____ .

   d. Amira's belt is _____ . Lisa's belt is _____ .

   e. Amira's blouse is _____-sleeved, but the sleeves are too _____ .

   f. Lisa's blouse is _____-sleeved too, but the sleeves are too _____ .

   g. Lisa's blouse is _____ .

   h. Both women are unhappy with the clothes. And at $500, they are much too _____ !

**3. Look at the pictures. Circle the words to complete the article.**

# Suitable Dressing

1500s

1700s

after 1789

end of 1800s

Men's formal business suits never seem to change very much these days. However, it took a long time for men to get to this basic piece of clothing.

During the 1500s in Europe, fashionable men wanted to look fat. Their pants were (short) / long and baggy / tight. They wore short / long, light / heavy jackets that were
a.                b.              c.          d.
sleeveless / long-sleeved, and they even stuffed their clothes to look bigger!
e.

In the 1700s, men preferred to look thinner and taller. The rich and stylish wore their pants shorter / longer and very tight / baggy, and they wore shoes with low / high heels.
f.                        g.                      h.
Jackets became longer / shorter and looser / tighter, and men wore fancy / plain shirts
i.                        j.                      k.
under them. After the French Revolution in 1789, it became dangerous to dress like the rich. Instead, many men dressed like workers in long / short pants and loose jackets.
l.
This outfit was a lot like the modern suit, but the parts did not match. The man in the picture, for example, is wearing striped / checked brown pants with a fancy
m.
polka-dotted / paisley vest and a solid / plaid green jacket.
n.                        o.

Finally, at the end of the 1800s, it became stylish to match the pants, jacket, and vest.

As you can see, today's business suit has not changed much since then.

**Challenge** Describe traditional clothing for men or women from a culture you know well.
**Example:** *In Oman, women wear long, baggy pants. The weather is very hot, so clothing is usually light.*

**1. Look in your dictionary. Cross out the word that doesn't belong. Write the category.**

a. <u>Parts of a sewing machine</u>    needle    bobbin    ~~velvet~~    feed dog

b. _____    wool    pattern    leather    linen

c. _____    fringe    zipper    snap    hook and eye

d. _____    beads    sequins    appliqué    buckle

**2. Write the name of the material.**

a.      b.      c.      d.

a. ____<u>linen</u>____ This was the first woven material. Ancient people learned how to make thread from the blue-flowered flax plant and weave it into cloth. Today it is often used to make light jackets and suits.

c. _____ This material is made from the hair of sheep and some other animals. It is soft, warm, and even waterproof! It is often used to make coats, sweaters, mittens, and scarves.

b. _____ Very early, people learned how to make animal skins into this strong material. They rubbed the skins with fat to make them soft. Today it is often used to make shoes, boots, jackets, coats, belts, purses, and briefcases.

d. _____ For thousands of years only the Chinese knew how to make clothing from this beautiful material. The thread is made from the eggs of worms. The fabric is often used to make underwear, blouses, and ties.

**3. Circle the words to complete the conversation in a fabric store.**

**Isabel:** I'm making a blouse for my daughter.

**Kim:** What type of material are you thinking of?

**Isabel:** (Lace)/ Thread or maybe <u>cotton / ribbon</u>. I'm not sure yet.
       **a.**               **b.**

**Kim:** OK. What kind of <u>fabric / closure</u> are you going to use?
               **c.**

**Isabel:** <u>Buttons / Beads</u>.
      **d.**

**Kim:** Do you need a <u>rack / pattern</u>?
             **e.**

**Isabel:** No. I always like to design clothes myself.

**Kim:** Really? That's great. Do you use a <u>sewing machine / bobbin</u>?
                               **f.**

**Isabel:** No. I don't have one. I sew by <u>hand / machine</u>. All I need is a needle and <u>thread / feed dog</u>!
                                **g.**                             **h.**

4. **Look in your dictionary.** *True* or *False*? **Correct the underlined words in the false sentences.**

a. The sewing machine operators are sewing by ~~hand~~. *machine*          _____false_____

b. There are seven <u>bolts of fabric</u> in the garment factory.          _____

c. The shirts on the <u>rack</u> in the garment factory are purple, green, and blue.          _____

d. The <u>bobbin</u> is above the presser foot.          _____

e. The women in the fabric store are looking at <u>hook and loop fasteners</u>.          _____

5. **Write the name of the material.**

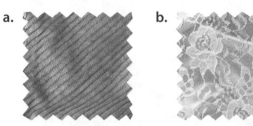

a.          b.          c.          d.

a. ___corduroy___ This material is made from cotton. It can have a wide or narrow pattern of raised ridges (vertical lines). It is often used to make jackets and pants.

c. _____ This strong material is usually made from cotton. In the 1800s, clothing maker Levi Strauss used it to make the first pair of blue jeans. Today this very popular material is worn all over the world, especially by young people.

b. _____ This material is usually made from linen thread. It has a beautiful open design, often of flowers or leaves. It is often sewn by hand, but it can also be made by machine. It is used for blouses, dresses, curtains, and tablecloths.

d. _____ This material comes from the chemistry laboratory, not from a plant or animal. It is very strong, and it is used to make stockings, panty hose, windbreakers, and many other items of clothing.

6. **What about you? What are you wearing today? Complete the chart.**

| Clothing Item | Material | Type of Closure | Type of Trim |
|---|---|---|---|
|  |  |  |  |
|  |  |  |  |
|  |  |  |  |
|  |  |  |  |

**Challenge** Design a piece of clothing. Draw it and write a description.

1. **Look in your dictionary. What can you use to do these things?**

   a. repair ripped clothing when you don't have needle and thread    _safety pin_

   b. cut material    _____

   c. hold pins and needles    _____

   d. remove threads from a hem    _____

   e. measure a sleeve or waistband    _____

   f. protect your finger when you sew    _____

   g. put clothes on while you make alterations    _____

2. **Circle the words to complete the instructions to the tailor.**

**TAILOR MADE**

Please make these alterations:

Take in the collar / (waistband).
　　　　　　　　　a.
Shorten / Lengthen the sleeves.
　　　　　　b.
The right cuff / pocket is
　　　　　　c.
missing—please sew it on.

Let out / Take in the skirt
　　　　d.
and lengthen / shorten it
　　　　　e.
so it's right at the knee.

**Challenge** Look at the sewing supplies in your dictionary. Choose five and describe their functions.
**Example:** *A thimble protects your finger.*

**1.** Look in your dictionary. What do you need to do the following?

a. make clothes softer ___*fabric softener*___

b. iron the clothes _____ and _____

c. sort the laundry _____

d. make clothes whiter _____

e. dry wet clothes without a dryer _____ and _____

f. dry wet clothes quickly _____

g. hang up clean clothes in your closet _____

**2.** Circle the words to complete the laundry room instructions.

**‖CLEANMACH**                                           ⚙ **QUICK WASH**

| **WASHING INSTRUCTIONS** | **DRYING INSTRUCTIONS** |
|---|---|

**WASHING INSTRUCTIONS**

**1.** Pour (laundry detergent)/ spray starch
      <u>                        </u>
                a.
into the <u>washer / dryer</u>.
            b.

**2.** <u>Load / Sort</u> the machine. DO NOT
        c.
OVERLOAD.

**3.** Choose the correct temperature.

**4.** Close door. <u>Hanger / Washer</u> will not
                    d.
operate with door open.

**5.** Insert coins or payment card into slot.

**6.** To add <u>bleach / dryer sheets</u>: wait until
                e.
<u>laundry basket / washer</u> has filled.
        f.

**7.** When the rinse light goes on, add

<u>fabric softener / laundry detergent</u> if
                g.
you want.

**DRYING INSTRUCTIONS**

**1.** Clean the <u>iron / lint trap</u> before
                h.
using the dryer.

**2.** <u>Load / Unload</u> the machine. DO NOT
        i.
OVERLOAD. Overloading causes

<u>dirty / wrinkled</u> clothes.
        j.

**3.** Add <u>dryer sheets / clothespins</u>
                k.
if you want.

**4.** Close door. <u>Dryer / Washer</u> will not
                    l.
operate with door open.

**5.** Choose the correct temperature.

**6.** Insert coins or payment card into slot.

Push *start* button.

**For service, call (800) 000-WASH**

**Challenge** Look at some of your clothing labels. Write the laundry instructions.

See page 288 for listening practice.

1. **Look in your dictionary.** *True* or *False*? **Correct the underlined words in the false sentences.**

   *electronics*

   a. The flyer advertises clothing, shoes, accessories, and ~~purses~~.   _____false_____

   b. A woman is <u>browsing</u> near the garage.   _____

   c. A <u>blue</u> sticker means the price is $2.00.   _____

   d. They have <u>new</u> clothing for sale.   _____

   e. A woman is bargaining for a <u>VCR</u>.   _____

2. **Complete the chart of items for sale at a garage sale.** ■ = $10.00, ● = $5.00, ★ = $2.00,

| Type of Item | Item | Price |
|---|---|---|
| Furniture | chair | $5.00 |
| | | |
| | jacket | |
| | | |
| Accessories | hat | |
| | | $2.00 |

3. **Circle the words to complete the conversations. Use information from Exercise 2.**

   **Donna:**   Hi. How much is this blue <u>jacket</u> / (sweatshirt)?
   **a.**

   **Eddy:**   It's <u>$2.00 / $5.00</u>.
   **b.**

   **Donna:**   But look, it's <u>stained / torn</u>.
   **c.**

   **Alya:**   Do you need a folding <u>chair / table</u>? This one's only $5.00.
   **d.**

   **Chen:**   Why don't you <u>bargain / browse</u> a little? They might take $2.00 for it.
   **e.**

   **Paz:**   What does the square <u>sticker / flyer</u> mean?
   **f.**

   **Lia:**   It means the price is <u>$10.00 / $5.00</u>.
   **g.**

   **Paz:**   That seems expensive for this <u>jacket / folding table</u>. It looks very old.
   **h.**

4. **What about you? Work with a partner. Imagine you are at a garage sale. Bargain for some of the items. Talk about the items in Exercise 2 or in your dictionary.**

5. **Look in your dictionary. Write the total for each group.**

| They bought . . . | They paid . . . . |
| --- | --- |
| **a.** an ironing board and a pair of cowboy boots | $10.00 |
| **b.** a pair of black shoes, two purses, and a pair of jeans | _____ |
| **c.** an iron, a grey coat, and a sports jacket | _____ |
| **d.** a pair of athletic shoes, a pink robe, and a purse | _____ |
| **e.** a hard hat, a pair of brown shoes, a blue T-shirt, and a sewing machine | _____ |

6. **Complete the article. Use the words in the box.**

| | | | | |
| --- | --- | --- | --- | --- |
| browse | clock radio | folding chair | used clothing | ~~garage sale~~ |
| bargain | stickers | flyers | folding card table | VCR |

# TIPS FOR A SUCCESSFUL ___Garage Sale___
a.

**1** Find things to sell. You have a new alarm clock, so you don't need that old

_____ anymore. You watch DVDs, so why keep that old
b.

_____?
c.

**2** Show the date, time, and address on your _____ .
d.

**3** Give information about sizes of _____—for example, size
e.

10 women's dresses.

**4** Set up your _____ and _____ early. People will arrive
f.                                       g.

before the sale starts.

**5** Use coloured _____ for prices. It's easier than price tags.
h.

**6** Let people just look around and _____ , but also ask them what they
i.

are looking for.

**7** People love to _____ , so don't insist on the full price. You want the
j.

money more than that old pair of shoes—that's why you're having the garage

sale, right?

**Challenge** Work with a group. Plan a garage sale for your class. Look at pages 53–56 and 86–87 in your
dictionary. Choose items to sell and decide on the prices. How will you use the money?

**1.** **Look in your dictionary. Complete the definitions.**

a. We use them to touch and to pick things up.       *fingers*

b. We use them to hear. _____

c. We use them to see. _____

d. We use it to smell. _____

e. It connects our head to our shoulders. _____

f. They are at the end of our feet. They help us walk. _____

g. It's the front part of our body, below the neck. _____

h. We use it to eat. _____

i. We have more than 100,000 of them on our head! They help keep our bodies warm. _____

**2.** **Complete. Read these as: "Hand is to finger as foot is to toe."**

a. hand : finger = foot : _____*toe*_____

b. leg : foot = arm : _____

c. hear : ears = see : _____

d. taste : tongue = smell : _____

e. pants : legs = shoes : _____

**3.** **What about you? What clothes or accessories do you use for these parts of your body?**

a. neck   *scarf, necklace, . . .* _____

b. head _____

c. eyes _____

d. ears _____

e. hands _____

f. legs _____

g. back _____

h. feet _____

4. **Look in your dictionary.** *True* or *False*?

a. The man sitting on the park bench has his left leg on his right knee. _____true_____

b. The man with the book is wearing a hat on his head. _____

c. The woman running has red hair. _____

d. The boy's arms are in front of him. _____

e. The boy isn't wearing anything on his feet. _____

5. **Circle the words to complete the article.**

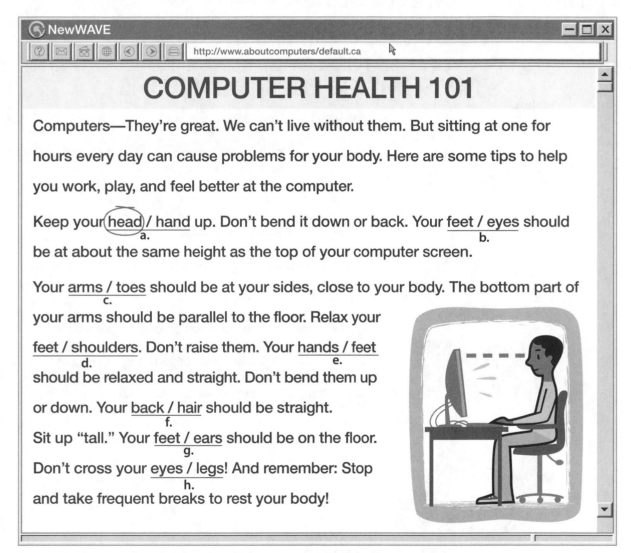

NewWAVE

http://www.aboutcomputers/default.ca

# COMPUTER HEALTH 101

Computers—They're great. We can't live without them. But sitting at one for hours every day can cause problems for your body. Here are some tips to help you work, play, and feel better at the computer.

Keep your (head) / hand up. Don't bend it down or back. Your feet / eyes should
a.                                                                b.
be at about the same height as the top of your computer screen.

Your arms / toes should be at your sides, close to your body. The bottom part of
c.
your arms should be parallel to the floor. Relax your

feet / shoulders. Don't raise them. Your hands / feet
d.                                                    e.
should be relaxed and straight. Don't bend them up

or down. Your back / hair should be straight.
f.
Sit up "tall." Your feet / ears should be on the floor.
g.
Don't cross your eyes / legs! And remember: Stop
h.
and take frequent breaks to rest your body!

---

**Challenge**  Which type of doctor should you see for problems with the following body parts?

feet  _____

eyes  _____

ears  _____

Look online or ask someone you know.

**1. Look in your dictionary. Cross out the word that doesn't belong. Write the category.**

a. <u>The Arm, Hand, and Fingers</u>    elbow   ~~shin~~   wrist

b. _____    ankle   heel   knuckle

c. _____    finger   see   hear

d. _____    gums   teeth   forehead

**2. Circle the words to complete the instructions.**

# YOGA IS A VERY OLD FORM OF EXERCISE AND MEDITATION.
## TRY SOME OF THESE POSITIONS.

**PALMING** Rub your (palms) / gums together until your
                         **a.**
hands feel warm. Then hold them over your mouth / eyes.
                                                **b.**

**BEE BREATH** Place your hands / legs gently on your
                            **c.**
knees / face: thumbs / teeth on your ears, first finger / knuckle
   **d.**         **e.**                       **f.**
on the eyelashes / eyebrows of your closed eyes, second on
                  **g.**
your nose, third and fourth on your top and bottom

lips / eyelids. When you breathe out, gently close your ears
      **h.**
with your thumbs and put your tongue / bone against the top
                                    **i.**
of your throat / mouth to make a "zzzz" sound.
           **j.**

**THE BOW** Lie on your abdomen / artery. Reach back and
                       **k.**
hold your shins / ankles. Pull your thighs / elbows and
         **l.**               **m.**
chest / buttocks off the floor. Your lip / pelvis is on the floor.
   **n.**                         **o.**

**THE MOON** Kneel with your buttocks / rib cage on your
                                **p.**
arms / heels. Put your hands / feet against your
   **q.**              **r.**
breast / lower back and hold your right wrist / vein. Bend
      **s.**                           **t.**
forward until your chin / forehead touches the floor.
                   **u.**

**3. Read the article. Label the foot with the matching parts of the body.**

Some people use reflexology to stay healthy. They believe that by pressing certain parts of the foot, you can help certain parts of the body. For example, if you have a headache, you should press the top of your big toe.

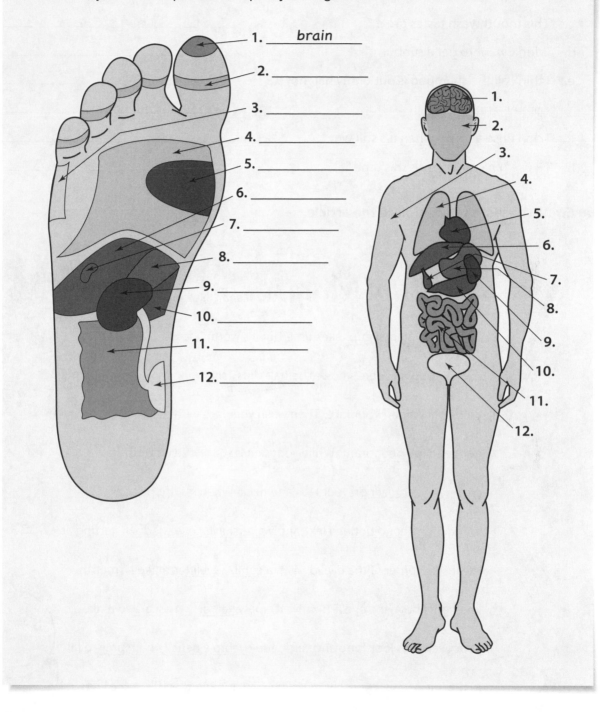

1. ___brain___
2. _____
3. _____
4. _____
5. _____
6. _____
7. _____
8. _____
9. _____
10. _____
11. _____
12. _____

1.
2.
3.
4.
5.
6.
7.
8.
9.
10.
11.
12.

**4. What about you? What activities do you do to relax and stay healthy? What parts of the body are these activities good for? Write at least five sentences.**

**Challenge** Write instructions for your favourite exercise.

1. **Look in your dictionary. What is each person doing?**

   a. "This air is really hot."                           _____drying her hair_____

   b. "This cap really keeps my hair dry!"                _____

   c. "This mouthwash tastes great."                      _____

   d. "I don't want to get a sunburn."                    _____

   e. "I think all the shampoo is out of my hair now."    _____

   f. "I prefer a razor."                                 _____

   g. "I don't use a brush when it's still wet."          _____

   h. "I'll use pink on my nails this time."              _____

2. **Circle the words to complete the article.**

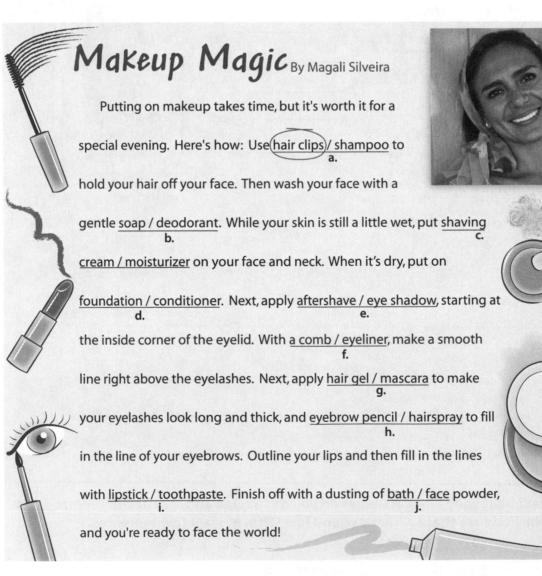

# Makeup Magic By Magali Silveira

Putting on makeup takes time, but it's worth it for a

special evening. Here's how: Use (hair clips) / shampoo to
                                      a.

hold your hair off your face. Then wash your face with a

gentle soap / deodorant. While your skin is still a little wet, put shaving
          b.                                                             c.

cream / moisturizer on your face and neck. When it's dry, put on

foundation / conditioner. Next, apply aftershave / eye shadow, starting at
       d.                                        e.

the inside corner of the eyelid. With a comb / eyeliner, make a smooth
                                              f.

line right above the eyelashes. Next, apply hair gel / mascara to make
                                                    g.

your eyelashes look long and thick, and eyebrow pencil / hairspray to fill
                                                   h.

in the line of your eyebrows. Outline your lips and then fill in the lines

with lipstick / toothpaste. Finish off with a dusting of bath / face powder,
        i.                                                 j.

and you're ready to face the world!

**3. Complete the crossword puzzle.**

|   |   |   |   |   |   |   | ¹r |   |   |   |   |   |   |   |
|---|---|---|---|---|---|---|---|---|---|---|---|---|---|---|
|   | ²◯ |   | ³ |   |   |   | a |   |   |   |   |   |   |   |
|   |   |   |   |   |   |   | z |   |   |   |   |   |   |   |
|   |   |   |   |   |   |   | o |   | ⁴ |   |   |   |   |   |
|   |   |   |   |   | ⁵ | r |   |   | ◯ |   |   |   |   |   |
|   | ⁶ |   |   |   |   |   |   |   |   |   |   |   |   |   |
| ⁷ |   |   |   | ◯ |   |   |   |   |   |   |   | ⁸ |   |   |
|   |   |   |   |   |   | ⁹ |   | ◯ |   |   |   |   |   |   |
|   |   |   |   |   |   |   |   |   |   |   |   |   |   |   |
|   | ◯ |   |   |   |   |   |   |   |   |   |   |   |   |   |
|   | ¹⁰ |   | ¹¹ |   |   |   |   |   |   |   |   |   |   |   |
|   |   |   |   |   |   |   |   |   |   | ¹² |   |   |   |   |
|   |   |   | ¹³ |   |   |   | ◯ |   |   |   |   |   |   |   |
|   |   | ◯ |   |   |   |   |   |   |   | ◯ |   |   |   |   |

**Across**

2. You can put this on your skin when you finish shaving.

5. Use this to make sure your hair is smooth and tangle-free.

7. You can keep your hair in place with this.

9. Try to use this after every meal.

10. At the end of the day, use makeup _____.

13. Use this in the shower after you have shampooed your hair.

**Down**

1. Be careful while using this _____ it's sharp.

3. This can make your eyes look bigger.

4. Use this to wash your hair.

6. This will make your eyelashes look longer and darker.

8. Put this on your skin to avoid getting burned.

11. Rinse with some of this after brushing your teeth.

12. Use this along with a brush to make sure your hair looks neat and tidy.

Now use the circled letters to answer this question:

What can you take to relax?  ___  ___ ___ ___  ___ ___ ___ ___

**4. What about you? What is your personal hygiene routine in the morning? List the steps.**

Example: *First, I . . .*

**Challenge** Write detailed instructions for one of the following tasks:

Washing and styling your hair          Flossing and brushing your teeth

Shaving          Doing your nails

**See page 289 for listening practice.**

1. **Look in your dictionary. Which symptom or injury are they talking about?**

   a. "This one in the back hurts."                          _toothache_

   b. "The thermometer says 39."                          _____

   c. "I ate too much ice cream."                          _____

   d. "Next time I'll wear gloves to rake the leaves."    _____

   e. "Press on it to stop the bleeding."                 _____

2. **Circle the words to complete the article.**

   http://www.abouthealthhints/default.ca

   # HOME HEALTH HINTS
   ### Sick or injured? Try some of these tips:

   ★ After a day in the sun, put oatmeal in your bath water for a swollen finger /(sunburn)
   **a.**

   ★ A sprained / cut ankle or wrist is a common sports injury. Use RICE—Rest, Ice,
   **b.**
   Compression (wrapping a tight elastic bandage), and Elevation (raising the injured part).

   ★ Rub deodorant on blisters / insect bites caused by bees or spiders.
   **c.**

   ★ Eating bad food can make you feel nauseous. You might even throw up / sneeze.
   **d.**
   Drinking warm cola helps you feel better.

   ★ It's hard to swallow with a backache / sore throat. Soft ice cream helps.
   **e.**

   ★ Put an ice pack on a rash / bruise the first day. After 24 hours,
   **f.**
   use a heating pad.

   ★ For headaches / nasal congestion, take hot baths and drink
   **g.**
   fluids to breathe more regularly.

   ★ It's not bad to cough / feel dizzy—it gets bacteria out of
   **h.**
   your lungs. But an over-the-counter syrup helps you stop
   when you want to sleep.

   FIRST AID KIT

   **Remember:** These problems can be serious. If you feel very bad or if the problem continues or gets worse, see your doctor or other health professional.

3. **What about you? What do you do when you have a stomach ache? an earache? a rash?**
   **Example:** *When I have a stomach ache, I drink tea.*

   **Challenge** Find out about blisters. What are they? Write about how to prevent and treat them.

**See page 290 for listening practice.**

**1. Look in your dictionary. Complete the chart.**

| Illness or Condition | What is it? | Contagious? | What are some symptoms? |
|---|---|---|---|
| a. *arthritis* | pain in the joints | No | painful, swollen, stiff joints, often in hands, feet, shoulders, and hips |
| b. | a medical condition | No | tight feeling or pain in chest, difficulty breathing, wheezing, coughing |
| c. | a common childhood disease | Yes | red, itchy rash on face, body, and inside throat that turns into blisters; fever |
| d. | a very common infection of the nose, throat, etc. | Yes | runny or stuffy nose, itchy or sore throat, cough, sneezing, low fever, tiredness, watery eyes |
| e. | an illness of the brain, more common in older people | No | confusion, problems with memory, language, and thinking; personality changes |
| f. | a condition caused by the pancreas not making enough insulin | No | tiredness, thirst, increased hunger, weight loss, blurred vision |
| g. | an infection most common in infants and children | No | nervousness, earache, "full" feeling in the ear, fever, difficulty hearing |
| h. | a condition often caused by hard and narrow arteries | No | (Often no symptoms in beginning) Later: chest pains, heart attack |
| i. | the virus that causes AIDS | Yes | (In the beginning) swollen glands, sore throat, fever, skin rash |
| j. | a common childhood disease | Yes | fever, dry cough, runny nose, red eyes, tiny spots inside mouth, red rash on forehead and around ears, and, later, whole body |
| k. | a childhood disease | Yes | painful, swollen glands (between ear and jaw) on one or both sides of face, fever, tiredness |

**Based on information from:** Mayoclinic.com (1998–2007 Mayo Foundation for Medical Education and Research).

**2. What about you? Check (✓) the illnesses or medical conditions you had as a child.**

☐ measles    ☐ mumps    ☐ chicken pox    ☐ ear infection    ☐ allergy

**Challenge** Find out about high blood pressure. What is it? Is it contagious? What are some symptoms?

1. **Look in your dictionary. What should the people buy at the pharmacy? Circle the answers.**

   a. "I need to keep my arm still."            Buy a cast / (a sling.)

   b. "I have a backache."            Try a heating pad / a humidifier.

   c. "I have a sore throat."            Get an antacid / throat lozenges.

   d. "My nose is stuffed."            Try an inhaler / nasal spray.

   e. "I'm coughing and sneezing a lot."            Buy cold tablets / eye drops.

   f. "I have a bad headache."            Get an air purifier / a pain reliever.

2. **Read the prescription labels. Write the type of medicine after each sentence. Use the words in the box.**

   | capsules | cough syrup | ointment |
   |---|---|---|

   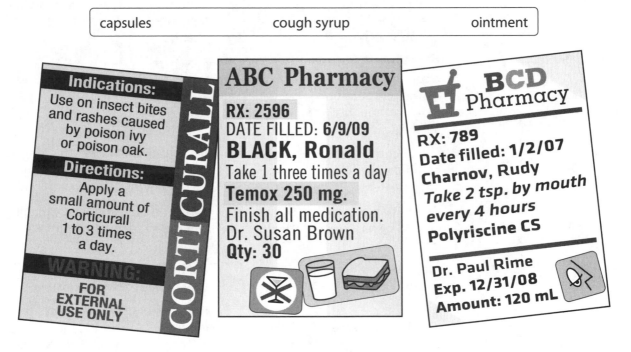

   a. You can use this three times a day. __ointment__

   b. It's a liquid. _____

   c. The dosage is one, three times a day. _____

   d. This is an over-the-counter medication. _____

   e. Take this for ten days. _____

   f. The expiration date has already passed. _____

   g. Don't take this by mouth. _____

   h. Don't take this on an empty stomach. _____

   i. Don't drive or operate heavy machinery when taking this medicine. _____

**3. Circle the words to complete the diary entries.**

Feb 11—Woke up in the hospital with crutches / (casts) on both my
    a.
legs! I can't remember anything about the accident. Jim's OK,
thank goodness. He has a sling / walker on his arm, but that's all.
    b.
Here comes the nurse . . .

Feb 14—Jim visited me today and pushed me around the hospital in
a wheelchair / humidifier.
    c.

March 24—They took off the casts / canes. Now I can hold my
    d.
air purifier / walker in front of me and move around on my own.
    e.
After a couple of weeks, I'll be ready for a pair of crutches / capsules.
    f.

April 8—I can stand, but I have to learn to use my legs again. The
exercises hurt a lot. I put an antacid / a heating pad on my painful
    g.
muscles after therapy. At first I used pain relievers / throat lozenges,
    h.
but I don't like to take medicine.

April 28—Tomorrow I go home! It's been more than two months!
I still need to use a cane / an inhaler to get around, but it won't be
    i.
long now until I can walk without any help.

**4. What about you? What over-the-counter medicines can you find at your local pharmacy?
Look at some labels and make a chart like the one below.**

| Type | Dosage | Indications | Warnings |
|------|--------|-------------|----------|
| tablets | 1–2 tablets every 4–6 hours | to prevent nausea | Do not take if you have a breathing problem. |

**1. Look in your dictionary. What are the people doing?**

a. "This book is good."                              _getting bed rest_

b. "I have to take one capsule two times a day."    _____

c. "This is hard exercise!"                          _____

d. "I need to see a doctor. My back really hurts."   _____

e. "I'd like some more salad."                       _____

f. "That's OK, Doctor. It only hurt for a second!"   _____

**2. Read the doctor's notes and look at the picture. Is the patient following medical advice? What is he doing? What is he NOT doing?**

**From the Desk of Dr. Wise**

a. Get bed rest.

b. Drink fluids.

c. Take medicine.

d. Eat a healthy diet.

e. Don't smoke!!!

a. _He isn't getting bed rest._

b. _____

c. _____

d. _____

e. _____

**3. Look in your dictionary. What's the problem?**

a. "I can't read this. Why are the words so small?"      <u>vision problems</u>

b. "Ow! My leg really hurts!"      _____

c. "I feel sad all the time."      _____

d. "What? Could you repeat that again, please?"      _____

e. "Help! I have too much to do, and no time to do it!"      _____

**4. Circle the words to complete the pamphlets.**

Do you have

(Vision Problems)/ Hearing Loss?
**a.**

Are you having trouble reading this?

It may be time for new

<u>glasses / hearing aids.</u>
**b.**
Or maybe you like <u>contact lenses / fluids.</u>
**c.**
Visit an <u>audiologist / optometrist</u> and have
**d.**
your eyes checked.

Are you feeling

tired and sad most of the time?

Maybe you are one of the more than

20 million people suffering from

<u>depression / stress.</u> Don't despair!
**e.**
See a <u>physical therapist / therapist</u> for
**f.**
<u>physical / talk</u> therapy. You can also
**g.**
<u>get immunized / join a support group.</u>
**h.**

**5. What about you? What do you do when you feel stress?**

**Example:** _When I feel stress, I exercise._

**Challenge** How do you take care of your health? What do you do? What don't you do?
Write two paragraphs.

See page 292 for listening practice.

1. **Look in your dictionary. What happened? Complete each sentence.**

   a. The little girl in the laundry room _____*swallowed poison*_____.

   b. The woman in the snow _____.

   c. The man with the toaster _____.

   d. The boy in the doctor's office _____.

   e. The man boiling water in the kitchen _____.

   f. After her car hit a tree, the woman on the ground _____.

   g. The woman near the ambulance _____ when the paramedics arrived.

2. **Circle the words to complete the article.**

   ## How Safe Are You At Home?

   Not very. As you probably know, most accidents occur at home. The chart below shows the

   number of people who were injured at home in just one year using everyday products. More than

   two million people (fell)/ were in shock while using stairs, steps, or bicycles. Falls also caused
         **a.**

   some of the 301,375 injuries in the bathtub or shower. How else are people getting hurt?

   Some people drowned / choked or burned themselves / got frostbite while bathing. More than
         **b.**          **c.**

   30,000 people cut themselves and bled / couldn't breathe while using razors, and other people
             **d.**

   burned themselves / overdosed on drugs or had a heart attack / an allergic reaction (such as a
         **e.**          **f.**

   skin rash) while taking medication.

   | Product | Estimated Injuries |
   |---|---|
   | stairs, steps | 2,028,968 |
   | bicycles | 539,642 |
   | bathtubs and showers | 301,375 |
   | TVs | 50,021 |
   | stoves and ovens | 43,347 |
   | razors and shavers | 33,532 |

**Challenge** Look at the chart in Exercise 2. How do you think people hurt themselves using TVs and irons?

**1. Look in your dictionary. Complete the information in the first aid manual.**

**Always keep your medicine chest or first aid kit well supplied.** Include:

a. _____gauze_____ for holding sterile pads in place, or (if sterile) for covering cuts

b. _____ for removing pieces of glass or wood from the skin

c. _____ for preventing movement of a broken or sprained arm, finger, etc.

d. _____ for covering large cuts and burns

e. _____ for holding pads and gauze in place

f. _____ for preventing infection of small cuts

g. _____ for covering small cuts

h. _____ for pouring on a new cut to help prevent infection

i. _____ for putting around a sprained ankle

j. _____ for treating rashes and allergic skin reactions

k. _____ for reducing pain and swelling

l. _____ for finding medical information

**Note:** A deep cut that continues to bleed may need _____ . Contact your doctor or go
m.
to a clinic or hospital emergency room. People with special medical conditions such as diabetes,
heart disease, or serious allergies, should wear a _____ to identify the problem.
n.

**2. Write the name of the life-saving techniques. Use the words in the box.**

| CPR | ~~Heimlich manoeuvre~~ | rescue breathing |
|-----|----------------------|------------------|

a. _Heimlich manoeuvre_ Named after the doctor who invented it, this technique is used on people who are choking on food or other objects.

b. _____ Performed mouth to mouth, this technique is used on people who have stopped breathing.

c. _____ Involves mouth-to-mouth breathing and chest compressions on people who have stopped breathing. Special training is needed.

**Challenge** Are there first aid items that you use that are not in your dictionary? Write about them.
**Example:** *I use vitamin E for small kitchen burns.*

1. **Look in your dictionary. What are the people talking about?**

   a. "Can you please fill <u>this</u> out for me?"                    <u>health history form</u>

   b. "According to <u>this</u>, your pressure is fine."              _____

   c. "Relax. <u>This</u> will only hurt for a second."              _____

   d. "According to <u>this</u>, you have a low fever."              _____

   e. "When I listen through <u>this</u>, your lungs sound clear."   _____

2. **Complete the pamphlet. Use the words in the box.**

   | | | |
   |---|---|---|
   | ~~appointment~~ | check your blood pressure | draw blood |
   | examination table | examine your eyes | examine your throat |
   | health history form | health card | listen to your heart |
   | patient | nurse | receptionist |

   # Dr. Gregory Sarett

   **What to Expect During Your** <u>Appointment</u>
   a.

   Before you see the doctor, the _____ will ask to see your
   b.

   _____. If you are a new _____, she will also ask you to
   c.                                         d.

   complete a _____ . Then a _____ will check your
   e.                                           f.

   height and weight. She will also _____ to see if it is too high or too low.
   g.

   Then Dr. Sarett, using a stethoscope, will _____ while you are on the
   h.

   _____. He will use the stethoscope to listen to your lungs and abdomen,
   i.

   too. Next comes the vision exam. Using an ophthalmoscope (an instrument with a light), the

   doctor will _____ . He will also _____ , nose, and ears.
   j.                                            k.

   He may do other tests, too. He may, for example, _____ and send it to a lab
   l.

   for testing. At the end of the exam, he will discuss the results and make recommendations.

**Challenge** Look in your dictionary. Write about Mr. Zolmar's doctor's appointment.
   **Begin:** *Andre had a doctor's appointment. First, the receptionist . . .*

See page 293 for listening practice.

**1. Look in your dictionary. What is the dentist or dental hygienist doing?**

a. "I'm getting all the plaque off."  _cleaning teeth_

b. "I'm almost finished. Then I'll fill it."  _____

c. "This will give us a good picture of that tooth."  _____

d. "You won't feel any pain after this."  _____

e. "It's almost out now."  _____

**2. Complete the pamphlet. Use the words in the box.**

| cavities | crown | dental instruments | dentist | dentures |
|----------|-------|--------------------|---------|----------|
| fillings | gum disease | hygienist | ~~plaque~~ | |

COMMON
DENTAL
QUESTIONS

**Q:** What is _____plaque_____ ?
a.

**A:** A substance that forms on your teeth.

After it gets hard, only a

_____ or dental
b.

_____ using special
c.

_____ can remove it.
d.

**Q:** I never get _____.
e.

Do I still need to make appointments

every year?

**A:** Yes. Dentists also check for other

problems, including cancer and

_____, the main
f.

reason for tooth loss. The goal is to keep

your own teeth and avoid needing

_____.
g.

**Q:** I have a lot of old silver and gold

_____. Is there
h.

anything I can do about their

appearance?

**A:** Yes. Dentists can place a

_____ over a tooth
i.

with old fillings.

**Challenge** Write two more questions about dental care like the ones in Exercise 2. Try to find the answers.

# Hospital

**1. Look in your dictionary. *True* or *False*? Correct the underlined words in the false sentences.**

RN

a. The ~~RPN~~ is checking the patient's IV drip. — false

b. The administrator is putting an ID bracelet on a new patient. — ____

c. The pediatrician's patient isn't wearing a hospital gown. — ____

d. The surgical nurse is discussing a patient's food. — ____

e. There's a medical waste disposal inside the lab. — ____

f. There's medication on the patient's over-bed table. — ____

g. The bed pan is next to the hospital bed. — ____

h. The volunteer is drawing blood for a blood test. — ____

**2. Circle the words to complete the information from a hospital pamphlet.**

## The Operation—What to Expect
### Surgery is stressful, but it can help to know what to expect.

In most cases, orderlies will take you to the hospital's emergency / (operating) room on an
**a.**
over-bed table / gurney. They will then carefully move you to the ambulance / operating table,
**b.**                                                                        **c.**
where the surgery will take place. Your surgical team (the anesthesiologist, surgical

nurses, and, of course, the dietician / surgeon) will be there. In order to avoid infection,
**d.**
they will wear surgical caps / gowns on their heads and sterile surgical gloves / stretchers
**e.**                                                            **f.**
on their hands. All the instruments will be sterilized, too. During

the operation, the administrator / anesthesiologist will monitor
**g.**
all your medical charts / vital signs (blood pressure, breathing,
**h.**
and heart rate). A call button / An IV, attached to a vein in
**i.**
your arm, will provide you with fluids, and, if necessary,

medication. Ask your doctor how long it will take to recover

from your operation. Remember: Knowing what to expect

will help you feel better!

120

3. **Look at the chart. Write the numbers to complete the sentences.**

| Doctors by Specialty and Sex in Canada | | |
|---|---|---|
| Specialty | Male | Female |
| anesthesiology | 2028 | 754 |
| cardiology | 934 | 174 |
| obstetrics / gynecology | 964 | 796 |
| ophthalmology | 903 | 218 |
| pediatrics | 1161 | 1112 |
| psychiatry | 2606 | 1639 |
| radiology | 1621 | 572 |

**Based on information from**: The Canadian Medical Association.

a. There are _____ *218* _____ female eye doctors in Canada.

b. The number of male eye doctors is _____.

c. There are _____ female doctors who are X-ray specialists.

d. _____ male doctors are heart specialists.

e. _____ males doctors specialize in mental illness (for example, depression).

f. _____ female doctors specialize in women's health care.

g. _____ male doctors specialize in children's medicine.

4. **What about you? Would you prefer a man or a woman? Check (✓) the columns.**

| | Male | Female | No Preference |
|---|---|---|---|
| **a.** internist | | | |
| **b.** cardiologist | | | |
| **c.** psychiatrist | | | |
| **d.** ophthalmologist | | | |
| **e.** orderly | | | |
| **f.** obstetrician | | | |
| **g.** pediatrician | | | |
| **h.** nurse | | | |

**Challenge** Find out the name of other kinds of medical specialists. What do they do?
    **Example:** *An orthopedist is a bone doctor.*

Go to page 247 for Another Look (Unit 6).  |  See page 294 for listening practice.

**1. Look in your dictionary. *True* or *False*?**

a. The <u>aerobics</u> class starts at 10:00.   <u>    true    </u>

b. There's a <u>fat-free</u> cooking demonstration.   <u>            </u>

c. The health fair opened at <u>9:00</u>.   <u>            </u>

d. An acupuncture treatment is <u>free</u>.   <u>            </u>

e. You can buy <u>vitamins</u> at the Good Foods booth.   <u>            </u>

f. The medical screening is <u>free</u>.   <u>            </u>

g. A nurse is <u>taking</u> a woman's <u>temperature</u>.   <u>            </u>

h. The eye exam is <u>$2.00</u>.   <u>            </u>

i. There's a nutrition label <u>demonstration</u>.   <u>            </u>

**2. Write the letter of the false sentences in Exercise 1. Make them true.**

<u>  b.  </u>   <u>There's a sugar-free cooking demonstration.                    </u>

<u>    </u>   <u>                                                                    </u>

<u>    </u>   <u>                                                                    </u>

<u>    </u>   <u>                                                                    </u>

<u>    </u>   <u>                                                                    </u>

**3. Circle the words to complete the journal entry.**

Today, I went to a <u>booth</u> / (<u>health fair</u>) at a local <u>clinic</u> / <u>demonstration</u>. I am so glad I went!
                    **a.**                                        **b.**
At the <u>hatha yoga</u> / <u>medical screening</u> booth, I found out that my <u>blood pressure</u> / <u>pulse</u> is a little
                **c.**                                                        **d.**
high—135 over 80. The nurse told me that exercise helps, so I watched a very interesting

<u>acupuncture</u> / <u>aerobic exercise</u> class. It looked easy and fun, and I'll ask my doctor if it's OK for me.
                **e.**
Next, I had an <u>ear</u> / <u>eye</u> exam and found out I can see perfectly—no problems there! I wanted to
                **f.**
try an acupuncture <u>exam</u> / <u>treatment</u>, but the needles scared me a little. Maybe next time.
                        **g.**
The last booth had a lecture about <u>nutrition labels</u> / <u>vitamins</u>—very interesting! I'm going to start
                                        **h.**
reading them when I shop for food.

**4. What about you? Do you exercise? Is exercise important to you? Why or why not? Tell a classmate.**

**5. Look in your dictionary. Complete the flyer.**

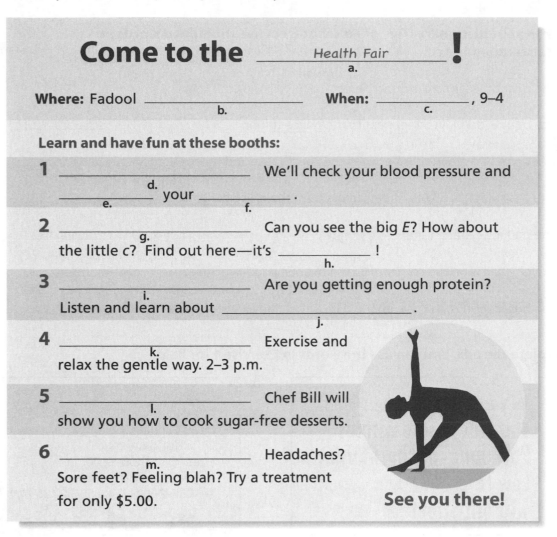

# Come to the ___Health Fair___ !
                          a.

**Where:** Fadool _____     **When:** _____ , 9–4
                          b.                                c.

**Learn and have fun at these booths:**

**1** _____ We'll check your blood pressure and
        d.
_____ your _____ .
   e.                    f.

**2** _____ Can you see the big *E*? How about
            g.
the little *c*? Find out here—it's _____ !
                                        h.

**3** _____ Are you getting enough protein?
            i.
Listen and learn about _____ .
                                    j.

**4** _____ Exercise and
            k.
relax the gentle way. 2–3 p.m.

**5** _____ Chef Bill will
            l.
show you how to cook sugar-free desserts.

**6** _____ Headaches?
            m.
Sore feet? Feeling blah? Try a treatment
for only $5.00.

**See you there!**

**6. Where can you hear the following things? Match.**

__2__ **a.** "Bend your left leg. Raise your right arm."      **1.** nutrition lecture

____ **b.** "Now cover your left eye, and read the first row."  **2.** yoga class

____ **c.** "Seventy-two beats per minute. Excellent."          **3.** acupuncture treatment

____ **d.** "You can make this delicious dessert with no sugar!"  **4.** medical screening

____ **e.** "Notice the serving size. It's only a half cup."     **5.** cooking demonstration

____ **f.** "Just relax. The needle won't hurt."                **6.** eye exam

**Challenge** Work with a classmate. Imagine you are planning a health fair. Look at the activities
in the word box below and the ones in your dictionary. What are some activities that you
will include? Why?

| | | |
|---|---|---|
| bicycle safety | talking to your doctor | quitting smoking |
| having a healthy back | making a first aid kit | having healthy teeth |

1. **Look in your dictionary. *True* or *False*? Correct the underlined words in the false statements.**

   a. The post office is across from the ~~bank~~. *courthouse*         _____*false*_____

   b. The bank is on Main Street next to the <u>police station</u>.      _____

   c. The Chinese restaurant is between the courthouse and the <u>fire station</u>.    _____

   d. The gas station is on 6th Street, across from the <u>office building</u>.     _____

   e. The parking garage is next to the <u>hotel</u>.     _____

   f. The <u>city hall</u> is on the corner of Grand Avenue and Main Street.     _____

   g. The <u>bus station</u> is on the corner of Elm Street and Grand Avenue.     _____

2. **Complete the ads. You can use the words in Exercise 1 for help.**

a.
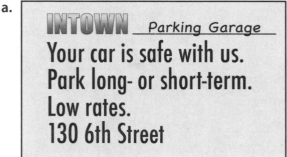

**INTOWN** _Parking Garage_
Your car is safe with us.
Park long- or short-term.
Low rates.
130 6th Street

b.

Down City _____
201 Elm Street
International Cooking
Open for dinner
Tues–Sun 6:00–9:00
Reservations suggested
Tel 555-2634   Fax 555-2635

c.

*Miram* _____
Medicine with a Heart
Patient information 555-4313
Emergency service 555-4310
Visit our website at www.mh.ca.

d.

*Parkside* _____
12 minutes from the airport
100 new non-smoking rooms
Free breakfast
Free cable TV and Internet connection
555-2956  www.ps.ca

e.
**Rick's** _____
Open every day from 6 a.m. to midnight.
Best car wash in town!
Just 2 minutes from the highway

f.

The People's Savings _____
"Where your money is our business!"
Downtown Branch:
210 Main Street
24-hour ATM
555-6666

3. **Look in your dictionary. Where can you go to do the following?**

   a. have lunch                              the restaurant

   b. borrow a book or DVD                    _____

   c. visit a sick friend                     _____

   d. rest for a night                        _____

   e. get on the 8:04 p.m. bus to Waterloo    _____

   f. apply for a driver's licence            _____

   g. report a crime                          _____

   h. get married                             _____

4. **Circle the words to complete the notes.**

   a.
   I went to the (bank) / city hall
   to get some money.
   I'll be home around 4:00.

   Dan

   b.
   I'm driving Suzie to the
   bus station / hospital.
   She's taking the 8:40 to
   Greenville. See you soon.

   Alicia

   c.
   It's now 3:00. I'm going to the
   gas station / parking garage.
   The tires need air.
   I'll be back soon.

   M

   d.
   I needed to go to the
   office building / post office
   to buy some stamps.
   Also, your Mom called.

   R

5. **What about you? Work with a partner. Complete the chart with information about your community.**

   | Place | Street Location |
   |---|---|
   | library | |
   | courthouse | |
   | bus station | |
   | city hall | |
   | fire station | |
   | police station | |
   | post office | |

**Challenge** Look in a phone book or at an online phone directory.
Find the names of a hotel, a bank, and a hospital in your community.

1.  **Look in your dictionary. Where can you find these things? (Do not use *supermarket* or *shopping mall*.)**

    **a.** a sandwich        _____coffee shop_____

    **b.** a cake        _____

    **c.** paper and pens        _____

    **d.** the best view of the city        _____

    **e.** tickets for a football game        _____

    **f.** English classes        _____ or _____

    **g.** a new couch        _____

    **h.** a used car        _____

    **i.** paint for your living room        _____

    **j.** a room for the night        _____

    **k.** a place to exercise        _____

2.  **Complete the tourist information. Use the words in the box.**

    | | | | |
    |---|---|---|---|
    | bakeries | stadium | ~~churches~~ | cemetery |
    | shopping mall | skyscraper | coffee shops | schools |

    # PLACES OF INTEREST IN
    # MONTRÉAL

    **Notre-Dame Basilica** Built in 1829, this is one of the city's most famous _churches_. Tourists
                        **a.**

    often visit to see the stained glass windows showing Montreal's history.

    **Olympic** _____ This sports centre was originally built for the 1976 Olympic Games. Now, you
          **b.**

    can go there to watch sporting events, take a tour of the building, or go for a swim in one of the pools.

    **Biosphere** With a height of 61 metres, this giant structure towers over Parc Jean-Drapeau. The

    sphere was originally the United States' contribution to the 1967 World Exhibition, and was later

    donated to the city of Montreal. It is now a science museum that is very popular destination for

    children from many Quebec _____.
                        **c.**

**Notre-Dame-des-Neiges** is the largest _____ in Canada and the third-largest in
<sub>d.</sub>
North America. Many notable people are buried within its beautiful park setting, including some
famous poets, artists, sports figures, and politicians. In order to preserve this historic place, the
Canadian government has declared it a national historic site.

**World Trade Centre Montreal** This centre is the size of an entire city block, and is made up of old
buildings that have been renovated and joined together into one large complex. Montreal is a city
known for its unique stores and boutiques, so it's no surprise that the centre contains a
_____ along with restaurants and a dining hall.
<sub>e.</sub>

**1000 de La Gauchetière** This _____ is the tallest building in Montreal, at 205 metres. It
<sub>f.</sub>
could not have been built any higher, because the city does not allow buildings to reach above the top
of Mount Royal.

**Saint Catherine Street** Take a walk down this busy street to get a sense of the city. You'll see lots
of interesting people and shops. Be sure to stop in at some of the _____ and _____
<sub>g.</sub>     <sub>h.</sub>
along the way to sample some fantastic desserts and cappuccinos.

3.   **What about you? Would you want to live near the following things? Check (✓) the boxes.**

| | Yes | No | Why? |
|---|---|---|---|
| construction site | ☐ | ☐ | _____ |
| school | ☐ | ☐ | _____ |
| supermarket | ☐ | ☐ | _____ |
| factory | ☐ | ☐ | _____ |
| Other: _____ | ☐ | ☐ | _____ |

**Challenge** Make a list of places for tourists to visit in your city or town. Include information about each
of the places.

**See page 295 for listening practice.**

**1. Look in your dictionary. Where can a shopper use these coupons?**

**BARGAIN PACK COUPON**
**FREE**
Burger, Fries, and Medium Drink
When you buy a lunch combo at the regular price.

a. _fast food restaurant_

**MANUFACTURER'S COUPON**
**SAVE $1.50** When you buy two boxes of Nuts 'n Bran or Apple Oatmeal Cereal
Apple Oatmeal **CEREAL**   **Nuts 'n Bran**

b. _____

**BRITE AID**
**CHILDREN'S COLD MEDICINES**
½ **PRICE** Savings Coupon
**This Month Only** Offer expires 11/30

c. _____

**STORE COUPON**
Men's Haircuts Just **$15**
with this coupon
(first time customers only)

d. _____

**BARGAIN PACK COUPON**
Fall Special
**20% OFF**
All shirts cleaned and pressed
Not valid after 11/30

e. _____

**Buy 12 Get 1 FREE** STORE COUPON
(with a FREE cup of coffee) Baked Fresh Daily!

f. _____

**2. Where can you hear these conversations? Use your dictionary if you need help.**

**Dad:** I can't read the menu.
**Tim:** Drive forward a little.
a. _drive-through window_

**Bob:** Where's the bleach?
**Kim:** On top of the dryer.
c. _____

**Anne:** How much change do I need?
**Clerk:** Two quarters for ten pages.
b. _____

**Pete:** Do you get Italian papers?
**Owner:** *Corriere della Sera* comes on Tuesdays.
d. _____

**3.** Look at the picture. <u>Underline</u> six more mistakes in the newspaper article.

### LOCAL NEWS

Last week, Fran Bates rode her bike into Mel Smith's <u>car</u>. There were no injuries. A pedestrian entered the video store with a dog and was asked to leave. Two children opened the mailbox on Elm Street. Fire Chief Dane closed it and called their parents. A shopper parked a car at the crosswalk on Main Street and received a parking ticket.

The town council met yesterday and voted to fix the parking space at Main and Elm. Pedestrians say they cannot cross the street safely. Officer Dobbs reported that the parking meter on that corner should also be fixed. Finally, the council voted for another street vendor. Shoppers complained about long lines for the only one in service in front of the photo shop.

**4.** Look at the picture in Exercise 3. Rewrite the article correctly.

Example: *Last week, Fran Bates rode her bike into Mel Smith's cart.*

**Challenge** Look at the picture in Exercise 3. Write about other problems.

See page 296 for listening practice.

1.  **Look in your dictionary. Check (✓) the activities you can do at this mall.
    Write the kind of store you can do them in. (Do not use *department store*.)**

    ☐ buy cough syrup     _____

    ✓ buy a birthday card     _____ *card store* _____

    ☐ look at DVD players     _____

    ☐ get clothes dry cleaned     _____

    ☐ plan a vacation     _____

    ☐ get new eyeglasses     _____

    ☐ get a hamburger     _____

    ☐ buy flowers     _____

    ☐ buy a dictionary     _____

    ☐ buy a dog     _____

    ☐ mail letters     _____

    ☐ buy chocolates     _____

2.  **Two teenagers are shopping at a mall. Look at the mall directory on page 131 of this
    book. Read the conversations and write the location of each one.**

    a. **Server:** What flavour?
       **Emma:** Strawberry, please.     _____ *ice cream shop* _____

    b. **Amy:** What do you think? Too curly?
       **Emma:** No. It's a terrific perm.     _____

    c. **Amy:** I love that new song by King.
       **Emma:** Let's go buy the CD.     _____

    d. **Emma:** Hey! Do you want to take the elevator?
       **Amy:** No. Let's take this instead. It'll be faster.     _____

    e. **Emma:** Let's go here for your high heels.
       **Amy:** Good idea. I usually don't like shopping at Crane's.     _____

    f. **Amy:** Do you like these earrings?
       **Emma:** Yeah. You look good in gold.     _____

    g. **Emma:** I need to get a new cellphone.
       **Amy:** Well, there's Cell Town right over there.     _____

    h. **Amy:** Excuse me. Where's the main entrance?
       **Clerk:** Right over there. Next to the washrooms.     _____

3. **Look at Exercise 2. Circle the numbers and symbols on the map and draw Amy and Emma's route.**

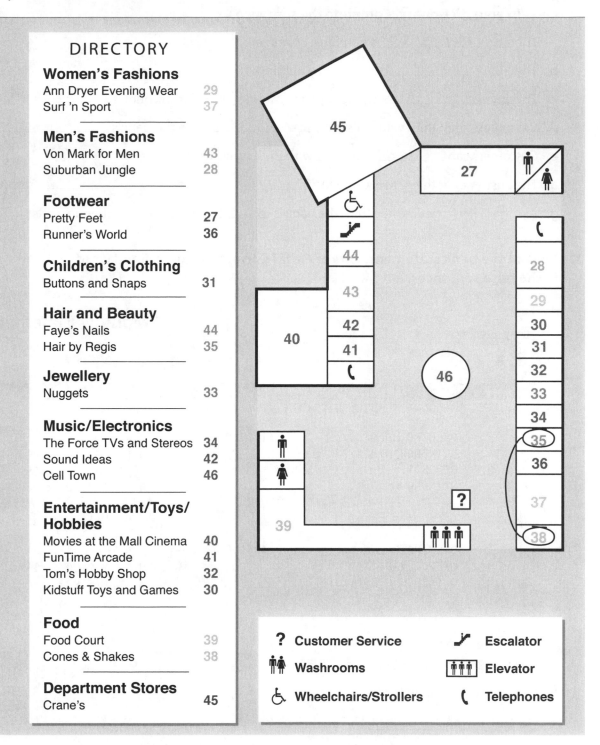

DIRECTORY

**Women's Fashions**
Ann Dryer Evening Wear ........ 29
Surf 'n Sport ........ 37

**Men's Fashions**
Von Mark for Men ........ 43
Suburban Jungle ........ 28

**Footwear**
Pretty Feet ........ 27
Runner's World ........ 36

**Children's Clothing**
Buttons and Snaps ........ 31

**Hair and Beauty**
Faye's Nails ........ 44
Hair by Regis ........ 35

**Jewellery**
Nuggets ........ 33

**Music/Electronics**
The Force TVs and Stereos ........ 34
Sound Ideas ........ 42
Cell Town ........ 46

**Entertainment/Toys/
Hobbies**
Movies at the Mall Cinema ........ 40
FunTime Arcade ........ 41
Tom's Hobby Shop ........ 32
Kidstuff Toys and Games ........ 30

**Food**
Food Court ........ 39
Cones & Shakes ........ 38

**Department Stores**
Crane's ........ 45

? Customer Service   ⌇ Escalator
Washrooms   Elevator
Wheelchairs/Strollers   ( Telephones

4. **What about you? Look at the mall in Exercise 3. Where would you like to go? Why?**

**Challenge** Where do you prefer to shop—downtown (the business centre of a town or city) or a shopping mall? Think about weather conditions, the transportation you can use to get there, the kinds of stores, prices, and entertainment. Write at least five sentences.

1. **Look in your dictionary. Complete the sentences.**

   a. The _____teller_____ is helping a customer.

   b. The _____ is wearing a uniform.

   c. The _____ is helping two customers open an account.

   d. Customers keep their valuables in a _____ in the bank's _____.

   e. Customers can _____ with their computers.

   f. The customer at the ATM is using his _____ to _____ cash.

   g. Another way to get money from the bank is to _____ a cheque.

2. **Look at the bank statement.** *True* or *False*? **Correct the <u>underlined</u> words in the false sentences.**

   ### Monthly Statement

   **FIRST BANK**

   JAMAL AL-MARAFI
   MARCH 31-APRIL 30, 2010

   | DATE | TRANSACTION | | AMOUNT | BALANCE |
   |------|-------------|---|--------|---------|
   | SAVINGS | ACCOUNT NUMBER: 0125-00 | | | |
   | | OPENING BALANCE:        $1117.20 | | | |
   | 3/31/10 | QUIKCASH ATM #123 | W | 50.00 | 1,067.20 |
   | 4/01/10 | DEPOSIT | D | 1,283.47 | 2,350.67 |
   | 4/20/10 | WITHDRAWAL | W | 100.00 | 2,250.67 |
   | CHEQUING | ACCOUNT NUMBER: 0135-08 | | | |
   | | OPENING BALANCE:        $849.00 | | | |
   | 4/05/10 | CHEQUE #431 | W | 732.00 | 117.00 |
   | 4/11/10 | QUIKCASH ATM #123 | W | 75.00 | 42.00 |

          *chequing*

   a. Jamal's ~~savings~~ account number is 0135-08.      _____false_____

   b. On 3/31, he <u>withdrew cash</u>.      _____

   c. On 4/01, he <u>made a deposit</u>.      _____

   d. On 4/05, he used his <u>chequebook</u>.      _____

   e. On 4/11, the balance in his chequing account was <u>$849.00</u>.      _____

   f. On 4/11, he used a <u>deposit slip</u>.      _____

   **Challenge** Compare the balances and transactions in Jamal's savings and chequing account.
   **Example:** *Jamal made one deposit in his ... .*

See page 297 for listening practice.

1. **Look in your dictionary. Complete the sentences.**

   a. You can find a map of the Nile River in an _____atlas_____.

   b. The little girl and her mother are looking at a _____.

   c. You'll need a _____ to check out library books.

   d. The library clerk is at the _____.

   e. If you keep a book too long, you have to _____.

2. **Complete the librarian's answers. Use the words in the box.**

   | author | biography | ~~DVD~~ | magazines | newspaper |
   |---|---|---|---|---|
   | online catalogue | periodicals | reference librarian | title | |

   **Natasha:** Do you have the movie *Crash* on video cassette?

   **Librarian:** No, but we have it on _____DVD_____.
                                                    **a.**

   **Riyaad:** I'm looking for a job. Do you have this weekend's job ads?

   **Librarian:** The Sunday _____ is over there
                                         **b.**
   along with the other _____.
                                                 **c.**

   **Ming:** Where can I find information about fashion and makeup?

   **Librarian:** We get several fashion _____ every month. Try those.
                                                 **d.**

   **Pupinder:** I'm looking for a novel by Jane Austen, but I can't remember what it's called.

   **Librarian:** You don't need the _____. Just type the name of the
                                         **e.**
   _____ into the _____ and press *Enter*.
                  **f.**                                  **g.**

   **Brad:** Can you recommend a good _____ about Pierre Elliot Trudeau?
                                                   **h.**
   I have to write a report about his life.

   **Librarian:** Sorry. I'm the library clerk. Ask the _____. She's over there.
                                                 **i.**

**Challenge** Look at the library in your dictionary. What is each person doing? **Example:** *The reference librarian is showing a man an atlas.*

**1. Look in your dictionary. Answer the questions.**

a. What comes in books of 8? _____ *stamps* _____

b. What says *Newton, New York*? _____

c. What has a London postmark? _____

d. What tells you the weight of a package? _____

e. Where can you buy stamps? _____

f. Who delivers the mail? _____

**2. Circle the words to complete the information about postal services.**

## HOW TO SEND YOUR MAIL

**Standard Lettermail / registered mail:**
                  a.

With this service, your letter will be delivered

locally within two days, anywhere in your

province within three days, or almost

anywhere in the country within four days.

Standard sized postmarks / envelopes that
                        b.

weigh 30 grams or less can be sent using one

Canadian address / stamp.
                c.

**Priority Courier:** Use this service when you

are in a rush. Your letter carrier / package can
                              d.

be delivered to Canada or the United States

as early as the next morning. If the mailing

address / postcard is in a very remote region
        e.

of the country, delivery could take as long

seven days.

**Xpresspost:** This isn't quite as fast as

Priority Courier / Lettermail, but your package
                  f.

will be delivered almost anywhere in the country

within three days. If you are mailing CDs or

DVDs, use a bubble envelope / greeting card to
                      g.

protect them.

**Surface / Registered mail:** Use this service
          h.

when you send important documents or packages

and you want to make sure they are delivered

safely. You will receive a confirmation when the

item has been delivered, and the person receiving

the item must sign for it.

**Regular parcel post:** This is the least expen-

sive way to send a parcel when you are not in a

hurry. You do not have to fill out any complicated

packages / postal forms, and your parcel will be
              i.

delivered within 2 to 13 days.

**3.** **What about you? What kinds of mail service do you use? How much do they cost?**

**4.** **Look at the information in Exercise 2. Answer the questions.**

    **a.** You are mailing a very important document to a school. What's the safest way to mail it?
       _registered mail_

    **b.** Your letter must arrive tomorrow. What's the fastest way to send it? _____

    **c.** You are mailing DVDs to your nephew. How should you send them? _____

    **d.** You are mailing gifts to your family. What's the cheapest way to send them? _____

    **e.** You are mailing a letter to a friend. It's OK if it doesn't arrive tomorrow.
       How should you send it? _____

**5.** **Complete this email. Use the words in the box.**

| addressed | delivered | envelope | ~~greeting card~~ | letter carrier | mailbox |
| mailed | put on | received | return address | stamp | wrote |

**My Mail**            `− □ ✕`

To: LibraGuy@iol.ca
Subject: Sorry!

Hi Sophie!

I really didn't forget your birthday on October 4! Two weeks ago, I went to the store and got you

a beautiful _____greeting card_____. I _____ a note in the card, put the card in
           **a.**            **b.**

the green _____, _____ the envelope, walked to the nearest
        **c.**       **d.**

_____, and _____ the card. Yesterday I was very surprised when the
    **e.**       **f.**

_____ _____ the card—to ME!!! Guess what? I forgot to _____
    **g.**       **h.**                  **i.**

a stamp! (Luckily, I didn't forget to write my _____ on the envelope!) So, long story
                                **j.**

short, that's the reason you never _____ a card from me this year.
                        **k.**

Next year I'll send you an e-card, so I won't need a _____!
                                   **l.**

1. **Look at the driver licensing office on page 136 in your dictionary. *True* or *False*? Correct the underlined words in the false sentences.**

   *handbook*
   a. You can get a form or a ~~photo~~ at the information stand.    *false*

   b. Three people are taking a test in the <u>testing area</u>.    _____

   c. A licensing clerk is taking a man's <u>photo</u>.    _____

   d. Another clerk is giving a man a <u>licence plate</u>.    _____

   e. One <u>window</u> is closed.    _____

2. **Look at the pictures. Answer the questions.**

| PROOF OF INSURANCE | KEEP IN VEHICLE AS EVIDENCE OF INSURANCE | |
|---|---|---|
| POLICY HOLDER:<br>ROSA RODRIGUEZ | POLICY NUMBER:<br>54323-45HG | |
| ADDRESS:<br>79 MAIN ST<br>HALIFAX, NS<br>B3K 4H8 | EXPIRATION DATE:<br>12/01/2012 | **ABC**<br>AUTO INSURANCE<br>14601 Young Street<br>Halifax, NS<br>B3H 1C8 |
| MAKE:<br>HONDA CIVIC | YEAR:<br>2009 | |

   a. What is Rosa's licence plate number?    *265 MAB*

   b. What is her driver's licence number?    _____

   c. When is the expiration date for her licence?    _____

   d. Are there registration stickers on her licence plate?    _____

   e. When is the expiration date for her proof of insurance?    _____

**3. Circle the words to complete the information from the website.**

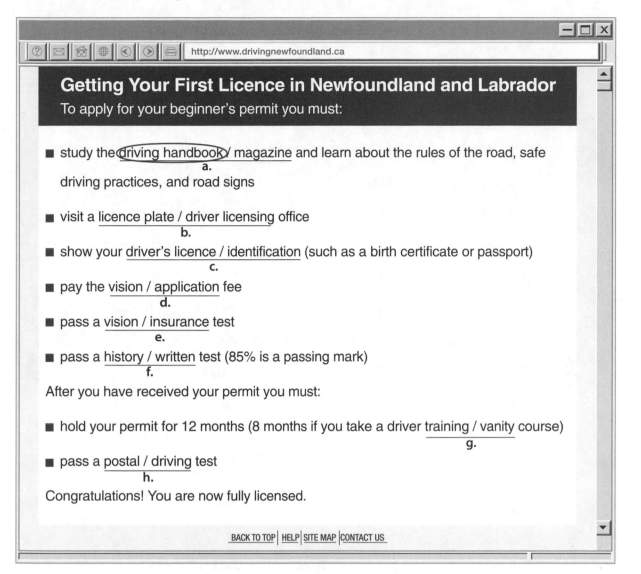

http://www.drivingnewfoundland.ca

## Getting Your First Licence in Newfoundland and Labrador
To apply for your beginner's permit you must:

- study the (driving handbook) / magazine and learn about the rules of the road, safe
  a.
  driving practices, and road signs

- visit a licence plate / driver licensing office
  b.

- show your driver's licence / identification (such as a birth certificate or passport)
  c.

- pay the vision / application fee
  d.

- pass a vision / insurance test
  e.

- pass a history / written test (85% is a passing mark)
  f.

After you have received your permit you must:

- hold your permit for 12 months (8 months if you take a driver training / vanity course)
  g.

- pass a postal / driving test
  h.

Congratulations! You are now fully licensed.

BACK TO TOP | HELP | SITE MAP | CONTACT US

**Challenge** Compare getting a licence in Newfoundland and Labrador to getting a licence in your native country or another province in Canada. **Example:** *In Germany, you can sometimes get your driver's licence when you are 17...*

**See page 299 for listening practice.**

137

**1. Look in your dictionary. Complete the information about Canada's government.**

The _____ is located on Parliament Hill in Ottawa. This is where many people work for the
    **a.**

federal government. The _____ is the meeting place for Canada's 308 _____
    **b.**     **c.**

Each of these individuals has been elected to represent a particular area of the country, or a "riding."

Canada's _____ is made up of 105 _____ who have been appointed to
    **d.**     **e.**

represent their region of the country.

The king or queen of England, also known as the _____, is Canada's head of state. This
    **f.**

person has a representative in Canada who is called the _____. The _____,
    **g.**     **h.**

however, is much more involved in the daily lives of Canadians. He or she is the head of the party that

received the most votes in a federal election. This person then selects _____ — each in
    **i.**

charge of a different area, such as Foreign Affairs or the Environment — to be in the _____.
    **j.**

A branch of the government called the Judiciary includes Canada's highest court, called the

_____. This court is made up of nine _____, one of whom is the
    **k.**     **l.**

_____. In the year 2000, this position was filled by a woman for the first time.
    **m.**

**2. Look at the pie chart. Circle the words to complete the sentences.**

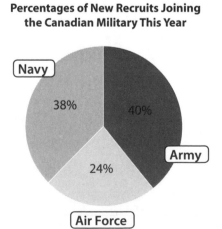

**Percentages of New Recruits Joining the Canadian Military This Year**

Navy 38%
Army 40%
Air Force 24%

a. Most new recruits are joining the (army)/ navy.

b. The fewest people are joining the army / air force.

c. Almost as many people are joining the
navy / air force as are joining the army.

3. **Look in your dictionary. Answer the questions.**

   a. What is the provincial capital of New Brunswick?     *Fredericton*

   b. Who is the head of the provincial government?     _____

   c. Who works in the Legislative Assembly?     _____

   d. What is another name for the Legislative Assembly?     _____

   e. Who is the head of the city government?     _____

   f. Who does he or she work with?     _____

4. **Complete the newspaper article. Use the words in the box.**

| | | | | |
|---|---|---|---|---|
| city council | councillor | ran for office | debated | elected officials |
| elected | opponent | political campaign | serve | ~~election results~~ |

ELECTION COVERAGE *A3*

# Dan Chen Wins!

**By Roland Cormier**
Smithfield, Wednesday, Nov 7

The ___election results___ are in. The city of Smithfield has a new _____ ,
    **a.**                                                 **b.**
forty-five–year–old Dan Chen. Mr. Chen, a Smithfield resident, was _____
                                                            **c.**
in yesterday's election. He beat his _____ , Martha Larson, by 35,000
                                                      **d.**
votes. This was the first time Chen _____ . He led an excellent
                                                         **e.**
_____ . Hundreds of people watched as he and Larson
                 **f.**
_____ the issues last month at the Smithfield University Auditorium.
                 **g.**
Mr. Chen will _____ on the Smithfield _____ for a
                            **h.**                            **i.**
term of four years. There are four other _____ on the council.
                                               **j.**

**Challenge** Compare the Canadian government with another country's government that you know about.
**Example:** *In Canada, a prime minister is the head of government. In Colombia a president is the head of government.*

**1.** **Look in your dictionary. Complete the sentences.**

**a.** To avoid a $500 fine, you must _obey Canada's laws_ .

**b.** Anne Johnson likes to _____. On Mondays, she makes sure her elderly neighbour gets to the supermarket safely.

**c.** Jack Smolka decided to _____ for Kofi Appiah in the election.

**d.** By encouraging different racial groups to work together in their community, Malcolm and Farrah helped to _____.

**e.** By learning about Canada's history, Shan is learning to _____ his heritage and environment.

**f.** Community meetings allow people to _____ while respecting the rights and freedoms of others.

**2.** **Read the sentences. Which right is each person talking about? Use the words in the box.**

| |
|---|
| freedom of thought, belief, opinion and expression          freedom of association |
| freedom of conscience and religion          ~~peaceful assembly~~ |

"We can march in the park."

"We can say what we want."

**a.** _peaceful assembly_          **b.** _____

"I can go to a church, synagogue, or mosque. It's *my* choice."

"We can work together to protect our rights."

**c.** _____          **d.** _____

**3.** **Read the information. Who can take a citizenship test? Check (✓) the correct box.**

**a.** ☐ Luisa is 17 years old. She has lived in Canada for 10 years.

**b.** ☐ Mehmet is 50 years old. He has lived in Canada for 4 years.

**c.** ☐ Mei-ling is 20 years old. She has lived in Canada for 3 of the last 6 years.

**Challenge** Which right is the most important to you? Why?

**1. Look in your dictionary. Who is doing the following things?**

a. wearing handcuffs _____the suspect_____

b. talking to the witness _____

c. typing _____

d. standing next to the defendant in the courtroom _____

e. sitting in jail _____

f. standing in a corner in the courtroom _____

**2. Circle the words to complete the interview with a former convict.**

# A HARD LESSON

**PS MAGAZINE:** Tell us about your experience with the legal system.

You (went to prison) / stood trial for several years, didn't you?
  a.

**DAN LEE:** Yes—for burglary. I was released / arrested three
  b.
years ago. It was the happiest day of my life.

**PS MAGAZINE:** You didn't have a job when you were arrested.

How did you hire a lawyer / stand trial?
  c.

**DAN LEE:** I didn't. The court gave me one. And she was good. In fact, when we appeared in

court / jail, she got the guard / judge to lower the bail to $1,000.
  d.                    e.

**PS MAGAZINE:** So what happened when you sentenced the defendant / stood trial?
  f.

**DAN LEE:** She did her best, but the Crown Counsel / defence lawyer had a lot of
  g.
evidence / handcuffs against me.
  h.

**PS MAGAZINE:** Were you surprised when the police officer / jury gave a verdict / witness
  i.                          j.
of "guilty"?

**DAN LEE:** No, but I *was* surprised when the judge sentenced / released me. Seven years!
  k.
Now I tell young people what it's like to spend years in jail / court.
  l.

---

**Challenge** Write the story of the man in the dictionary who was arrested.

# Crime

1.  **Look in your dictionary. Put each crime in the correct category.**

| Crimes Against People | Crimes Against Property (buildings, cars, etc.) | Substance Abuse Crimes (drugs and alcohol) |
|---|---|---|
| _____ | _____*vandalism*_____ | _____ |
| _____ | _____ | _____ |
| _____ | _____ | |
| _____ | _____ | |
| _____ | | |

2.  **Look at the line graph. Complete the sentences. Use the words in the box. (You will use two words more than once.)**

| arson | assaults | burglaries | murders |
|---|---|---|---|

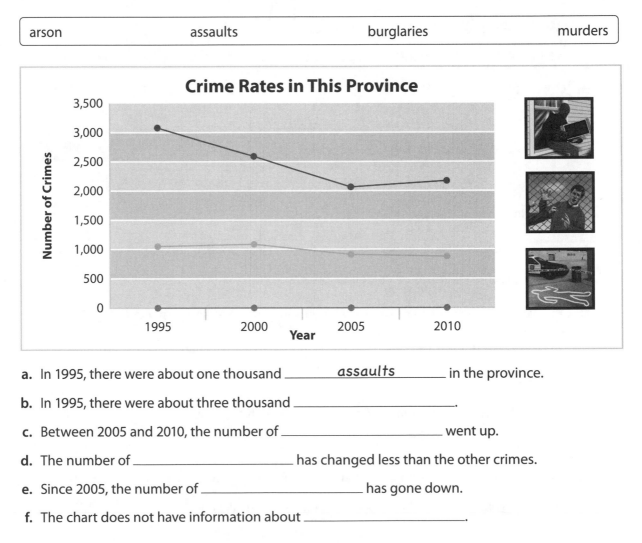

**Crime Rates in This Province**

a.  In 1995, there were about one thousand _____*assaults*_____ in the province.

b.  In 1995, there were about three thousand _____.

c.  Between 2005 and 2010, the number of _____ went up.

d.  The number of _____ has changed less than the other crimes.

e.  Since 2005, the number of _____ has gone down.

f.  The chart does not have information about _____.

**Challenge** Look at page 258 in this book. Follow the instructions.

1. **Look in your dictionary. Complete the poster with the correct advice.**

## Neighbourhood Lookout  *Safety Tips*

a. _____Lock your doors._____ A dead bolt is your best protection. Door chains are also good.

b. _____ Always ask, "Who's there?" If you don't know them, don't let them in!

c. _____ Who else is on the street? Notice other people.

d. _____ For men, the best place is an *inside* jacket pocket. For women, keep it *closed* and *close* to your body at all times.

e. ATMs are great, but be careful using one. _____

f. _____ There's safety in numbers. Remember: muggers usually look for *easy* victims.

g. _____ Remember: Criminals don't want witnesses, so lights are your friends.

h. _____ Whose suitcase is that? If its owner isn't there, contact the police.

i. Be careful on the Internet too. Only _____ where you see the 🔒 symbol.

j. _____ If you witness a crime or become a crime victim, dial 911 immediately!

*The Birch Hills Neighbourhood Lookout — Looking Out for You!*

2. **Look at the picture. What safety mistakes is the man making? Use the information in Exercise 1.**

   a. _He isn't staying on well-lit streets._

   b. _____

   c. _____

   d. _____

   e. _____

3. **What about you? Which of the safety tips in Exercise 1 do you follow? Make a list.**

**Challenge** Interview five people. Find out about the safety tips they follow.

**1. Look in your dictionary. Which disaster is the news reporter talking about?**

a. "The same one erupted five years ago."                           <u>volcanic eruption</u>

b. "All homes near the beach were destroyed by the ocean water."    _____

c. "The two vehicles were badly damaged, but the drivers
were not hurt in the crash."                                        _____

d. "Store detectives found the little girl sitting on the floor."   _____

e. "The twister destroyed several farms in its path."               _____

f. "The search and rescue team arrived at the house quickly."       _____

**2. Complete the news articles. Use the words in the box.**

| | | | |
|---|---|---|---|
| airplane crash | avalanche | blizzard | drought |
| ~~earthquake~~ | explosion | fire | firefighters |
| hurricane | search and rescue team | | |

a.

# DISASTER STRIKES KOBE, JAPAN

TOKYO, JAN 17 —An ___earthquake___ measuring 7.1 on the Richter scale hit the
city of Kobe, Japan killing more than 5,000 people and injuring 26,500 others. More
than 100,000 buildings were destroyed.

b.

# _____ KILLS 109

**Vancouver, May 11**—A DC-9 jet on its way to Edmonton went down in the
Rockies just a few minutes after takeoff from Vancouver. All 109 passengers were
killed. The cause of the disaster is not yet known.

c.

# INFERNO IN LONDON UNDERGROUND

London, November 18—Thirty died and thirty-one were seriously injured in a
_____ in one of the busiest subway stations in the world. "As soon as
I got on the escalator, I could smell burning," said one witness. Seconds later she saw
the red flames and dark smoke. _____ rushed to the scene.

**d.**

# BOMB _____ in Oklahoma City Kills 169

**Oklahoma City, April 19**—A car bomb went off outside a federal office building, killing 168 people. A member of the _____ also died while trying to save the victims. The bomb destroyed most of the nine-storey building and damaged many other buildings in the area.

**e.**

# HIGH WINDS HIT THE YUCATAN

**Cancun, October 22**—_____ Wilma, the most powerful Atlantic storm ever recorded, struck the popular tourist resorts of Mexico's Yucatan Peninsula, leaving 8 dead and destroying many beach hotels. Winds of 240 kilometres per hour broke windows and caused trees to fall.

**f.**

# THE _____ OF '93

**Halifax, March 22**—Described as a "hurricane with snow," the giant storm hit the eastern third part of Canada and the United States. The winds created snow drifts as high as 10 metres in some areas.

**g.**

**A LONG DRY WINTER**

**Santa Barbara, March 23**—As a result of 73% less rain than usual over the last year, California is experiencing its worst _____ since the 1930s. The state is going to stop water deliveries to farms in an effort to save water.

**h.**

# MAN RESCUED FROM _____

**Banff, March 27**—An employee at Sunshine Village ski resort was buried when a 200-metre-wide wall of snow hit him and caused him to fall. A rescue team reached him in less than four minutes. The employee is fine.

**Challenge** Write a paragraph about an emergency or natural disaster.

# Emergency Procedures

1. **Look in your dictionary. Complete the sentences.**

    a. The Azzopardi family _is planning for an emergency_ .

    b. Their _____ is Aunt Maria in British Columbia.

    c. If there is a flood, they have two _____ out of their house.

    d. Their _____ is Cartier Drive, a road near their house.

    e. Their _____ is at the corner of Oak and Elm.

    f. The _____ is in their basement.

2. **Complete the disaster kit checklist. Use the words in the box.**

| batteries | blankets | bottled water | can opener | canned food |
|-----------|----------|---------------|------------|-------------|
| coins | important papers | packaged food | towelettes | ~~warm clothes~~ |

---

### EMERGENCY CHECKLIST

**Clothing and Bedding**

☐ _____warm clothes_____ (hat, gloves, etc.)
    **a.**

☐ _____ or sleeping bags
    **b.**

**Tools and Supplies**

☐ flashlight and extra _____
                                                **c.**

☐ non-electric _____
                            **d.**

☐ _____ (4 litres per person per day)
        **e.**

**Food**

☐ ready-to-eat _____ (cereal, granola bars)
                                    **f.**

☐ _____ (soup, juice)
        **g.**

**Sanitation**

☐ toilet paper          ☐ moist _____
                                                **h.**

**Special Items**

☐ medication          ☐ extra eyeglasses

☐ cash and _____          ☐ copies of _____
                    **i.**                                              **j.**

146

**3. Look in your dictionary. What are people doing? Write sentences.**

a. Gino is looking at the sky.          He's watching the weather.

b. Rosa is packing her suitcase.          _____

c. The Azzopardis are listening to the radio and leaving.          _____

d. Gino is carrying a woman's suitcase to the shelter.          _____

e. The family is leaving their home.          _____

f. They are entering a neighbourhood shelter.          _____

g. Kenji and his son are under the table.          _____

h. They are not looking outside at the weather.          _____

i. Rosa is on the phone with Aunt Maria.          _____

j. Kenji and Rosa are in their basements.          _____

k. Kenji is in his front yard.          _____

**4. What about you? Are you ready? Look at the checklist in Exercise 2. Complete the chart.**

| Things I have | Things I don't have | Things I'm going to get |
|---|---|---|
|  |  |  |
|  |  |  |
|  |  |  |
|  |  |  |
|  |  |  |
|  |  |  |
|  |  |  |
|  |  |  |
| Other: | Other: | Other: |

**Challenge** What things should you have in a first aid kit? Make a list.

Go to page 248 for Another Look (Unit 7).  |  See page 303 for listening practice.

# Community Cleanup

1. **Look at the top row of pictures on pages 148 and 149 in your dictionary. Complete the chart. Check (✓) the columns.**

|  | Doughnuts | Hammers & More | Pharmacy | Flowers |
|---|---|---|---|---|
| **a.** This store has broken windows. | ✓ | ✓ | ✓ | ✓ |
| **b.** There is a streetlight in front. |  |  |  |  |
| **c.** There is litter in front. |  |  |  |  |
| **d.** There is graffiti on the store. |  |  |  |  |
| **e.** It is next to the hardware store. |  |  |  |  |
| **f.** It is across the street from the pharmacy. |  |  |  |  |

2. **Complete the conversation. Use the words in the box.**

| streetlights | hardware store | litter | graffiti | street |
|---|---|---|---|---|
| change | free | give a speech | ~~petition~~ |  |

**Marta:** Excuse me. Would you please sign this ___*petition*___?
a.

We really need to _____ things here.
b.

Main Street is a mess. There's a lot of _____
c.

painted on the stores.

**Customer:** Yes, there is. And there's a lot of _____
d.

in the street. Is that what the petition is for?

**Marta:** No. I am going to talk about those things when I _____ to the city council,
e.

but the petition is to repair the _____. They don't work.
f.

**Customer:** Oh, of course, I'll sign it. This _____ is a mess.
g.

**Marta:** Thanks. And can you give some of your time?

We need volunteers to do the rest of the work.

**Customer:** Sure. I can help plant some flowers. And I work right next door

at the _____. I can ask the manager to give some _____ paint.
h.                                                                                    i.

**Marta:** Oh, great! Thank you.

**3. Look in your dictionary. How many of the following things do you see?**

a. stores on the street         _4_

b. signatures on the petition    ____

c. broken streetlights          ____

d. city councillors who are applauding    ____

e. people who are giving a speech    ____

**4. Read Amar's web post. Circle the words to complete the sentences.**

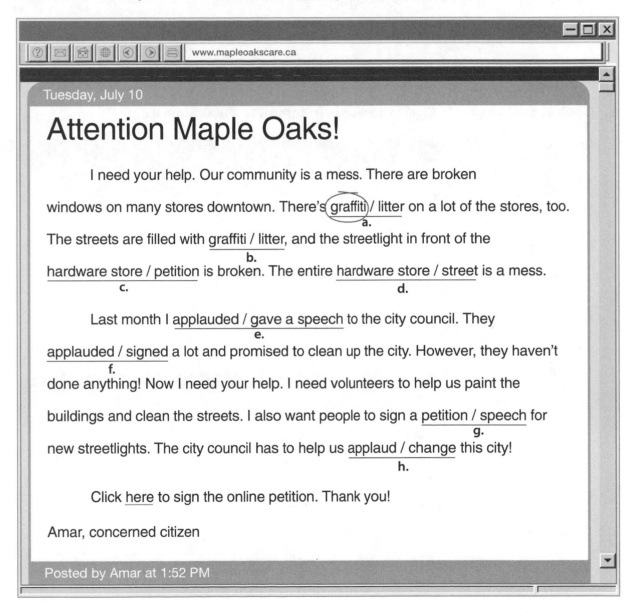

www.mapleoakscare.ca

Tuesday, July 10

# Attention Maple Oaks!

I need your help. Our community is a mess. There are broken

windows on many stores downtown. There's (graffiti) / litter on a lot of the stores, too.
                                                     **a.**

The streets are filled with graffiti / litter, and the streetlight in front of the
                                         **b.**

hardware store / petition is broken. The entire hardware store / street is a mess.
                **c.**                                   **d.**

Last month I applauded / gave a speech to the city council. They
                                 **e.**

applauded / signed a lot and promised to clean up the city. However, they haven't
      **f.**

done anything! Now I need your help. I need volunteers to help us paint the

buildings and clean the streets. I also want people to sign a petition / speech for
                                                              **g.**

new streetlights. The city council has to help us applaud / change this city!
                                                 **h.**

Click here to sign the online petition. Thank you!

Amar, concerned citizen

Posted by Amar at 1:52 PM

**Challenge** Imagine there are problems in your community. Write a web post. Tell people about the problems and ask for help. Use Exercise 4 as a model.

1. **Look in your dictionary. *True* or *False*? Correct the <u>underlined</u> words in the false sentences.**

   a. A passenger is getting into the ~~truck~~. *taxi*            _____*false*_____

   b. There is one <u>motorcycle</u> on the street.            _____

   c. The <u>helicopter</u> is flying over the airport.            _____

   d. The subway station is around the corner from the <u>bus stop</u>.            _____

   e. A <u>bicycle</u> rider is wearing a jacket.            _____

   f. There are four people at the <u>subway station</u>.            _____

2. **Look at the bar graph. Circle the words to complete the sentences.**

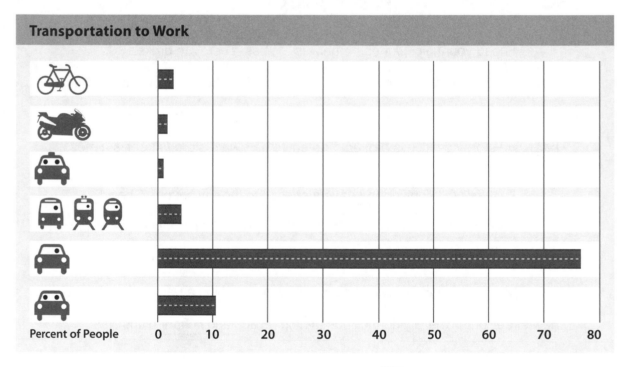

   a. Almost 5% of people gets to work by bus, train, or car /(subway).

   b. Most people go to work by <u>car / train</u>.

   c. The least popular way to get to work is by <u>motorcycle / taxi</u>.

   d. More people go to work by <u>bicycle / taxi</u> than by motorcycle.

   e. More than 75% of people ride to work <u>alone / as a passenger</u> in a car.

3. **What about you? How do you get to work? school? the market? the airport? Use your own paper.**

**4. Compare these types of transportation. Write sentences with *than* and the words in parentheses ( ).**

a. _The plane is safer than the car._
   (plane / car / safer)

b. _____
   (bus / subway / faster)

c. _____
   (plane / bus / more expensive)

d. _____
   (bicycle / motorcycle / more dangerous)

e. _____
   (bus / taxi / cheaper)

f. _____
   (car / truck / more comfortable)

**5. Look at the chart. Complete the sentences.**

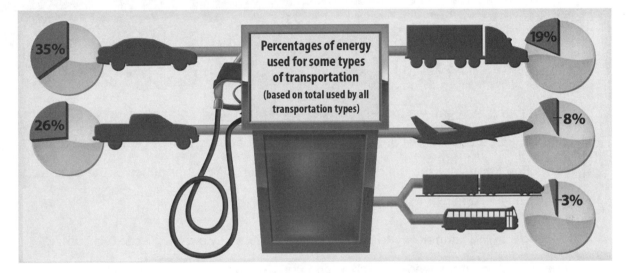

a. Small ____trucks____ use 26% of the total energy for all types of transportation.

b. At 19%, large _____ use less energy than small ones.

c. _____ use the most energy of all types of transportation.

d. _____ use only 8% of the total energy for transportation.

e. _____ and _____ together use just 3% of the total energy for transportation.

**Challenge** What are the advantages (positive points) and disadvantages (negative points) of different types of transportation? Compare your answers with a classmate's list.
**Example:** *Riding a bicycle is good exercise. Bikes don't use gas, but they aren't very fast.*

1. **Look in your dictionary. What are the people talking about? Where are they?**

|  | **What?** | **Where?** |
|---|---|---|
| a. "It goes in this way." | fare card | subway station |
| b. "This says there's one at 6:30." | _____ | _____ |
| c. "Use this, Miss, to change at Avenue A." | _____ | _____ |
| d. "It says $22.00, so I'll tip $3.30." | _____ | _____ |
| e. "Is it for a one-way trip or a round trip?" | _____ | _____ |

2. **Circle the words to complete the pamphlet.**

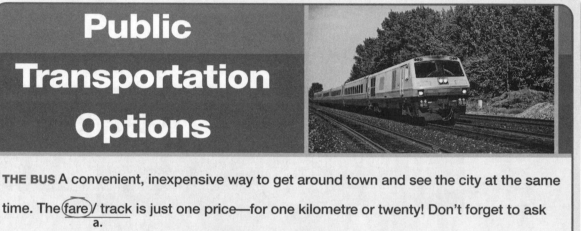

# Public Transportation Options

**THE BUS** A convenient, inexpensive way to get around town and see the city at the same

time. The (fare) / track is just one price—for one kilometre or twenty! Don't forget to ask
     **a.**

for a token / transfer from the driver, so you can change to other buses or the subway
     **b.**

without paying again.

**THE SUBWAY** The fastest way to get around town. Just buy a token / schedule from an
     **c.**

automatic conductor / vending machine and put it in the meter / turnstile.
     **d.**      **e.**

**TAXIS** Convenient, but expensive. Watch the meter / shuttle as your driver / rider takes
     **f.**      **g.**

you to your destination. The further you go, the more you pay!

**TRAINS** For longer distances, a good form of public transportation. A round-trip ticket is

sometimes less expensive than two one-way / round-trip tickets, so plan ahead! Buy
     **h.**

one at the subway car / ticket window and then wait on the platform / track for your train.
     **i.**      **j.**

**Challenge** Describe the advantages and disadvantages of different types of public transportation.
     **Example:** *The subway is fast, but you can't see the street from it.*

      See page 304 for listening practice.

1. **Look in your dictionary. *True* or *False*? Correct the <u>underlined</u> words in the false sentences.**

   a. A woman is walking ~~down~~ <sup>up</sup> the steps.     *false*

   b. A man is running <u>across the street</u>.     _____

   c. The red truck is going to <u>drive through the tunnel</u>.     _____

   d. The blue car is <u>getting off</u> the highway.     _____

2. **Look at the map of Toronto. Circle the words to complete the directions.**

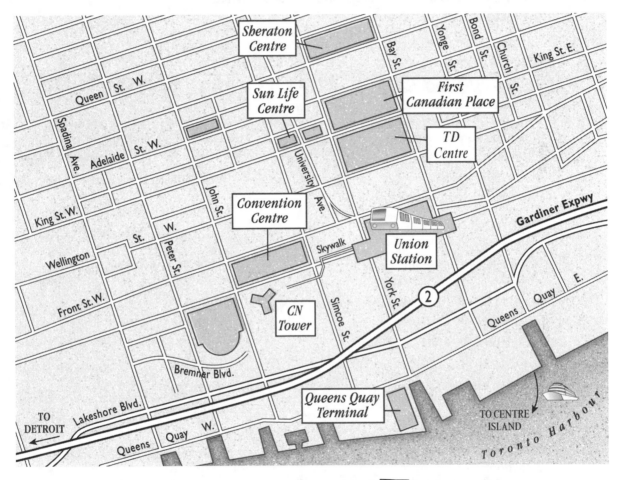

   a. To go from Union Station to Toronto Harbour, <u>get off / go under</u> the Expressway on Yonge St.

   b. To go from the Convention Centre to the Sun Life Centre, get <u>into / out of</u> the taxi on King St.

   c. To go from Queens Quay Terminal to Centre Island, go <u>across / around</u> Toronto Harbour.

   d. To go from Union Station to Detroit, get <u>on / off</u> the Expressway at York Street.

   e. To go from the CN Tower to Union Station on foot, go <u>over / under</u> the Skywalk.

   **Challenge** Write directions from your home to:
       school     the bus station     Other: _____

1. **Look in your dictionary. Which signs have the following things?**

   **a.** numbers     _speed limit_ and _____

   **b.** letters, not words     _____ and _____

   **c.** pictures of people     _____, _____, _____, and _____

   **d.** arrows (→)     _____, _____, _____, _____

       and _____

2. **Complete the written part of a test for a driver's licence.**
   **Circle the letters of the answers.**

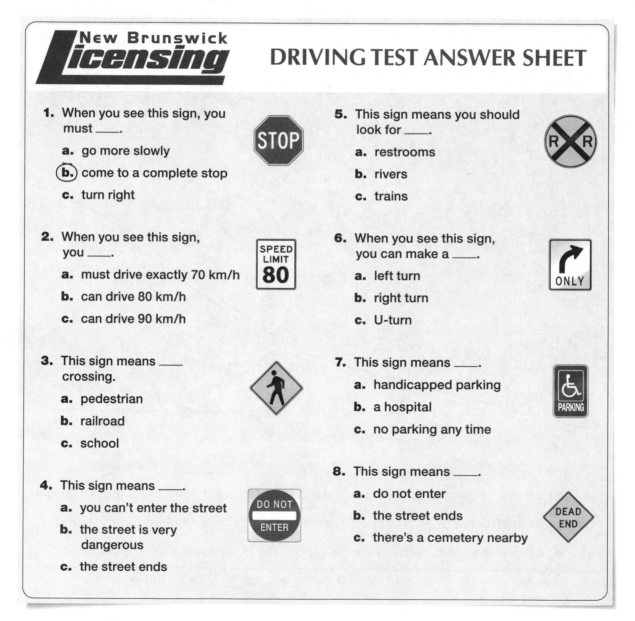

**New Brunswick**
**Licensing**     **DRIVING TEST ANSWER SHEET**

**1.** When you see this sign, you must ____.
   **a.** go more slowly
   **(b.)** come to a complete stop
   **c.** turn right

**2.** When you see this sign, you ____.
   **a.** must drive exactly 70 km/h
   **b.** can drive 80 km/h
   **c.** can drive 90 km/h

**3.** This sign means ____ crossing.
   **a.** pedestrian
   **b.** railroad
   **c.** school

**4.** This sign means ____.
   **a.** you can't enter the street
   **b.** the street is very dangerous
   **c.** the street ends

**5.** This sign means you should look for ____.
   **a.** restrooms
   **b.** rivers
   **c.** trains

**6.** When you see this sign, you can make a ____.
   **a.** left turn
   **b.** right turn
   **c.** U-turn

**7.** This sign means ____.
   **a.** handicapped parking
   **b.** a hospital
   **c.** no parking any time

**8.** This sign means ____.
   **a.** do not enter
   **b.** the street ends
   **c.** there's a cemetery nearby

**Challenge** Draw some other traffic signs. Explain their meanings.

1. **Look in your dictionary. *True* or *False*? Correct the <u>underlined</u> words in the false sentences.**

   *east*
   a. The car went ~~west~~ on Elm Street.                     _____false_____

   b. It <u>didn't stop at the corner</u> of Elm and Main.     _____

   c. It turned <u>right</u> on Pine.                          _____

   d. It continued to drive <u>south</u> on Oak.               _____

2. **Look at the Internet map. Circle the words to complete the sentences.**

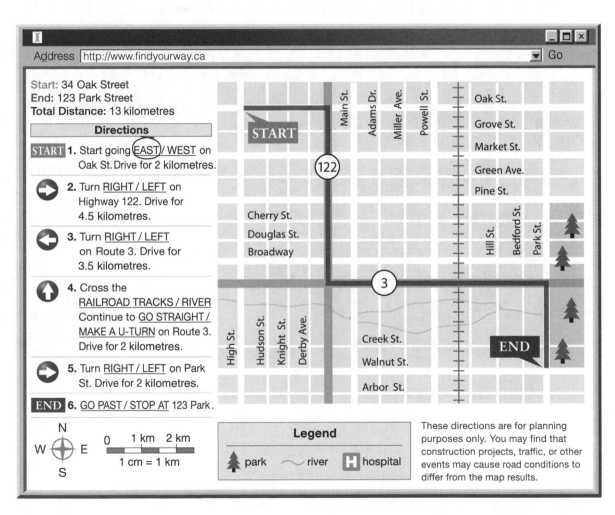

3. **Look at the map in Exercise 2. Circle the words to complete the sentences.**

   a. The <u>Internet map</u> / (river) is blue.

   b. According to the <u>scale</u> / GPS, one centimetre is one kilometre.

   c. The map has a <u>symbol</u> / key for parks.

   d. The <u>streets</u> / highways are orange.

**Challenge** Look at the map in Exercise 2. Give directions from 123 Park Street to 34 Oak Street.

**See page 305 for listening practice.**

1. **Look in your dictionary. Which car or truck does the following things?**

   a. takes furniture from one place to another _____moving van_____

   b. takes children to school _____

   c. helps move your car if it's in an accident _____

   d. uses both gas and electricity _____

   e. transports oil from one place to another _____

   f. can pour sand on the ground _____

2. **Look at the bar graph. Circle the words to complete the sentences.**

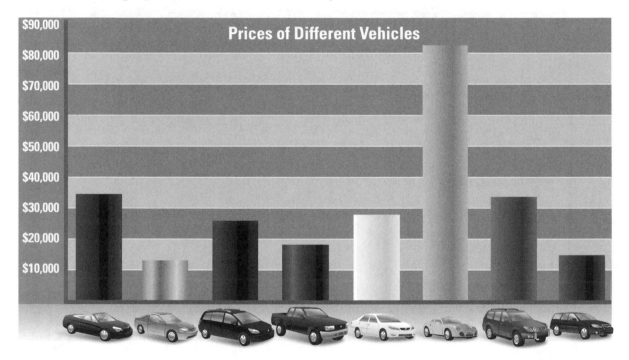

**Prices of Different Vehicles**

   a. The (convertible) / minivan costs about $34,000.

   b. The sedan is more expensive than the <u>convertible / coupe</u>.

   c. The SUV is a little less expensive than the <u>convertible / pickup truck</u>.

   d. The <u>sports car / coupe</u> is the most expensive car.

   e. The <u>pickup truck / coupe</u> is the least expensive vehicle.

   f. The <u>minivan / station wagon</u> costs about $28,000.

3. **What about you? Look in your dictionary. Which car would you choose? Why?**
   **Example:** *I would choose a pickup truck. I carry a lot of things, but not many passengers.*

**Challenge** Look at newspaper or online ads. Find the price range of the car you chose in Exercise 3.

1. **Look in your dictionary. Complete the sentences.**

   a. Juan wanted to buy _a used car_____.

   b. He _____ in the newspaper and online.

   c. When he _____, he learned how many kilometres were on the car.

   d. When he _____, he learned that it was in good condition.

   e. He _____ of $2,000.

   f. After he got the title from the seller, he _____.

2. **Look at the checklist. What did Juan do? What didn't he do? Write sentences.**

   ## Car Maintenance
   - ☑ Fill the tank with gas.
   - ☑ Check the oil.
   - ☐ Put in coolant.
   - ☐ Go for an emissions test.
   - ☐ Replace the windshield wipers.
   - ☑ Fill the tires with air.

   a. _He filled the tank with gas._____

   b. _____

   c. _He didn't_____

   d. _____

   e. _____

   f. _____

**Challenge** List other things people do to maintain their cars. **Example:** *They check the spare tire and add air if necessary.*

1. **Look in your dictionary. How many of the following parts does the car have?**

   **a.** hubcaps    _4_

   **b.** licence plates    ___

   **c.** gauges    ___

   **d.** power outlets    ___

   **e.** side-view mirrors    ___

   **f.** tail pipes    ___

   **g.** rear-view mirrors    ___

   **h.** spare tires    ___

2. **Complete the conversations. Use the words in the box.**

   | air conditioner | front seat | ~~gas gauge~~ | gas pedal | glove compartment |
   |---|---|---|---|---|
   | licence plate | radio | rear-view mirror | stick shift | temperature gauge |

   **a. Passenger:** Look, the ____ _gas gauge_ ____ is almost on empty.
       **Driver:** There's a gas station. I'll stop there.

   **b. Driver:** Where would you like to sit?
       **Passenger:** In the _____, next to you.

   **c. Driver:** It would be good to hear a traffic report.
       **Passenger:** I'll turn on the _____.

   **d. Passenger:** It's getting hot in here.
       **Driver:** We can turn on the

       _____.

   **e. Passenger:** Do we have a map?
       **Driver:** There should be one in

       the _____.

   **f. Passenger:** That truck is getting very close!
       **Driver:** Don't worry. I'm watching it in

       the _____.

   **g. Passenger:** Step on the _____! You're going much too slow.
       **Driver:** OK.

   **h. Passenger:** Look at the _____.
       **Driver:** Oh. The radiator needs coolant. It's much too hot.

   **i. Passenger:** That car is leaving the accident scene!
       **Driver:** Quick! Let's call the police. Write down the _____ number!

   **j. Passenger:** Do you like using a _____?
       **Driver:** Yes. I've always driven a car with a manual transmission.

**3. Circle the words to complete the information from a driver's manual.**

## BASIC DRIVING

a. The bumper / steering wheel gives you control over your car.

b. Always have the correct amount of air in your hubcaps / tires. Check the air pressure.

c. When you step on your brake pedal / clutch, your car should stop quickly and smoothly.

d. Jumper cables / Turn signals tell other drivers which direction you are going to go.

e. Brake lights / Tail lights tell other drivers that you are slowing or stopping.

f. Your hood / horn lets other drivers and pedestrians hear that you are there.

g. Lug wrenches / Headlights are important in night driving, rainy weather, and fog.

h. The heater / windshield should be free of cracks and breaks. Use your gearshift / windshield wipers to clean it.

## PREVENTING INJURIES

i. Check your odometer / speedometer to see how fast you are going.

j. All new cars come with airbags / spare tires that open in case of an accident. They keep you from hitting your head against the dashboard / trunk or steering wheel.

k. Back seats / Seat belts help prevent injury or death in case of an accident. Always use them.

l. Use your jacks / door locks to keep your doors from opening in an accident.

m. Buy child safety seats / hazard lights for small children and always use them. It's the law!

## AIR AND NOISE POLLUTION CONTROL

n. Make sure there is enough coolant in the battery / radiator.

o. If your car is making a lot of noise, you may need to replace your ignition / muffler.

**Challenge** Look in your dictionary. Choose five parts of the car that are not described in Exercise 3. What are they for? **Example:** *heater—to keep the inside of the car warm.*

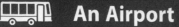 

**1. Look in your dictionary. Who's speaking? What is he or she speaking about?**

|  | | Who? | What? |
|---|---|---|---|
| **a.** | "My other bag isn't on <u>it</u>! " | *passenger* | *baggage carousel* |
| **b.** | "Put your keys in <u>it</u>, too, with your briefcase." | | |
| **c.** | "You didn't fill <u>it</u> out." | | |
| **d.** | "Put <u>it</u> over your face." | | |

**2. Circle the words to complete the travel trips.**

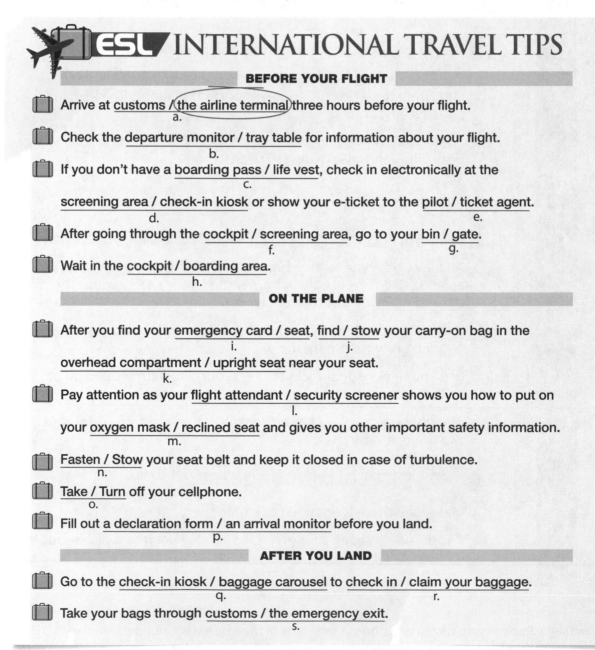

# ESL INTERNATIONAL TRAVEL TIPS

### BEFORE YOUR FLIGHT

- Arrive at <u>customs / (the airline terminal)</u> three hours before your flight.
  a.
- Check the <u>departure monitor / tray table</u> for information about your flight.
  b.
- If you don't have a <u>boarding pass / life vest</u>, check in electronically at the
  c.
  <u>screening area / check-in kiosk</u> or show your e-ticket to the <u>pilot / ticket agent</u>.
  d.                                                                  e.
- After going through the <u>cockpit / screening area</u>, go to your <u>bin / gate</u>.
  f.                                                          g.
- Wait in the <u>cockpit / boarding area</u>.
  h.

### ON THE PLANE

- After you find your <u>emergency card / seat</u>, <u>find / stow</u> your carry-on bag in the
  i.                                          j.
  <u>overhead compartment / upright seat</u> near your seat.
  k.
- Pay attention as your <u>flight attendant / security screener</u> shows you how to put on
  l.
  your <u>oxygen mask / reclined seat</u> and gives you other important safety information.
  m.
- <u>Fasten / Stow</u> your seat belt and keep it closed in case of turbulence.
  n.
- <u>Take / Turn</u> off your cellphone.
  o.
- Fill out <u>a declaration form / an arrival monitor</u> before you land.
  p.

### AFTER YOU LAND

- Go to the <u>check-in kiosk / baggage carousel</u> to <u>check in / claim your baggage</u>.
  q.                                             r.
- Take your bags through <u>customs / the emergency exit</u>.
  s.

3. **Look at Taking a Flight on page 160 in your dictionary.** *Before* or *After*? **Circle the words to complete the sentences.**

    **a.** The passenger checked his bags <u>before</u> /(after)he checked in electronically.

    **b.** He stowed his carry-on bag <u>before</u> / after he found his seat.

    **c.** He turned off his cellphone <u>before</u> / after the plane took off.

4. **Look at the flight information.** *True* or *False*? **Write a question mark (?) if the information isn't there.**

| HAPPY Travel | MERLIN, JARED<br>PAGE 1 OF 1 FILE #142-34-02-54-2 |
|---|---|

Reconfirm reservations 72 hours prior to each flight. Failure to do so may result in missing your flight or having the space cancelled by the airline.

```
AIRWAY AIRLINES     FLIGHT 613            10 MAR SUN
DEPART 0755A        TORONTO               CHECK-IN REQUIRED
ARRIVE 1048A        MIAMI INTERNATIONAL   MEALS: SNACK

AIRWAY AIRLINES     FLIGHT 695            10 MAR SUN
DEPART 1115A        MIAMI INTERNATIONAL   SEAT 23D NON-SMOKING
ARRIVE 1215P        SAN JUAN              MEALS: SPECIAL LOW-SALT
```

    **a.** The passenger bought his ticket from Happy Travel.       \_\_\_\_true\_\_\_\_

    **b.** This is an e-ticket.    _____

    **c.** The arrival time in Miami is 11:15 a.m.    _____

    **d.** The departure time from Toronto is 7:55 a.m.    _____

    **e.** Passengers will board flight 613 at 7:35 a.m.    _____

    **f.** Passengers can have two carry-on bags.    _____

    **g.** Flight 613 takes off on Sunday morning.    _____

    **h.** It lands on Sunday afternoon.    _____

    **i.** The passenger doesn't have to check in for flight 613.    _____

    **j.** He is in seat 23D on flight 695.    _____

    **k.** The seat is next to an emergency exit.    _____

    **l.** The passenger requested a special meal.    _____

    **m.** Passengers will claim their baggage at carousel 4.    _____

**Challenge** Write a paragraph about a plane trip you or someone you know took.

**See page 306 for listening practice.**

1. **Look in your dictionary. Number the sentences in the correct order.**
   **(Number 1 = the first thing that happened)**

   ____ **a.** They have a flat tire.

   ____ **b.** They get lost.

   ____ **c.** They run out of gas.

   ____ **d.** They look at scenery.

   ____ **e.** They arrive at their destination.

   ____ **f.** They ask a gas station attendant for directions.

   ____ **g.** They get a speeding ticket.

   _1_ **h.** Joe and Rob leave Vancouver, which is their starting point.

   ____ **i.** Their car breaks down.

2. **What's happening? Match.**

   _2_ **a.** "Where are we? Was that our turn?"          **1.** They're calling a tow truck.

   ____ **b.** "Go straight one kilometre. Then turn right."          **2.** They're getting lost.

   ____ **c.** "The car is stopping. We forgot to buy gas!"          **3.** They're running out of gas.

   ____ **d.** "You were way over the speed limit."          **4.** They're getting a speeding ticket.

   ____ **e.** "Our bags are in the car. Let's go to New York!"          **5.** They're packing.

   ____ **f.** "The mountains are beautiful!"          **6.** They're getting directions.

   ____ **g.** "There's smoke coming out of the engine!"          **7.** They're leaving their starting point.

   ____ **h.** "Please send a truck. We're ten kilometres west of Denver."          **8.** They're looking at scenery.

   ____ **i.** "I'm going to bring my bathing suit and suntan lotion."          **9.** Their car is breaking down.

   ____ **j.** "I'll take the flat tire off. Would you get the spare tire?"          **10.** They're changing a flat tire.

3. **What about you? Check (✓) the things that have happened to you. Tell a classmate about your experiences.**

   ☐ I forgot to pack something important.          ☐ I ran out of gas.

   ☐ I got a speeding ticket.          ☐ I got a flat tire.

   ☐ My car broke down.          ☐ I got lost.

4. **Complete the story. Use the words in the box.**

| | | | |
|---|---|---|---|
| pack | get a speeding ticket | breaks down | get lost |
| ~~destination~~ | scenery | gas station attendant | run out of gas |
| road trip | tow truck | mechanic | |

_____Destination_____ : NANAIMO
a.

"I'm tired of Red Deer," Jane says. "Let's take a

_____ on spring break and visit Lia in Nanaimo." "Let's
b.

_____ our bags!" says Tonya. "I can't wait." A week later, Jane and Tonya
c.

are driving through the beautiful _____ in Banff National Park.
d.

But problems are still in front of them. They _____ in Kamloops, and they stop
e.

to ask a _____ for directions. They _____ in Ashcroft
f.                                                        g.

because they are driving too fast. In Whistler, they _____. Jane walks to a
h.

gas station and buys some. Finally, their car _____ only thirty kilometres
i.

from the ferry to Nanaimo. Tonya calls a _____, and the truck takes the car
j.

to a mechanic. "Your car will be ready in two days," says the _____. The
k.

friends rent a car. Two hours later, they're at Lia's door.

5. **Complete the sentences about Jane and Tonya's trip home. Use the words in the box.**

| | | |
|---|---|---|
| get a speeding ticket | ~~have any problems~~ | run out of gas |
| break down | get lost | have a flat tire |

a. Jane and Tonya had a great trip home because they didn't _have any problems_____.

b. They always obeyed the speed limit, so they didn't _____.

c. A mechanic checked their car, so their car didn't _____.

d. They remembered to buy gas, so they didn't _____.

e. They bought some new tires, so they didn't _____.

f. They got good directions on the Internet, so they didn't _____.

**Challenge** Write a story about a road trip. Use your own experience or your imagination.

1. **Look in your dictionary. Who does the following things? Check (✓) the columns.**

| | The Employer | The Receptionist | The Payroll Clerk | The Supervisor | All Employees |
|---|---|---|---|---|---|
| **a.** uses a time clock | | | | | ✓ |
| **b.** greets customers | | | | | |
| **c.** signs paycheques | | | | | |
| **d.** receives paycheques | | | | | |
| **e.** hands out paycheques | | | | | |
| **f.** gives instructions | | | | | |

2. **Complete the conversations. Use the words in the box.**

| | | | |
|---|---|---|---|
| customer | deductions | employee | entrance |
| payroll clerk | ~~receptionist~~ | time clock | pay stub |

_____Receptionist_____: Irina's Computer Service. How can I help you?
**a.**

_____: I need to bring in my computer. Could you tell me your address?
**b.**

_____: This is my first day. I need to clock in, but I can't find the
**c.**

_____.
**d.**

**Supervisor:** It's over there. To the right of the _____ where you
**e.**

come in.

**Employee:** I don't understand my _____. Why are there so
**f.**

many _____?
**g.**

_____: Well, this one is for federal. This is for GPP. This is for EI.
**h.**

3. **What about you? Look in your dictionary. Answer the questions. Discuss your answers with a classmate.**

a. Would you like to work at Irina's Computer Service? Why or why not?

_____

b. Would you prefer to work in the office or the room with the time clock? Why?

_____

4. **Look in your dictionary. *True* or *False*? Correct the underlined words in the false sentences.**

       *A customer*

   **a.** ~~An employee~~ is standing in the entrance.      _____*false*_____

   **b.** Employees can find the <u>safety regulations</u> near the door    _____
       that says *Employees Only*.

   **c.** Irina Sarkov is in <u>the office</u>.                  _____

   **d.** The <u>payroll clerk</u> is giving Kate Babic a paycheque.    _____

   **e.** The supervisor is talking to <u>the employer</u>.        _____

5. **Look at the pay stub and paycheck. Answer the questions.**

   **a.** What is the employee's name?

        _____*Asif Ahmad*_____

   **b.** What is the employer's name?

        _____

   **c.** What are the wages before deductions?

        _____

   **d.** How many deductions are there?

        _____

   **e.** Which is more, the GPP or the
       EI deduction?

        _____

   **f.** What is the amount of the paycheque?

        _____

| IRINA'S COMPUTER SERVICE | 10/17/11 to 10/23/11 |
| --- | --- |
| 7000 Main Street Cape Breton, NS B1X 1J6 | |

**Asif Ahmad**
600-23-5473

| | |
| --- | --- |
| **Salary** | **$860.00** |
| Deductions | |
| Federal | $94.60 |
| GPP | $23.65 |
| EI | $12.47 |
| **Net** | **$729.28** |

| IRINA'S COMPUTER SERVICE | Cheque number: 123456789 999999999 124 |
| --- | --- |
| 7000 Main Street Cape Breton, NS B1X 1J6 | |

Pay to the order of ____Asif Ahmad____ **$729.28**

Seven hundred twenty-nine and 28/100 dollars

Town Bank                  *Irina Sarkov*

**Challenge** Look at the pay stub in Exercise 5. What is *EI*? Look up *EI* online or ask someone you know.

**1. Look in your dictionary. Write the job titles.**

### HELP WANTED  JOBS A3

**a.** _Baker_  to make bread, pies, and cakes at our midtown restaurant. $10.67/hr. 555-2343

**b.** _____  to prepare and sell meat at our busy counter. S & W Supermarket. $28,000/yr. Call 555-4345

**c.** _____  to receive payment, give change and receipts to customers. Amy's Foods. Mineral Springs Road. 555-2243

**d.** _____  to plan and design public buildings at our growing firm. MCKAY, BROWN, & PETRILLO. 555-3451

**e.** _____  to watch our two preschoolers. Good storytelling skills a must! Excellent references required. $15/hr. 555-3406

**f.** _____  to put together parts in radio factory. On-the-job-training. $450/wk. Call Frank Collins. 555-9922.

**g.** _____  to repair and maintain cars at small garage. Part-time, weekends. 555-7396

**h.** _____  to help build shelves and doors in new building. $525/wk., 555-4345. Ask for Mr. Heller.

**i.** _____  to perform in plays for a small theatre company. TV, stage, or movie experience. 555-8299

**j.** _____  to plan and organize appointments for busy business executive. H. Thomas & Sons. 555-8787

**2. Circle the words to complete the sentences.**

a. A carpenter / childcare worker works with children.

b. An auto mechanic / accountant needs to be good with numbers.

c. An appliance repair person / assembler can fix refrigerators.

d. An architect / artist enjoys painting.

e. Many business owners / businesspeople have their own stores.

**3. What about you? Look at the ads in Exercise 1. Which job would you like? Which job wouldn't you like? Why?**

**Challenge** Look at page 258 in this book. Follow the instructions.

1. **Look in your dictionary. *True* or *False*? Correct the underlined words in the false sentences.**

   a. The home health care aide and the ~~customer service representative~~ work with patients.

      *dental assistant*

      *false*

   b. The <u>graphic designer</u> uses a computer.

      _____

   c. The delivery person works for a <u>gardener</u>.

      _____

   d. The firefighter and the <u>dockworker</u> wear hard hats.

      _____

2. **Look at the bar graph. Circle the words to complete the sentences.**

   ## How Stressful* is the Job?

   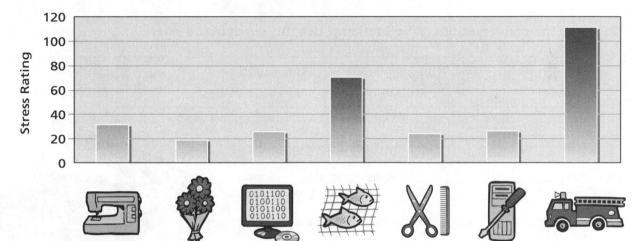

   * A *stressful* job can make you feel nervous and not relaxed.

   **Based on information from**: Krantz, L.: *Jobs Rated Almanac* (NJ: Barricade Books, 2002).

   a. A <u>computer technician / (firefighter)</u> has the job with the most stress.

   b. A <u>florist / computer software engineer</u> has the job with the least stress.

   c. A garment worker's job is less stressful than a <u>computer technician's / commercial fisher's</u> job.

   d. A hairdresser and a <u>computer software engineer / commercial fisher</u> have about the same amount of job stress.

   e. A hairdresser has less job stress than a <u>florist / garment worker</u>.

3. **What about you? Look in your dictionary. Which job do you think is the most stressful? the least stressful? Why?**

**Challenge** Look at pages 166–169 in your dictionary. Find five other stressful jobs. Tell a classmate. Do you and your classmate agree?

1. **Look in your dictionary. Cross out the word that doesn't belong. Give a reason.**

   **a.** homemaker ~~musician~~ housekeeper

   _A musician doesn't work in the home._

   **b.** machine operator nurse occupational therapist

   _____

   **c.** (house) painter medical records technician manicurist

   _____

   **d.** police officer messenger homemaker

   _____

   **e.** physician assistant nurse model

   _____

2. **Read the conversations. Who's talking? Use the words in the box.**

   | interpreter | ~~lawyer~~ | manicurist | model |
   |---|---|---|---|
   | mover | musician | physician assistant | police officer |

   **a.** _____Lawyer_____ : "Your honour, I object! My client is not guilty!"

   _____ : "Monsieur le juge, je récuse! Mon client n'est pas coupable!"

   **b.** _____ : "Where should we put this couch?"

   _____ : "Over there. That way our patients can look out the window while they're waiting."

   **c.** _____ : "I'll be wearing a red dress at the fashion show."

   _____ : "Well, this colour nail polish will look great with it."

   **d.** _____ : "Where were you yesterday between 11:00 and 11:30 p.m.?"

   _____ : "I was at the Blue Note Club, detective. I was playing the piano."

**Challenge** Write three short conversations between a police officer and a house painter, a homemaker and a mover, and a messenger and a physician assistant. Use the conversations in Exercise 2 as an example.

**1. Look in your dictionary. Who said these things?**

a. "These shoes are very comfortable. Would you like to try them on?" _____retail clerk_____

b. "It can be difficult being a single mom, but we can help you." _____

c. ". . . 18, 19, 20 . . . . That's 20 boxes of desk lamps." _____

d. "You can get a very special offer, but you must order today!" _____

e. "Ms. Davidson's office is through the glass doors to your left." _____

**2. Look at the chart. *True* or *False*?**

| Occupation | Hours worked per week | $ a year |
|---|---|---|
| | 45 | 35,000 |
| | 42.5 | 50,000 |
| | 42.5 | 28,000 |
| | 47.5 | 47,000 |
| | 35 | 20,000 |
| | 40 | 49,000 |
| | 45 | 60,000 |
| | 45 | 50,000 |

a. A truck driver works more hours per week than a sanitation worker. _____true_____

b. A server works as many hours as a security guard. _____

c. A veterinarian works the most hours and makes the most money. _____

d. A server works the fewest hours and makes the least money. _____

e. A welder works as many hours as a writer and makes almost
as much money. _____

f. A reporter makes the same amount of money as a security guard. _____

**Challenge** Look at job ads online or in the newspaper. Find four jobs. Make a chart like the one in
Exercise 2. Then write four sentences comparing the jobs.

**1. Look in your dictionary. Complete the job descriptions.**

a. A cashier ___*uses a cash register*___.

b. A childcare worker _____.

c. A garment worker _____.

d. A carpenter _____.

e. A server _____.

f. An interpreter _____.

**2. What about you? Complete the questionnaire. Check (✓) the job skills you have.**

| Can you…? | Kim | Alexis | Hassan | Diana | Your name: _____ |
|---|---|---|---|---|---|
| solve math problems | ✓ | | | | |
| program computers | ✓ | | | ✓ | |
| type | ✓ | | ✓ | ✓ | |
| sell cars | | ✓ | | ✓ | |
| repair appliances | | | | ✓ | |
| operate heavy machinery | | | ✓ | | |
| drive a truck | | ✓ | | | |
| teach | ✓ | | | | |
| do manual labour | ✓ | | ✓ | | |
| assemble components | | ✓ | ✓ | | |

**3. Look at the chart in Exercise 2. *True* or *False*?**

a. Kim could apply for a job as a teacher.                                          ___*true*___

b. Hassan could get a job as a truck driver.                                       _____

c. Only Diana could apply for a job as a repair person.                    _____

d. Both Kim and Alexis could get jobs as assemblers.                       _____

e. Alexis could apply for a job as a salesperson, but not as a repair person. _____

f. Kim, Hassan, and Diana could be administrative assistants.          _____

g. You and Kim could work as accountants.                                        _____

h. You and Hassan can both work with your hands.                           _____

**Challenge** Look at page 258 in this book. Follow the instructions.

1. **Look in your dictionary. What does the administrative assistant need to do to follow the boss's instructions?**

    a. "Please put these files in alphabetical order."          _organize materials_

    b. "I'd like to meet with Mr. Ghosh next Friday, if possible."    _____

    c. "Could you send this report to Amy Ma at 555-3523?"    _____

    d. "We need enough copies for thirty people."    _____

2. **Read the conversations. Circle the words to complete the sentences.**

    a. **Muniza:** J & R Associates. Good morning.
       **Caller 1:** Hello. Can I speak to John Smith, please?

       Muniza is <u>putting the caller on hold</u> /<u>greeting the caller.</u>

    b. **Caller 2:** Is Marta Rodriguez there?
       **Muniza:** Yes. I'll connect you.

       Muniza is <u>checking messages</u> / <u>transferring the call</u>.

    c. **Caller 3:** Can I speak to Tom Chen, please?
       **Muniza:** I'm sorry. Mr. Chen isn't in.
       **Caller 3:** OK. Please tell him that I called.
       **Muniza:** Sure. What is your name and number, please?

       Muniza is <u>leaving a message</u> / <u>taking a message</u>.

Muniza

3. **Look at the pictures. Write what the office assistant can do.**

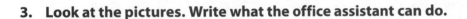

    a. ___He can transcribe notes.___    c. _____

    b. _____    d. _____

**Challenge** Look in your dictionary. Make a list of the office and telephone skills you have.

**1. Look in your dictionary. Complete the sentences.**

a. __Vocational training__ gives you hands-on experience.

b. One woman is taking an _____ in medical transcription.

c. One man is getting _____ from his supervisor.

d. Ms. Diaz recently got a _____. Now she's a manager.

**2. Complete the FAQs (Frequently Asked Questions) from a website. Use the words in the box.**

| | | | |
|---|---|---|---|
| career counsellors | internship | interest inventory | job fair |
| on-the-job training | resource centre | recruiters | skill inventory |
| vocational training | | | |

---

**Career Counselling Centre**

**Q.** I'm not really sure about the kind of job I want. Can you help me?

**A.** Yes! Come and talk to one of our __career counsellors__. An _____ will
a.                                              b.
help you find out the kinds of jobs you will enjoy. A _____ will show you the
c.
kinds of jobs you will be good at.

**Q.** What if I'm interested in a job but don't have the necessary skills?

**A.** Many jobs offer _____. You learn the skills <u>after</u> you are hired.
d.

**Q.** How can I learn skills <u>before</u> I'm hired?

**A.** There are several possibilities. _____ teaches practical skills for a specific
e.
job, for example a car mechanic or a computer programmer. But you can also get an

_____ with a company before you graduate from school.
f.

**Q.** How can I get more information about a specific job?

**A.** Our _____ has hundreds of books and brochures about different jobs.
g.
And you can speak to _____ from various companies at our yearly
h.

_____ .
i.

---

**Challenge** When is it good to have vocational training? List four jobs. Tell a classmate.

**See page 308 for listening practice.**

1. **Look in your dictionary. *Before* or *After*? Circle the words to complete the sentences.**

   a. Dan checked Internet job sites (before) / after he went to an employment agency.

   b. He wrote a cover letter before / after he wrote a resume.

   c. Before / After he looked in the classifieds, he talked to friends.

   d. Before / After he went on an interview, he filled out an application.

2. **Complete the information. Use the words in the box.**

   | | | |
   |---|---|---|
   | set up an interview | check Internet job sites | send in your resume |
   | write a resume | ~~talk to friends~~ | go on the interview |
   | fill out an application | get hired | go to an employment agency |
   | look in the classifieds | look for help wanted signs | |

   ---

   http://www.jobtips/default.ca

   # Looking for a Job
   **It can take a lot of time—and work—to find a job. Here are some tips.**

   Tell everyone that you are looking for work. Begin close to home. ___Talk to friends___,
   a.

   relatives, teachers, and classmates. Keep your eyes open. When you're walking down the street,

   _____ in store windows. Get the newspaper every day and be sure to
   b.

   _____. Go online to _____. If you want someone to help
   c.                                         d.

   you with the process, _____. They can even help you _____ by
   e.                                                    f.

   listing all your work experience and education.

   **Applying for a job:** When you apply for a job, _____ and a cover letter. Interested
   g.

   employers will call you to _____. Then, you will probably have to
   h.

   _____. This gives the employer basic information about your skills and experience.
   i.

   When you _____, you will have the chance to talk about your experience in more
   j.

   detail. It's a long process. Remember: Be patient and don't give up. You may have to try many different

   approaches before you finally _____ and get that first paycheque!
   k.

**Challenge** Look at page 259 in this book. Follow the instructions.

1. **Look in your dictionary. Write the interview skill.**

   a. "I worked there for four years."  <u>talk about your experience</u>

   b. "What is the dress code?"  _____

   c. "Nice to meet you."  _____

   d. "Hmm. This website says GBG has 100 employees."  _____

2. **Look at the pictures. Circle the words to complete the interviewer's notes.**

🌐 **GLOBAL IMPORTERS**          Amy Cho Interview                    4/23

Ms. Cho (dressed appropriately) / prepared in a suit, and she <u>was / wasn't</u> very
　　　　　　　　　　a.　　　　　　　　　　　　　　　　　　　　　　b.

neat. The interview was at 10:00, but she was <u>late / on time</u>. She didn't
　　　　　　　　　　　　　　　　　　　　　　　　　　　c.

<u>bring her resume / turn off her cellphone</u>. Ms. Cho <u>greeted me / shook hands</u>,
　　　　　　d.　　　　　　　　　　　　　　　　　　　　　　　　　　e.

but she didn't <u>listen carefully / make eye contact</u>. She <u>asked questions / talked</u>
　　　　　　　　　　f.　　　　　　　　　　　　　　　　　　　　　　　g.

about her work experience. I liked that she <u>asked / brought</u> questions about
　　　　　　　　　　　　　　　　　　　　　　　　h.

our company. At the end of the interview, she <u>didn't thank / thanked</u> me, but
　　　　　　　　　　　　　　　　　　　　　　　　i.

a few days later she <u>brought her resume / wrote a thank-you note</u>.
　　　　　　　　　　　　　　　　　　　j.

**Challenge** Look at Exercise 2. Would you give Amy Cho a job? Why or why not?

**1. Look in your dictionary. Complete the factory newsletter.**

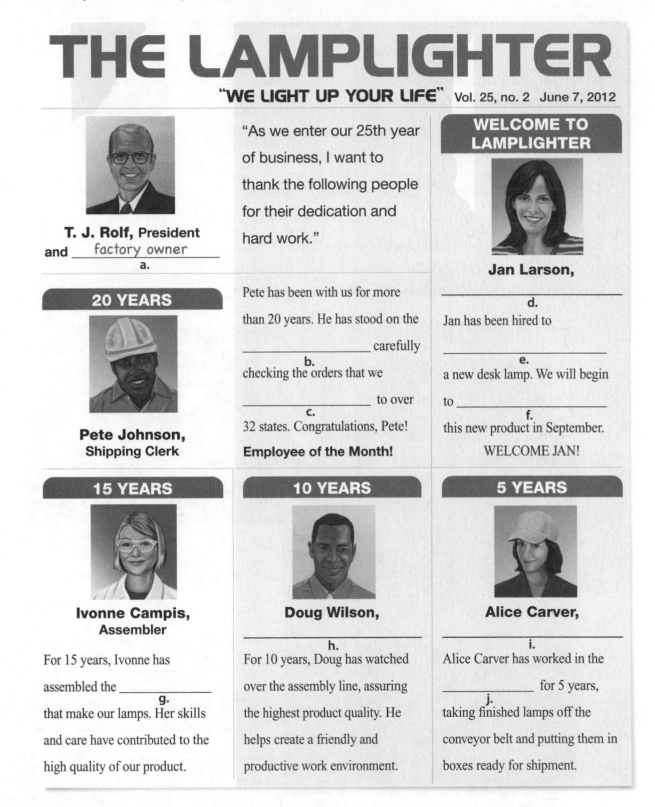

# THE LAMPLIGHTER

**"WE LIGHT UP YOUR LIFE"** Vol. 25, no. 2 June 7, 2012

**T. J. Rolf, President**
and _factory owner_
a.

"As we enter our 25th year of business, I want to thank the following people for their dedication and hard work."

### WELCOME TO LAMPLIGHTER

**Jan Larson,**
_____
d.
Jan has been hired to
_____
e.
a new desk lamp. We will begin
to _____
f.
this new product in September.
WELCOME JAN!

**20 YEARS**

**Pete Johnson,**
**Shipping Clerk**

Pete has been with us for more than 20 years. He has stood on the _____ carefully
b.
checking the orders that we _____ to over
c.
32 states. Congratulations, Pete!
**Employee of the Month!**

**15 YEARS**

**Ivonne Campis,**
**Assembler**

For 15 years, Ivonne has assembled the _____
g.
that make our lamps. Her skills and care have contributed to the high quality of our product.

**10 YEARS**

**Doug Wilson,**
_____
h.
For 10 years, Doug has watched over the assembly line, assuring the highest product quality. He helps create a friendly and productive work environment.

**5 YEARS**

**Alice Carver,**
_____
i.
Alice Carver has worked in the _____ for 5 years,
j.
taking finished lamps off the conveyor belt and putting them in boxes ready for shipment.

**Challenge** Look in your dictionary. Write short paragraphs about the shipping clerk and the order picker for the factory newsletter in Exercise 1. Use your imagination.

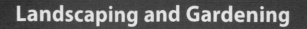
1. **Look in your dictionary. Complete the sentences.**

   a. The _____ <u>trowel</u> _____ is to the left of the hedge clippers.

   b. The gardening crew leader is talking to the _____.

   c. You can use a _____ or a _____
      to remove leaves from your lawn.

   d. You can use a _____ to remove weeds.

   e. You need a _____ to plant a tree.

   f. You can cut the grass with a _____.

   g. You can use a _____ to move dirt or plants.

   h. You can water the lawn by hand, or you can install a _____.

2. **Look at the picture. Complete the note to the gardening crew.**

Eric,

I ___<u>fertilized</u>___ the plants and
    **a.**
_____ the hedges, but please:
    **b.**
_____
    **c.**
_____
    **d.**
_____
    **e.**
_____
    **f.**
_____
    **g.**
                        Thanks!!

PLANT STARTER

**Challenge** Compare a shovel to a trowel and hedge clippers to pruning shears. How are they the same? How are they different? What can you use them for?

1. **Look in your dictionary. Cross out the word that doesn't belong. Write the category.**

   a. _Place for animals_     barn     corral     ~~vegetable garden~~

   b. _____     hired hand     field     orchard

   c. _____     vineyard     soybeans     wheat

   d. _____     farmer     rancher     tractor

   e. _____     hay     livestock     cattle

2. **Circle the words to complete the blog.**

   ---

   ● ● ●    m myspot.ca       <<back     MySpot.ca | rss 🔊 | sign in | sign out

   ### SAMANTHA'S TRAVELS

   JULY 10: **My First Day on the Farm**

   When I got up, it was still dark. John Johnson, the
   (farmer) / hired hand who owns the place, was already
       a.
   in the corral / barn. He was harvesting / milking the
       b.               c.
   cows. My job was to feed / plant the chickens and
                d.
   other cattle / livestock.
       e.

   Breakfast here is great! We have fresh eggs and ham along with tomatoes from

   the vegetable garden / vineyard and fruit from the barn / orchard. After breakfast, it
       f.                            g.
   is time to work in the fence / field. John says that in the old days horses pulled most
                  h.
   of the farm equipment / cattle. Today, a hired hand / tractor does the job. John and
            i.                     j.
   his farm workers / ranchers planted rows of corn and other crops / wheat. They also
       k.                            l.
   grow alfalfa / cotton for animal feed. I'd like to come back when they harvest / milk
       m.                                   n.
   the corn in the summer. I like life on the farm.

                  POSTED BY SAMANTHA AT 1:52 PM     [REPLY TO THIS]

   ---

   **Challenge** Would you like to spend some time on a farm or a ranch? Write a paragraph explaining your opinion.

**1.** Look in your dictionary. *True* or *False*? Correct the <u>underlined</u> words in the false sentences.

       *thirteen*

a. There are ~~eight~~ construction workers on the site.      <u>   *false*   </u>

b. One worker is climbing a <u>ladder</u>.      <u>        </u>

c. Two construction workers are helping move the <u>plywood</u>.      <u>        </u>

d. The worker in the <u>cherry picker</u> is not hammering.      <u>        </u>

e. One worker is using a <u>sledgehammer</u>.      <u>        </u>

**2.** Complete the sentences. Use the words on the bricks.

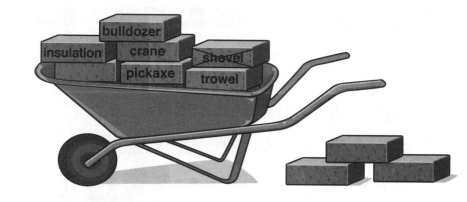

a. You can use a _____*shovel*_____ to dig a small hole in the ground.

b. A _____ moves earth or large rocks from one place to another.

c. _____ keeps a house warm.

d. A _____ can lift and place beams on high floors.

e. A _____ is used to lay bricks.

f. A _____ is used to dig in very hard ground.

**3.** What about you? Check (✓) the materials that your school and home are made of.

| | School | Home |
|---|---|---|
| bricks | | |
| shingles | | |
| stucco | | |
| wood | | |
| Other: | | |

**Challenge** Look for pictures of buildings in your dictionary, newspaper, or in a magazine. What building materials are used? **Example:** *The condominium on page 52 is made of brick.*

1. **Look in your dictionary. *True* or *False*?**

   a. The man listening to music is a careful worker. _____*false*_____

   b. The frayed cord is near the slippery floor. _____

   c. There's a fire extinguisher near the flammable liquids. _____

   d. Poisonous fumes are coming from the radioactive materials. _____

2. **Circle the words to complete the safety poster.**

   ⚠ **WARNING**

   # PROTECT YOURSELF
   ## from Head to Toe!

   Protect your head: A (hard hat) / respirator can protect you from falling objects. Don't forget
                                              a.
   your hair. If it's long, wear your hair back so it won't get caught in machinery.

   Protect your eyes: Always wear safety glasses / work gloves or earmuffs / safety goggles.
                                                       b.                 c.

   Protect your ears: Noise can cause hearing loss. Wear ear plugs / safety goggles or safety
                                                           d.

   earmuffs / particle masks if you work near loud machinery.
             e.

   Protect your hands: Always wear work gloves / back support belts when handling
                                                   f.

   knee pads / radioactive materials.
                g.

   Protect your feet: Knee pads / Safety boots protect you from falling objects.
                       h.

   Avoid dangerous situations: Don't use power tools in wet locations or near

   radioactive / flammable liquids or gases. Keep a fire extinguisher / respirator on the wall in
             i.                                        j.

   case of fire. And have a frayed cord / two-way radio so you can communicate with other
                              k.

   workers. Remember: Better safe than sorry!

3. **What about you? What safety equipment do you use? When do you use it?**

   **Example:** *I wear ear plugs when I go to a loud concert.*

**Challenge** Look at page 259 in this book. Follow the instructions.

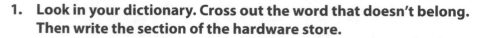
**1. Look in your dictionary. Cross out the word that doesn't belong. Then write the section of the hardware store.**

a. _____Hardware_____    nail     bolt     ~~C-clamp~~     wood screw

b. _____    axe     plunger     pipe     fittings

c. _____    circular saw     2 × 4     router     electric drill

d. _____    paintbrush     paint roller     spray gun     chisel

e. _____    wire stripper     drill bit     extension cord     wire

f. _____    hacksaw     chain     adjustable wrench     mallet

**2. Complete the conversations. Use the words on the toolbox.**

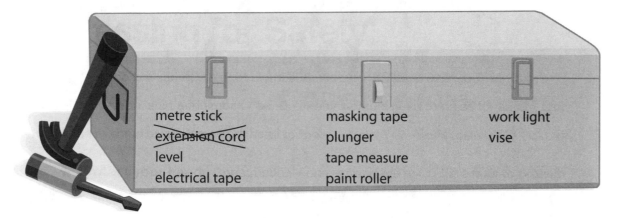

metre stick     masking tape     work light
~~extension cord~~     plunger     vise
level     tape measure
electrical tape     paint roller

a. **Ty:** I want to use this electric drill over there, but the cord is too short.
    **Jade:** No problem. Use this _____extension cord_____.

b. **Ian:** I've been painting for hours, and I still have three more walls to do.
    **Tina:** Why don't you use this _____? It's faster than a paint brush.

c. **Lily:** Oh, no. The toilet is stopped up again.
    **Dan:** Here. Use this _____. It always works.

d. **Kim:** Do you know how long the shelf in the dining room is?
    **Lian:** No. Use the _____ or _____ to find out.

e. **Eva:** Help! I could use a third hand here!
    **Jana:** Use the _____ to hold the wood in place.

f. **Jules:** Don't get paint on the glass!
    **Lyle:** I won't. I always put _____ around the panes before I start.

g. **Nico:** That wire doesn't look very safe.
    **Iris:** Don't worry. I'll put some of this _____ on before using it.

h. **Olga:** Does this shelf look straight?
    **Boris:** Hmm. I'm not sure. Let's use the _____. Then we'll know for certain.

i. **Enzo:** It's so dark behind here. I can't see what I'm doing!
    **Pia:** Here. Use the _____.

3. **Look at the pictures. Each situation shows a mistake. Describe the mistake and tell the people what they need to do the job right.**

a.

_You can't paint on that wall._
_You need to use a scraper first._

b.

_____

_____

c.

_____

_____

d.

_____

_____

e.
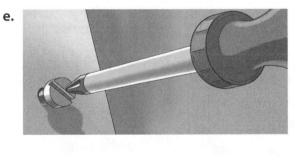

_____

_____

f.
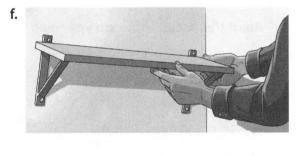

_____

_____

4. **What about you? Check (✓) the tools you or someone you know has used. What did you use them for?**

☐ hammer _____

☐ axe _____

☐ handsaw _____

☐ screwdriver _____

☐ pliers _____

☐ plane _____

☐ wrench _____

☐ vise _____

☐ electric drill _____

☐ Other: _____

**Challenge** Imagine you can have only three tools from the ones in Exercise 4. Which would you choose? Explain your choice.

See page 310 for listening practice.

**1. Look in your dictionary. Answer the questions.**

a. Who is in the reception area?            _the receptionist_

b. Who is working in the cubicle next to the conference room?  _____

c. Who is walking to the supply cabinet?  _____

d. Who is cleaning the floor?  _____

e. Where is the presentation?  _____

f. Who is standing at the file cabinet?  _____

**2. Match the word parts.**

_5_ a. paper          1. bands

___ b. correction     2. book

___ c. postal         3. scale

___ d. rubber         4. pad

___ e. appointment    5. shredder

___ f. legal          6. fluid

**3. Read the notes. What do you need to do the job? Use the words from Exercise 2.**

> Please collate these pages, but don't staple them.
> Thanks.
> L.

> There are some mistakes in this report. Please correct them before you make copies.

> * This is for your eyes only!
> Please read and destroy.

a. _rubber bands_     b. _____     c. _____

> Please let me know when my next meeting with L. J. Inc. is.

> I'll be out of the office on Friday. Please take notes at the staff meeting.
> Thanks.
> R.F.

> Mail two packages to Anne Miles.

d. _____     e. _____     f. _____

**4. Look in your dictionary. Cross out the word that doesn't belong. Give a reason.**

a. janitor    file clerk    ~~mailer~~    receptionist    _A mailer isn't a person._

b. scanner    desk    file cabinet    supply cabinet    _____

c. envelope    ink pad    letterhead    sticky note    _____

d. rubber band    paper clip    paper cutter    staples    _____

e. calculator    computer    fax machine    stapler    _____

**5. Circle the words to complete the instructions.**

# MEMO

**To:**  Alice Rader

**From:** Margaret Lu  ML

---

\* The electric pencil sharpener /(photocopier) is broken again. Please call the repair
  **a.**
  person. You'll find the phone number in the laser printer / rotary card file under "p."
                                              **b.**

\* The book on my desk goes to A. Olinski at 354 Main Street. The mailing label /stamp
                                                                 **c.**
  is already filled out. Please use glue / clear tape so you can read the address through it.
                            **d.**

\* The Thompson report is more than 500 pages. Use the stapler / laser printer so it prints
                                                        **e.**
  out faster. Before you file it, use the paper cutter / shredder to make it 8 × 10 inches.
                                          **f.**
  The paper in the printer is too long now.

\* Please stamp all letters to Japan "air mail." (The legal / ink pad is in the top
                                                       **g.**
  left drawer.)

\* Please order more rubber bands / clear tape. (I like the ones that come in different
                          **h.**
  colours and sizes.)

Thanks.

---

**Challenge** Look at the office supplies in your dictionary. Which items can you use for the same job?

**Example:** *You can use an inkjet printer or a laser printer to print out computer files.*

See page 311 for listening practice.

1. **Look in your dictionary. Read these job descriptions. Write the job.**

   a. Register and check out guests: _____desk clerk_____

   b. Carry the guests' luggage on a luggage cart: _____

   c. Take care of the guests' cars: _____

   d. Clean the guests' rooms: _____

   e. Repair and service hotel equipment: _____

2. **Circle the words to complete the hotel website.**

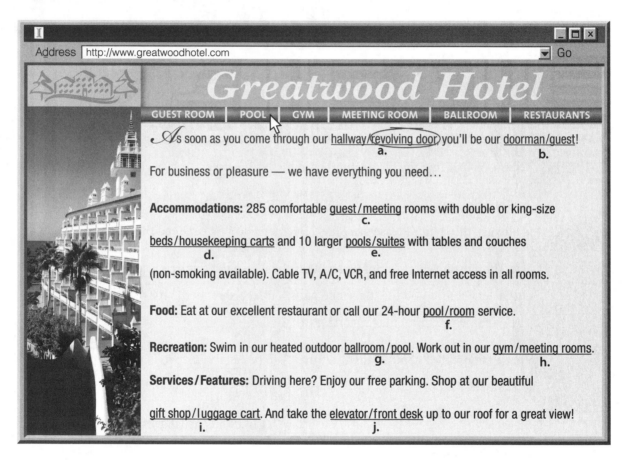

Address http://www.greatwoodhotel.com    Go

# Greatwood Hotel

| GUEST ROOM | POOL | GYM | MEETING ROOM | BALLROOM | RESTAURANTS |

As soon as you come through our hallway/(revolving door) you'll be our doorman/guest!
   **a.**                                                                      **b.**

For business or pleasure — we have everything you need...

**Accommodations:** 285 comfortable guest/meeting rooms with double or king-size
                                                 **c.**

beds/housekeeping carts and 10 larger pools/suites with tables and couches
      **d.**                                    **e.**

(non-smoking available). Cable TV, A/C, VCR, and free Internet access in all rooms.

**Food:** Eat at our excellent restaurant or call our 24-hour pool/room service.
                                                                    **f.**

**Recreation:** Swim in our heated outdoor ballroom/pool. Work out in our gym/meeting rooms.
                                                     **g.**                          **h.**

**Services/Features:** Driving here? Enjoy our free parking. Shop at our beautiful

gift shop/luggage cart. And take the elevator/front desk up to our roof for a great view!
      **i.**                                **j.**

---

**Challenge** Imagine you are staying at the hotel in your dictionary. Write a postcard.
Describe the hotel.

1. **Look in your dictionary. Read these job descriptions. Write the job.**

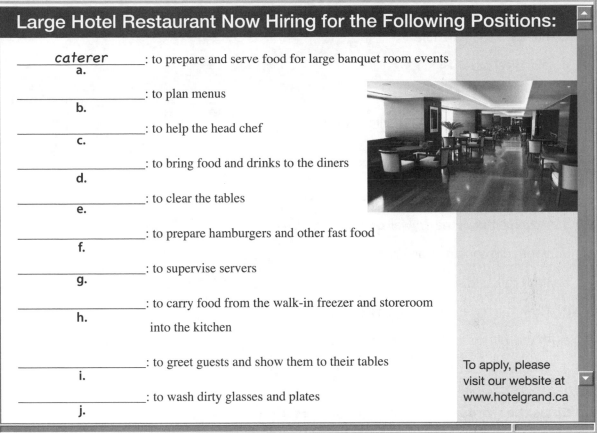

http://www.restaurantopening.ca

## Large Hotel Restaurant Now Hiring for the Following Positions:

_____caterer_____ : to prepare and serve food for large banquet room events
a.

_____ : to plan menus
b.

_____ : to help the head chef
c.

_____ : to bring food and drinks to the diners
d.

_____ : to clear the tables
e.

_____ : to prepare hamburgers and other fast food
f.

_____ : to supervise servers
g.

_____ : to carry food from the walk-in freezer and storeroom
h. into the kitchen

_____ : to greet guests and show them to their tables
i.

_____ : to wash dirty glasses and plates
j.

To apply, please visit our website at www.hotelgrand.ca

2. **What about you? Would you like to work as the following? Check (✓) _Yes_ or _No_. Give a reason.**

| | Yes | No | |
|---|---|---|---|
| a. short-order cook | ☐ | ☐ | _____ |
| b. dishwasher | ☐ | ☐ | _____ |
| c. food preparation worker | ☐ | ☐ | _____ |
| d. sous chef | ☐ | ☐ | _____ |
| e. server | ☐ | ☐ | _____ |
| f. head waiter | ☐ | ☐ | _____ |
| g. bus person | ☐ | ☐ | _____ |
| h. caterer | ☐ | ☐ | _____ |
| i. runner | ☐ | ☐ | _____ |

**Challenge** Write a job ad for a restaurant worker. Use the job descriptions in Exercise 1 as an example.

1. **Look in your dictionary. How many of the following do you see?**

   a. accidents that have happened or will happen    _7_

   b. bricklayers    ____

   c. dates on the schedule    ____

   d. electrical hazards    ____

   e. budgets    ____

   f. notes about people who called in sick    ____

   g. floor plans    ____

2. **Look in your dictionary. Answer the questions.**

   a. How much will the drywall cost?    _$200,000_

   b. When did construction start?    _____

   c. Who called in sick?    _____ and _____

   d. How much will the wiring cost?    _____

   e. When will the walls be put up?    _____

   f. Who is the contractor?    _____

3. **Circle the words to complete the conversation.**

   **Sam:** Hello. Lopez Contracting.

   **Pat:** Hello, Mr. Lopez. It's Pat. I'm (calling in sick) / worried today.
                                                     **a.**

   **Sam:** Oh, no. I need you to help me with the budget / floor plan. We're over by $50,000.
                                                    **b.**

   **Pat:** Could you email the budget? I can look at it at home. I think it would be

   an electrical hazard / dangerous for me to come to work today. I'm really sick.
                                   **c.**

   **Sam:** OK. I'll send it right now. See if we can cut costs with the wiring / bricklayer.
                                                               **d.**

   **Pat:** Hmm . . . Well, I don't think so. That could be a contractor / an electrical hazard.
                                                                    **e.**

   I'll look at the budget. Maybe we can pay the bricklayers / clinics less.
                                                      **f.**

   **Sam:** No, we can't do that! They're the best.

   **Pat:** Maybe we could pay the floor plan / contractor less.
                                                    **g.**

   **Sam:** You know what, you're sick and need to rest. I'll ask Sue to help me.

**4. Complete the notes. Use the words in the box.**

| | | | |
|---|---|---|---|
| called in sick | budget | wiring | electrical hazard |
| floor plan | ~~bricklayer~~ | clinic | |

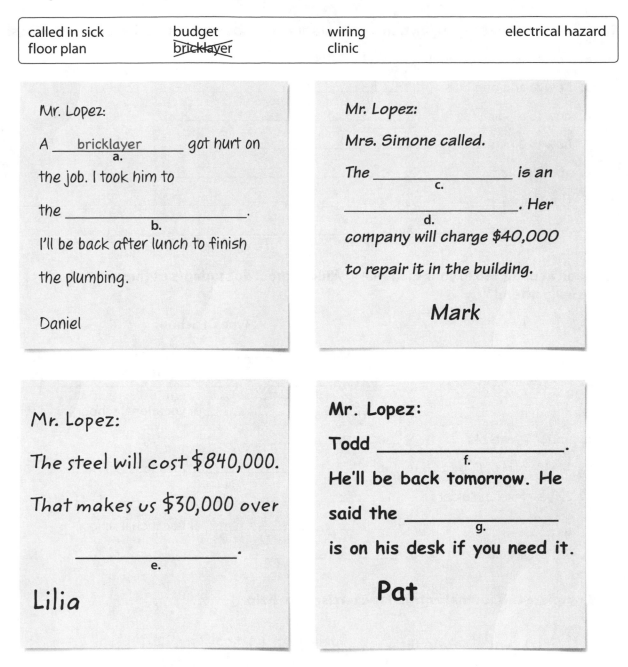

Mr. Lopez:

A ___bricklayer___ got hurt on
         a.
the job. I took him to

the _____.
         b.
I'll be back after lunch to finish

the plumbing.

Daniel

---

Mr. Lopez:

Mrs. Simone called.

The _____ is an
         c.
_____. Her
         d.
company will charge $40,000

to repair it in the building.

      **Mark**

---

Mr. Lopez:

The steel will cost $840,000.

That makes us $30,000 over

_____.
         e.

Lilia

---

Mr. Lopez:

Todd _____.
         f.
He'll be back tomorrow. He

said the _____
         g.
is on his desk if you need it.

   **Pat**

---

**5. What about you? Look in your dictionary. Which job do you think would be the hardest? the easiest? the most dangerous? Why?**

**Challenge** Write a report about the construction site in your dictionary. Write about the problems that happened that day.

# Schools and Subjects

1. **Look at page 188 in your dictionary. Where are the students learning the following things?**

   a. how to teach preschool    _in college_

   b. how to add numbers    _____

   c. how to repair a car    _____

   d. how to count to four    _____

   e. about biology    _____

   f. about history    _____, _____,

   and _____

2. **Look at page 188 in your dictionary. Which school do students of these ages usually attend?**

   | Age | Type Of School |
   |---|---|

   a. 11–14 years old    _middle school_

   b. 18–22 years old    _____, _____,

   _____, or vocational school

   c. under 5 years old    _____

   d. 14–18 years old    _____ or vocational school

   e. 22 years old and older    _____, _____,

   _____, or vocational school

   f. 5–11 years old    _____

3. **Complete this journal entry. Use Exercise 2 for help.**

   It's the end of Tommy's first week in _elementary school_! It seems like yesterday that I

   a.

   took him to _____ . His grade one class went to a farmers' market this week

   b.

   and brought home things beginning with the letters A and B—apples, beans, bananas. He's

   learning to read! In just six years, he'll be in _____ studying geography and history.

   c.

   After that, he'll be a teenager in _____, and we'll really have to think about his

   d.

   future. After graduation, will he go to _____ like his Dad? Or go to

   e.

   _____ and study computers, like I did? Wait a minute. He's just starting his second

   f.

   week of grade one now. Let's just enjoy this year.

**4.** **Look at page 189 in your dictionary. In which class are students doing the following things?**

a. painting _____arts_____

b. exercising _____

c. singing _____

d. learning about World War I _____

e. doing experiments in a group _____

f. studying the novel *Moby Dick* _____

g. speaking French and Spanish _____

h. repeating words in English _____

**5.** **Look at the things Katia needs for school. Complete her schedule.**

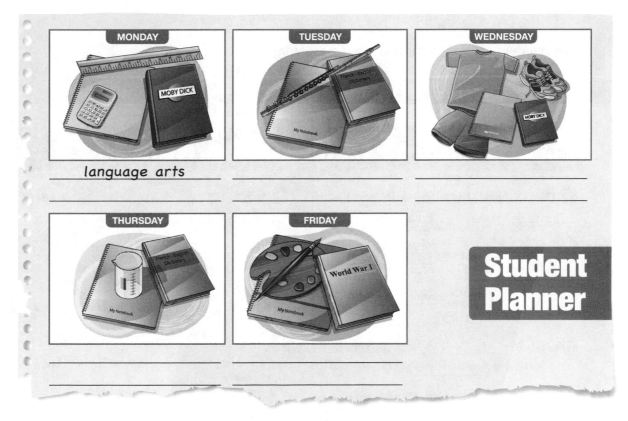

**6.** **What about you? Check (✓) the classes you would like to take.**

☐ math          ☐ music

☐ science         ☐ world languages     If *yes*, which?_____

☐ history         ☐ arts    If *yes*, which type?_____

☐ physical education   ☐ Other:_____

**Challenge** Explain your choices in Exercise 6.
**Example:** *I would like to take history because I like to learn about the world.*

1.  **Look in your dictionary. *True* or *False*? Correct the <u>underlined</u> words in the false sentences.**

    a.  The ~~conclusion~~ *body* of the essay has two paragraphs.      ____*false*____

    b.  The <u>title</u> of the essay has four words.      _____

    c.  The student indented the first <u>sentence</u> in each paragraph.      _____

    d.  There's a quotation in the <u>introduction</u>.      _____

    e.  The period comes <u>after</u> the last quotation mark.      _____

    f.  The student capitalized <u>names</u>.      _____

    g.  The <u>footnote</u> tells us where the student got his information.      _____

    h.  The student used parentheses in the first <u>sentence</u>.      _____

2.  **Look at the punctuation rules. Complete the sentences.**

    # Some Punctuation Rules

    **a** Use a ___question mark___ at the end of a question. *Where do you come from?*

    **b** Use a _____ at the end of a statement. *I come from Ecuador.*

    **c** Use an _____ to show a strong feeling. *I love Quito!*

    **d** Use an _____ in a contraction. *It's a beautiful city.*

    **e** Use a _____ before a list. *I miss a lot of things: my home, my friends, my school.*

    **f** Use a _____ between items in a list. *I email Luan, Enrique, and Kim every week.*

    **g** Use _____ around additional information. *I like Vancouver (especially the beach), and I'm beginning to feel more at home here.*

    **h** Use a _____ between parts of some words. *We live in a three-year-old building.*

    **i** Use _____ around a person's exact words. *My mother says, "There's no place like home."*

3.  **What about you? Write three sentences about your experience in this country. Use . . .**

    a.  a period      _____

    b.  quotation marks      _____

    c.  an exclamation mark      _____

**4. Look in your dictionary. What is Erdem doing?**

a. "For this draft, I'll just use my notebook."  ___writing a first draft___

b. "Oh, it should be *came*, not *come*!"  _____

c. "Here it is, Mr. Wilson."  _____

d. "I'll write *work* in this circle."  _____

e. "What do you think of the title, Mindy?"  _____

f. "Hmmm . . . Maybe I could write about my first day at work."  _____

g. "For this draft, I'll use my computer."  _____

h. "Paragraph 3 will be about success."  _____

**5. Find and circle seven more mistakes in this student's essay.**

## Things Get Better

I arrived in (whitehorse) in 2004. I came with my parents: my brother, and my little sister. At first I wasn't very happy. I didn't know anyone besides my family, and I missed my friends a lot. My mother told me, "Dont worry! Things will get better.

When I began school; things improved a little. I made friends right away? Because we were all from different countrie's we had to speak English. That really (helped) a lot! Now I can even write a composition in English. I guess my mother was right.

**6. Look at the essay in Exercise 5. Describe the mistakes.**

a. _The student didn't capitalize Whitehorse._

b. _The student used a colon after "parents" instead of a comma._

c. _____

d. _____

e. _____

f. _____

g. _____

h. _____

**Challenge** Write an essay about how you felt when you came to this country or started attending school. Write a first draft, edit it, get feedback, rewrite it, and turn in the essay to your teacher.

**1. Look in your dictionary. Cross out the word that doesn't belong. Write the category.**

a. _Types of math_     algebra     calculus     geometry     ~~solution~~

b. _____     even     negative     numerator     odd

c. _____     add     divide     equation     subtract

d. _____     circle     curved     perpendicular     straight

e. _____     acute     diagonal     obtuse     right

f. _____     cone     cylinder     parallelogram     sphere

g. _____     cube     rectangle     square     triangle

**2. Complete the test. Circle the letter of the correct answer.**

## Mathematics test

Name: _____

Date: _____

School: _____

**1.** The number 12 is ___.
   (a.) even
   b. odd
   c. negative

**2.** The ___ of 8 × 3 = 24.
   a. sum
   b. difference
   c. product

**3.** An equation always has ___.
   a. an equal (=) sign
   b. a fraction
   c. pi

**4.** In an equation, _x_ is called ___.
   a. an endpoint
   b. a graph
   c. a variable

**5.** The first odd number after 7 is ___.
   a. 5
   b. 8
   c. 9

**6.** The number 20 is ___.
   a. positive
   b. negative
   c. odd

**7.** You can use ___ to solve a word problem.
   a. a dictionary
   b. an equation
   c. a ruler

**8.** In the fraction 2/3, 3 is the ___.
   a. denominator
   b. numerator
   c. quotient

**3. What about you? Which operations or types of math do you use? When do you use them?**
**Example:** _I multiply to change dollars to Mexican pesos._

**4. Look in your dictionary. Complete the sentences.**

a. A _____ *triangle* _____ has three straight lines.

b. Perpendicular lines meet at _____ angles.

c. An _____ angle is bigger than a right angle.

d. A square is a _____ with four equal sides.

e. A cube has six _____.

f. The diameter of a circle is two times longer than the _____.

g. The distance between two _____ lines is always equal.

h. _____ lines can look like the letter *T*.

**5. Complete the analogies.**

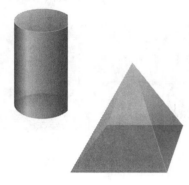

a. circle : sphere = square : _____ *cube* _____

b. triangle : three = rectangle : _____

c. add : subtract = multiply : _____

d. triangle : shape = pyramid : _____

e. divide : quotient = subtract : _____

f. circle : circumference = rectangle : _____

g. straight line : square = curved line : _____

**6. Follow the instructions.**

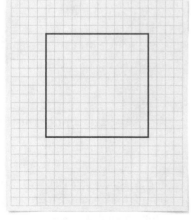

a. Draw a circle inside the square.

b. Draw a line showing the diameter.

c. Draw a diagonal line from the top left corner of the square to the bottom right corner.

d. Draw a line parallel to the left side of the square.

e. Draw a line parallel to the right side of the square.

f. Draw a line perpendicular to the top line of the square. Begin your line at the middle point of the top line of the square, and end your line at the bottom line of the square.

**Compare your drawing with a classmate's. Are they the same?**

**Challenge** Look at page 101 in your dictionary. Find examples of lines, shapes, and solid forms.
   **Example:** *The dryer door is a circle.*

1. **Look in your dictionary. Complete each sentence.**

   a. The _____biologist_____ is using a microscope to examine a leaf.

   b. The nucleus is in the centre of the _____.

   c. Plants make oxygen through the process of _____.

   d. Many _____ live in the desert.

   e. Many _____ live in the ocean.

   f. The ocean is the _____ of many invertebrates.

2. **Look at this page from a science book. Complete the definitions.**

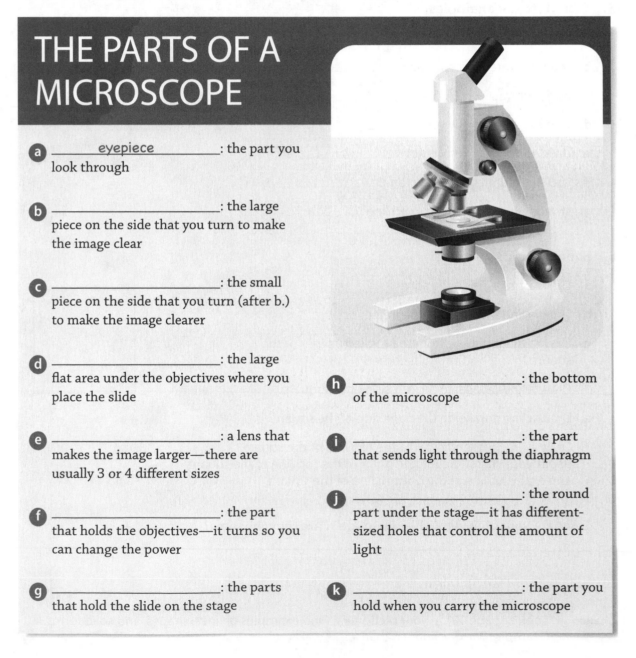

# THE PARTS OF A MICROSCOPE

**a** _____eyepiece_____: the part you look through

**b** _____: the large piece on the side that you turn to make the image clear

**c** _____: the small piece on the side that you turn (after b.) to make the image clearer

**d** _____: the large flat area under the objectives where you place the slide

**e** _____: a lens that makes the image larger—there are usually 3 or 4 different sizes

**f** _____: the part that holds the objectives—it turns so you can change the power

**g** _____: the parts that hold the slide on the stage

**h** _____: the bottom of the microscope

**i** _____: the part that sends light through the diaphragm

**j** _____: the round part under the stage—it has different-sized holes that control the amount of light

**k** _____: the part you hold when you carry the microscope

3. **Look in your dictionary. *True* or *False*? Correct the underlined words in the false sentences.**

a. The ~~physicist~~ chemist is discussing a molecule.          _____false_____

b. An electron is part of a prism.          _____

c. The protons and electrons are in the nucleus.          _____

d. The neutron is in the centre of the atom.          _____

e. The physicist is using the periodic table to explain something.          _____

f. The physicist drew a picture of a prism and a molecule on the board.          _____

4. **Look at the lab experiment. Complete the student's notes.**

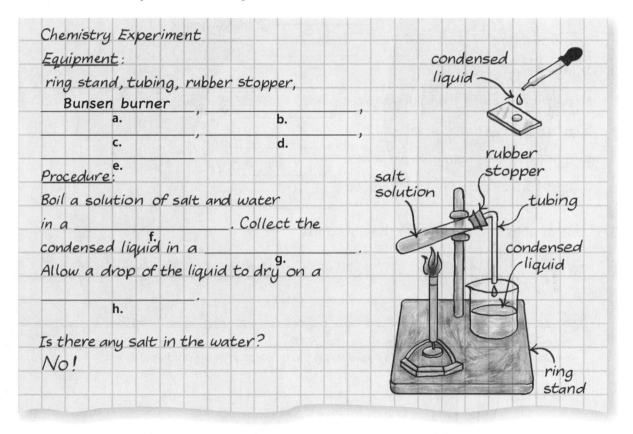

Chemistry Experiment
Equipment:
ring stand, tubing, rubber stopper,
  Bunsen burner _____ , _____ ,
         a.                              b.
_____ , _____ ,
         c.                              d.
         e.
Procedure:
Boil a solution of salt and water
in a _____ . Collect the
         f.
condensed liquid in a _____ .
Allow a drop of the liquid to dry on a
         g.
_____ .
         h.

Is there any salt in the water?
No!

condensed liquid

rubber stopper

salt solution

tubing

condensed liquid

ring stand

5. **Look at the student's notes in Exercise 4. Check (✓) the things the student did.**

[✓] use a Bunsen burner          [ ] observe

[ ] state a hypothesis          [ ] record the results

[ ] do an experiment          [ ] draw a conclusion

**1. Look in your dictionary. Complete the sentences.**

    **a.** There are two _____USB ports_____ on the front of the tower.

    **b.** The DVD and CD-ROM drive is in the _____.

    **c.** A _____ drive is in one of the ports.

    **d.** The microprocessor, _____, and _____ are inside the tower.

    **e.** The power cord goes from the tower into the _____.

    **f.** The webcam is on top of the _____.

    **g.** Cables go from the monitor to the _____ and to the _____.

    **h.** The _____ is to the right of the keyboard.

**2. *True* or *False*?**

    **a.** A laptop is smaller than a desktop computer. _____true_____

    **b.** A laptop has a tower. _____

    **c.** Both types of computers have keyboards. _____

    **d.** Both computers use the same software. _____

**3. Look at Alan's email. Answer the questions.**

| My Mail |     – □ X |
|---|---|
| To: tyler2@iol.ca | |
| Subject: New computer | |

Guess what? I'm typing this on my new laptopp! I love it. It's so much more practical than my old desktop computer. And it's easier to set up, too! Not so many cords cords and cables to connect.

Now all I need is a webcam! A. ☺

    **a.** What did Alan use to type this email? _____laptop_____

    **b.** What words did he select? _____

    **c.** What word does he need to delete? _____

    **d.** What letter does he need to delete? _____

    **e.** How many times did he go to the next line? _____

**Challenge** Give one or two examples of software that you use. What does the software do?

1. **Look in your dictionary. Circle the words to complete the sentences.**

   a. You can find "File" in the (menu bar) / search box.

   b. You start typing at the pointer / cursor.

   c. To return to a website you just visited, click on the back / forward button.

   d. A drop-down menu / URL begins with http://.

   e. To move up and down a webpage, use the scroll bar / tab.

   f. To watch a movie, you need a search engine / video player.

   g. To research information on the Internet, you use a search engine / link.

   h. When you sign in, you type your password into a search / text box.

2. **Look at Jason's email. What did he do right (☺) ? What did he do wrong (☹) ?**
   **Use the words in the box.**

   | | | |
   |---|---|---|
   | address the email | attach a file | attach a picture |
   | check the spelling | type the message | ~~type the subject~~ |

   **My Mail**  — ☐ ✕

   Send To:
   Subject: tomorro night          Attachment: ☐

   Hi. I'm haveing a few freinds over tomorro night.
   Can you come? We can play som video games
   on my new computter. I love it. I'm attaching
   a photo of it. I'm also attaching a file of vidoe
   titles. Hope you can come. Jason

   ☺                                    ☹

   a. _He typed the subject._          d. _____

   b. _____                   e. _____

   c. _____                   f. _____

**Challenge** Do you think it's important to check your spelling in an email? Why or why not?
Write a paragraph about your opinion.

**See page 312 for listening practice.**

**1. Look in your dictionary. Complete the information.**

# DID YOU KNOW...?

Most of Canada's early _____Settlers_____ came from Britain and
                              **a.**
France.

Many people were living in Canada for centuries before the Europeans arrived.

These native peoples, _____ and
                              **b.**

_____, have a long and rich history.
        **c.**

On July 1, 1867, the _____ came into effect, establishing
                              **d.**
the country of Canada. The _____ had spent years
                                    **e.**
working on this act. In honour of that day, we now celebrate Canada Day on July 1.

The four original _____ were Ontario, Québec,
                          **f.**
New Brunswick, and Nova Scotia. The newest one is Newfoundland and Labrador,

which joined Canada in 1949 (although at that time, it was simply called

"Newfoundland").

Canada's _____ was Sir John A. Macdonald, who served
                  **g.**
from 1867 to 1873.

From _____ to _____, Canada participated in Word War I (WWI). 21 years later, from
      **h.**    **i.**
1939 to 1945, Canada also fought in _____.
                                          **j.**

The _____, which lasted from 1929 to 1934, was a difficult time for
        **k.**
people who lived and worked in Canada.

In 1994, Canada signed the _____ (NAFTA), which allows
                                  **l.**
Canada, the United States, and Mexico to trade goods between the three countries.

In 1918, women won the _____ in federal elections. In 1929,
                              **m.**
women were declared persons by the Privy Council, which gave women the ability to

hold office in the Senate.

**See page 313 for listening practice.**

1. **Look in your dictionary. Circle the words to complete the sentences.**

   a. The Egyptian pyramids are a product of (an ancient) / a modern civilization.

   b. An emperor / A president is the ruler of an empire.

   c. A dictator / prime minister is a leader who controls everything and has all the power in a country.

   d. A dictator / monarch is a king or a queen.

   e. An activist / army fights during a war.

   f. Invention / Immigration is the process of moving to a new country.

2. **Complete the chart.**

| Category | Person | Country | Famous for... |
|---|---|---|---|
| composition | J.S. Bach (1685–1750) _composer_ **a.** | Germany | He is considered the greatest writer of Baroque music. |
| invention | Alessandro Volta (1745–1827) _____ **b.** | Italy | In 1800, he invented the first electric battery. |
| _____ **c.** | Vasco da Gama (1469?–1524) explorer | Portugal | In the late 1400s, he was the first to sail from Europe to India, around the Cape of Good Hope in Africa. |
| _____ **d.** | Rosa Parks (1913–2005) _____ **e.** | United States | Known as the "Mother of the Civil Rights Movement," in 1955 she refused to give up her seat on a bus to a white passenger. |
| architecture | I.M. Pei (1917– ) architect | United States _____ **f.** (from China) | He is famous for his modern skyscrapers, museums, and government buildings. |

**Challenge** Do an Internet search or use an encyclopedia or history book. Find another example of an explorer, an inventor, a composer, an immigrant, or an activist. Write information like the information in the chart in Exercise 2.

1. **Look in your dictionary. Cross out the word that doesn't belong. Complete the chart.**

| | | | | | |
|---|---|---|---|---|---|
| **a** | States in Mexico | ~~Louisiana~~ | Durango | Sonora | Jalisco |
| **b** | _States_ in the United States | Florida | Hawaii | Michigan | Baja California |
| **c** | Provinces in _____ | Alberta | Alaska | Nova Scotia | Québec |
| **d** | _____ in Central America | Belize | Guatemala | Ontario | Panama |
| **e** | Regions in Mexico | Atlantic Provinces | Yucatan Peninsula | Chiapas Highlands | Gulf Coastal Plain |
| **f** | _____ of Canada | Atlantic Provinces | Prairie Provinces | Nebraska | Ontario |
| **g** | Bodies of Water | Gulf of Mexico | Southern Uplands | Atlantic Ocean | Caribbean Sea |
| **h** | _____ | Costa Rica | Puerto Rico | Cuba | Bahamas |

2. **Look in your dictionary. Complete the sentences.**

a. Nunavut is in the region known as ___Northern Canada___.

b. Nicaragua lies between _____ and _____ in Central America.

c. _____ and the Dominican Republic share the same Caribbean island.

d. _____ is the smallest Canadian province.

e. _____, Mexico is northwest of Coahuila.

f. The west side of the American state of _____ lies on the Gulf of Mexico.

g. _____ is south of the Canadian province of Alberta.

h. The American state of _____ is made up of many islands.

i. Campeche lies in the _____ region of Mexico.

j. Bermuda is in the _____ Ocean.

3. **What about you? What state, province, or country are you in? Where is it?**

**Example:** *I'm in British Columbia. It's in the southwest part of Canada. It's north of the United States and south of Yukon.*

**4. Look at the map. It shows where some Mexican products come from. *True* or *False*? Correct the <u>underlined</u> words in the false sentences.**

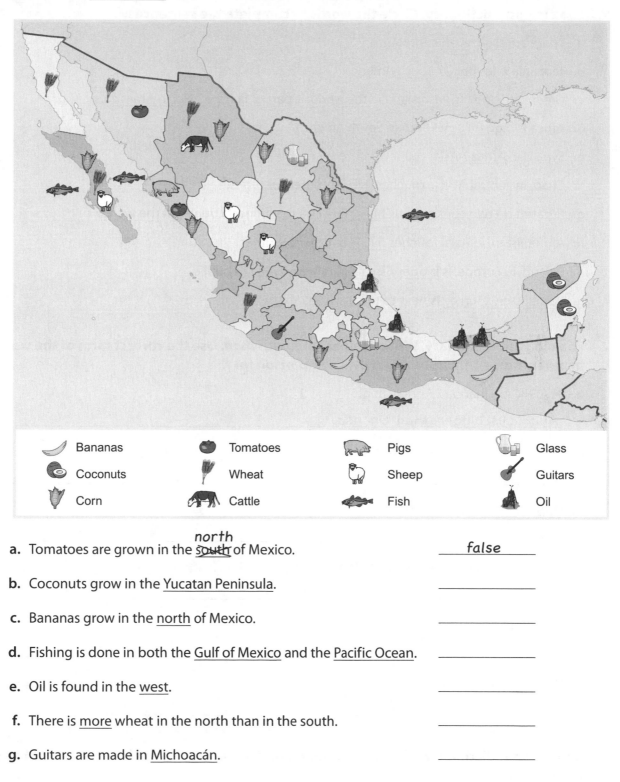

| | Bananas | | Tomatoes | | Pigs | | Glass |
|---|---|---|---|---|---|---|---|
| | Coconuts | | Wheat | | Sheep | | Guitars |
| | Corn | | Cattle | | Fish | | Oil |

                              *north*

**a.** Tomatoes are grown in the ~~south~~ of Mexico.             _____*false*_____

**b.** Coconuts grow in the <u>Yucatan Peninsula</u>.             _____

**c.** Bananas grow in the <u>north</u> of Mexico.             _____

**d.** Fishing is done in both the <u>Gulf of Mexico</u> and the <u>Pacific Ocean</u>.    _____

**e.** Oil is found in the <u>west</u>.             _____

**f.** There is <u>more</u> wheat in the north than in the south.             _____

**g.** Guitars are made in <u>Michoacán</u>.             _____

**5. What about you? Draw a map showing some of the products from your native country. Write eight sentences.**

**Challenge** Look at the map in Exercise 4. Write five more sentences about Mexican products.

1. **Look in your dictionary. Circle the words to complete the sentences.**

   a. There are six / (seven) continents.

   b. Tanzania is in Africa / South America.

   c. Greenland, the biggest island in the world, is part of Europe / North America.

   d. Africa is bigger / smaller than South America.

   e. Syria is in Africa / Asia.

   f. Chad, in central Africa, touches five / six other countries.

   g. Located on two continents, China / Russia is the biggest country in the world.

   h. Afghanistan, in Asia, touches five / six other countries.

   i. Poland, in Europe, is bigger / smaller than the Czech Republic.

   j. Kazakhstan / Turkey is next to the Black Sea.

2. **Look in your dictionary. Write comparisons with *than*. Use the correct form of the words in parentheses ( ). Choose your own comparison for *f*.**

   a. IN AFRICA:  Uganda / Angola (big)

   _Angola is bigger than Uganda._

   b. IN EUROPE:  Italy / Finland (warm)

   _____

   c. IN ASIA:  Thailand / Laos (small)

   _____

   d. IN SOUTH AMERICA:  Chile / Argentina (wide)

   _____

   e. AUSTRALIA / ANTARCTICA (cold)

   _____

   f. IN NORTH AMERICA: _____ / _____ (_____)

   _____

3. **Look in your dictionary. For each continent, find a country that is "landlocked" (it has no ocean around it).**

   Africa: _____Chad_____          South America: _____

   Europe: _____          Asia: _____

4. **Look in your dictionary. Complete these world facts. Write the names of the continents, countries, and bodies of water.**

a. _____ Mexico _____

**Location:** southern North America
**Borders:** U.S. to north, Gulf of Mexico to east, Belize and Guatemala to south, _____ Ocean to west

b. _____

**Location:** island off southeast Africa in western _____ Ocean
**Borders:** doesn't border any other countries; about 300 miles (500 km) east of Mozambique

c. _____

**Location:** central Europe
**Borders:** Germany and Czech Republic to north, Hungary and Slovakia to east, Slovenia and _____ to south, Switzerland and Liechtenstein to west

d. Laos

**Location:** southeast Asia
**Borders:** Burma to northwest, _____ to north, Vietnam to east, Cambodia to south, _____ to southwest

e. _____

**Location:** western Africa
**Borders:** Guinea to north, Atlantic Ocean and _____ to west, Ivory Coast to east

f. _____

**Location:** northwestern South America
**Borders:** Colombia to north, Peru to east and south, _____ to west

g. Belarus

**Location:** northeastern Europe
**Borders:** Lithuania and _____ to north and northwest; Russia to north, northeast, and east; _____ to south, Poland to west

h. _____

**Location:** southwestern Asia
**Borders:** Turkmenistan to northwest, Uzebekistan and Tajikistan to north, China to northeast, Pakistan to east and south, _____ to west.

5. **What about you? Write a description of your country like the ones in Exercise 4. (If your country is in Exercise 4, choose a country you have visited.) Use your own paper.**

**Challenge** Choose five other countries. Write descriptions like the ones in Exercise 4.

1. **Look in your dictionary. *True* or *False*? Correct the underlined words in the false sentences.**

    *rainforest*
    a. There's a waterfall in the ~~forest~~.          _____false_____

    b. An ocean is larger than <u>a pond or a bay</u>.          _____

    c. There's a <u>beach</u> around the lake.          _____

    d. There's a canyon between the <u>mountain ranges</u>.          _____

    e. There are flowers in the <u>valley</u>.          _____

    f. Hills are lower than <u>mountain ranges</u>.          _____

2. **Complete the descriptions. Use the words in the box. Look at the world map on pages 202 and 203 in your dictionary if you need help.**

    | desert | island | lake | mountain peak | ocean | river | ~~waterfall~~ |
    |---|---|---|---|---|---|---|

    # WORLD FACTS

    a. **Angel Falls** (980 metres) is the highest _____waterfall_____ in the world. It is located on the Churun River in southeast Venezuela.

    b. The **Pacific** is the largest (169.2 million square kilometres) and the deepest (10,911 metres) _____ in the world. It covers almost one third of the earth's surface.

    c. Located in Tibet and Nepal, **Everest** (8,848 metres) is the highest _____ in the world. In 1953, Hillary and Norgay were the first to reach the top.

    d. At 6,650 kilometres, the **Nile**, in Africa, is the longest _____ in the world. Its water supplies electricity and helps agriculture in Egypt and Sudan.

    e. The **Sahara** in Africa is the biggest _____ in the world. At 9 million square kilometres, it is almost as large as the United States. It gets only five to ten inches of rain per year and sometimes has dry periods that last for years.

    f. Surrounded by water, **Greenland** (2.2 million square kilometres) is the largest _____ in the world. It lies in the Arctic Circle and is a part of Denmark, although it is 2,000 kilometres away.

    g. The **Caspian Sea** (370,000 square kilometres) is the largest _____ in the world. It's called a sea because its water is salty.

**Challenge** Look online or in an encyclopedia. Write some facts about a rainforest, a canyon, and plains.

**1. Look in your dictionary. Complete the chart.**

| PLANET NAME | DISTANCE FROM THE SUN (IN KILOMETRES) | SYMBOL | DIAMETER (IN KILOMETRES) |
|---|---|---|---|
| a. Mars | 229 million | ☿ | 6,791 |
| b. | 108 million | ♀ | 12,104 |
| c. | 150 million | ⊕ | 12,756 |
| d. | 1429 million | ♄ | 120,660 |
| e. | 779 million | ♃ | 142,800 |
| f. | 2.9 billion | ♅ | 51,118 |
| g. | 4.5 billion | ☿ | 49,495 |
| h. | 58 million | ♄ | 4,878 |

**2. Circle the words to complete the sentences. You can use your dictionary for help.**

a. There are eight moons /(planets)/ stars in the solar system.

b. Uranus was the first planet discovered using a comet / solar system / telescope.

c. The astronaut / astronomer / space station William Herschel first observed Uranus in 1781.

d. Constellations / Observatories / Comets look like pictures in the sky.

e. The Earth's galaxy / orbit / space (a group of billions of stars) is called the Milky Way.

f. It takes 27 days for the moon to go from a new moon to a full moon and then back to a crescent moon / new moon / quarter moon again.

**3. What about you? Describe what you can see when you look at the night sky. Use your own paper.**

Example: *I can see the constellation called the Big Dipper, . . .*

**Challenge** Look online, in an encyclopedia, or in a science book. Find out more about three planets. How long does a day last on these planets? How long do they take to orbit the sun?

# A Graduation

1. **Look in your dictionary. *True* or *False*?**

   a. Adelia is wearing a cap and gown in <u>six</u> photos.     <u>false</u>

   b. Adelia's <u>mother</u> is taking pictures.     _____

   c. The guest speaker is <u>the mayor</u>.     _____

   d. The photographer is taking a picture of <u>ten</u> people.     _____

   e. <u>The photographer</u> is crying.     _____

   f. <u>Adelia</u> is speaking at the podium.     _____

2. **Look in your dictionary. Write the letters of the false sentences from Exercise 1. Make them true.**

   <u>a.</u>     <u>Adelia is wearing a cap in five photos.</u>_____

   ____     _____

   ____     _____

   ____     _____

   ____     _____

3. **Look in your dictionary. Who said these things? Match each quotation with the person who said it.**

   <u>3</u>  a. "Adelia, I want to take a photo of you with your diploma."       1. Adelia

   ____  b. "OK, everyone. I want this one to be a serious photo."       2. Adelia's mother

   ____  c. "Adelia, you look so beautiful in your cap and gown. It makes me cry."       3. Adelia's father

   ____  d. "Welcome, students, teachers, and parents. I am happy to speak at this year's ceremony."       4. Adelia's classmate

   ____  e. "I'll miss being in the band with you, Adelia!"       5. the guest speaker

   ____  f. "I graduated!"       6. the photographer

**4. Complete the comments on Adelia's webpage. Use the words in the box.**

| celebrate | funny | caps | guest speaker | ~~takes~~ |
|---|---|---|---|---|
| cry | gown | photographer | podium | |

| People | Comments |
|---|---|
| Tamara | Congratulations! Your Dad ___*takes*___ great pictures.<br>**a.**<br>You look great in your cap and _____!<br>**b.** |
| Jeff | Hey, Adelia. What a great day. I like the _____ photo.<br>**c.**<br>The _____ was so upset, but it's a great memory!<br>**d.** |
| Wendy | I thought the _____ gave a great speech.<br>**e.**<br>Of course, she's my mother. I'm glad she didn't _____<br>**f.**<br>until after her speech! |
| Dan | We finally graduated! I almost fell when I got my diploma at the<br>_____ . Now it's time to _____! I'm<br>**g.**                **h.**<br>having a party on Saturday. |
| Marcos | Great pictures! I love the one where we are throwing our<br>_____ in the air!<br>**i.** |

**5. What about you? Imagine you were at the graduation. Tell a partner about it. Answer the following questions.**

a. Were you a graduate or a friend or relative of one of the graduates?

b. How did you feel? Did you cry?

c. What photos did you take?

d. Who did you talk to?

e. How did you celebrate?

**Challenge** Write some comments to Adelia. Tell her what you think of the photos on her webpage (on pages 206 and 207 of the dictionary). Write at least six sentences.

**1.** Look in your dictionary. *True* or *False*? Correct the underlined words in the false sentences.

a. A man is painting a picture of ~~rocks~~. *trees*      *false*

b. Seven people are on the <u>path</u>.     _____

c. The <u>sun</u> is in the sky.     _____

d. There's a nest on a <u>rock</u> in the water.     _____

e. A man is examining four kinds of <u>fish</u>.     _____

f. There's a sign with pictures of five different types of <u>insects</u>.     _____

**2.** Complete the pamphlet. Use the words in the box.

| birds | ~~fish~~ | flowers | insects | mammals | plants | rocks | trees |
|-------|------|---------|---------|---------|--------|-------|-------|

## Did you know...?

a. _____*fish*_____ These animals are vertebrates (they have spines). They live in the water and can swim. Most of them lay eggs. There are more than 20,000 types, and many of them can live for ten to twenty years.

b. _____ These animals are invertebrates (they don't have spines) and there are more than a million types! They have six legs and most of them eat plants.

c. _____ There are about 260,000 types, and you can find them on land, in the ocean, and in rivers and lakes. They have chlorophyll, a green material that helps them make oxygen that people and animals breathe.

d. _____ They are warm-blooded, and when they are babies they drink their mothers' milk. Most of these animals have hair on all or part of their bodies. We belong to this animal group!

e. _____ They are combinations of minerals (solid material that is not living). They come from deep inside the earth or from the oceans, rivers, and lakes. Many are millions of years old!

f. _____ These are very large plants! The rings in their trunks tell us their age. They provide oxygen, food, wood, and other important products.

g. _____ They are the parts of plants that help the plant reproduce (make new plants). People like to grow them because of their beautiful colours and nice smell.

h. _____ They can walk on their back legs, and almost all of them can fly. There are more than 8,000 types of these feathered animals, and each type sings a different song!

## ❀ LILLO ❀
## Nature Centre

**3. Look in your dictionary. Cross out the word that doesn't belong.**

a. Things that need water      trees      plants      ~~rocks~~

b. Things that can fly      insects      nests      birds

c. Things above the earth      soil      sun      sky

d. Things that can swim      mammals      flowers      fish

e. Things you can stand on      path      water      rocks

f. Things with legs      insects      mammals      fish

**4. Circle the words to complete the pamphlet.**

❈ LILLO ❈
Nature Centre

PLANTS

**Please . . .**

❀ walk on our paths / soil.
               **a.**

❀ take pictures of our beautiful flowers / sun.
                             **b.**

❀ read about our many different types of
trees / water.
    **c.**

❀ buy plants / nests to take home.
           **d.**

**Please don't . . .**

❀ feed the fish / insects or mammals / rocks.
                    **e.**             **f.**

❀ pick the flowers / trees.
             **g.**
(Leave them so everyone can enjoy them!)

❀ throw bottles or trash on the paths / birds.
                           **h.**
(Use the garbage cans and recycling bins.)

**5. What about you? Look in your dictionary. Imagine you are at the Lillo Nature Centre. What will you do? Compare answers with a classmate.**

Example: *I'll take pictures of the trees and flowers.*

**Challenge** Try to list three types of each of the following: birds, flowers, mammals, fish, and insects.

1. **Look in your dictionary. What has the following features? You will use some answers more than once.**

| Flowers | Berries | Needles | Leaves That Can Give You a Rash |
|---|---|---|---|
| _dogwood_ | _____ | _____ | _poison ivy_ |
| _____ | _____ | _____ | _____ |
| _____ | _____ | _____ | _____ |
| _____ | | | |

2. **Circle the words to complete the article. You can use your dictionary for help.**

# Trees

Trees are the biggest vines / (plants) in the world. As long as they live, they never stop
    a.
growing. The tallest tree, the pine / redwood, can reach a height of 112 metres. Its
    b.
pinecone / trunk can have a diameter of 4.6 metres.
    c.

The limbs / roots, which grow underground, are the fastest-growing part of a tree.
    d.
They collect water and send it up the berries / trunk to the leaves / vines.
    e.    f.

There are two main categories of trees. Broad-leaf trees, such as the maple / pine,
    g.
have leaves that turn beautiful colours and then drop to the ground in the fall. These

trees often have many large, thick branches / twigs that grow from the lower trunk.
    h.

Needle-leaf trees, such as the birch / pine, stay green all year and are called
    i.
*evergreens*. They carry seeds in pinecones / berries. The trunk / twig usually goes to
    j.    k.
the top of the tree.

A third, smaller category of tree is the elm / palm. It is almost all leaves / limbs and
    l.    m.
does not have branches / roots.
    n.

All trees have flowers. Some are very big and beautiful like those of the

magnolia / willow. Others, such as those of some types of dogwood / oak, can be
    o.    p.
so small that many people do not notice them.

**Challenge** Make a list of five tree products. **Example:** *apples*

**1. Look in your dictionary. Complete the order form for this bouquet.**

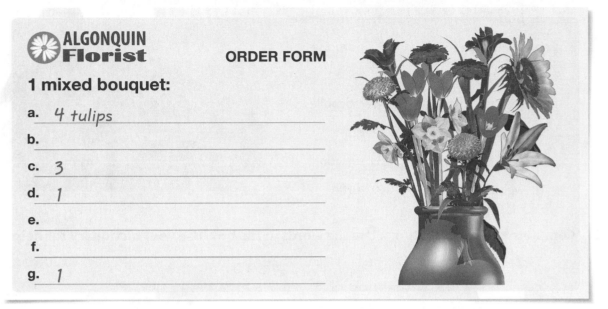

**⚙ ALGONQUIN**
**Florist**          ORDER FORM

**1 mixed bouquet:**

a. _4 tulips_

b. _____

c. _3_

d. _1_

e. _____

f. _____

g. _1_

**2. Look in your dictionary. Complete the sentences with information from the chart.**

| Flower | Grown from | Season | Comments |
|---|---|---|---|
|  |  | spring–fall | remove thorns for bouquets |
|  |  | late spring–late summer | water often |
|  |  | summer–early winter | plant seedlings in June |
|  |  | early spring | very short stems |
|  |  | winter–spring | good houseplant |
|  |  | spring–summer | lovely perfume |

a. _____Lilies_____ and _____ grow from bulbs.

b. _____, _____, and _____
   grow from seeds.

c. _____ have thick white petals and smell very nice.

d. Don't hurt your finger when you make a bouquet of _____!

**Challenge** Write about flower traditions in your country. **Example:** *In Canada, people often give red roses to their loved ones on Valentine's Day.*

1. **Look in your dictionary. Match the animals that look similar.**

   _3_ **a.** frog          **1.** garter snake

   ____ **b.** salamander    **2.** porpoise

   ____ **c.** dolphin       **3.** toad

   ____ **d.** tortoise      **4.** crocodile

   ____ **e.** alligator     **5.** lizard

   ____ **f.** eel           **6.** sea lion

   ____ **g.** walrus        **7.** turtle

2. **Complete the conversations. Use the words in the box. Use your dictionary for help.**

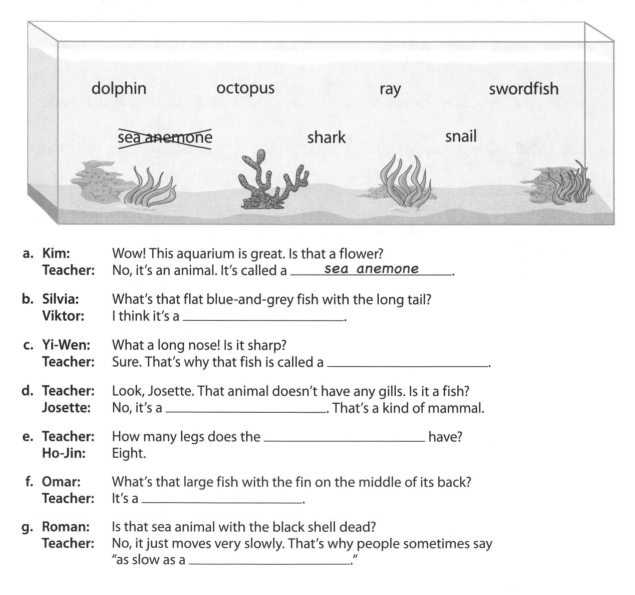

dolphin        octopus            ray            swordfish

~~sea anemone~~            shark            snail

   **a. Kim:**      Wow! This aquarium is great. Is that a flower?
   **Teacher:**  No, it's an animal. It's called a _____ *sea anemone* _____.

   **b. Silvia:**   What's that flat blue-and-grey fish with the long tail?
   **Viktor:**   I think it's a _____.

   **c. Yi-Wen:**  What a long nose! Is it sharp?
   **Teacher:**  Sure. That's why that fish is called a _____.

   **d. Teacher:**  Look, Josette. That animal doesn't have any gills. Is it a fish?
   **Josette:**  No, it's a _____. That's a kind of mammal.

   **e. Teacher:**  How many legs does the _____ have?
   **Ho-Jin:**   Eight.

   **f. Omar:**    What's that large fish with the fin on the middle of its back?
   **Teacher:**  It's a _____.

   **g. Roman:**   Is that sea animal with the black shell dead?
   **Teacher:**  No, it just moves very slowly. That's why people sometimes say
              "as slow as a _____."

**3.** Circle the words to complete the article.

# Animal Defences

Animals have many ways of protecting themselves. One fish, the cobra /(flounder) can
a.
change its colour. Two sea animals, the squid / starfish and the sea otter / octopus, squirt ink into
b.                                              c.
the water and hide in the dark cloud.

Some poisonous amphibians / seals and reptiles warn enemies to keep away. The bright
d.
colours of some cod / frogs tell other animals they are not safe to eat. The garter snake / rattlesnake
e.                                                                        f.
makes a loud sound with its tail before it bites. The turtle's / tuna's hard shell and the sharp needles
g.
of the sea urchin / scallop are other kinds of protection.
h.
Sea mammals like dolphins / newts use language to warn each other of danger. Scientists
i.
have recorded the songs that whales / worms sing to each other. Other members of this group,
j.
such as walruses and sea lions / seahorses, live in large groups to protect their babies.
k.

**4.** Circle the correct letter for each sentence. Write the circled letters on the blank lines.

|   |                                  | True | False |
|---|----------------------------------|------|-------|
| **a.** | Mussels are sea mammals.      | A    | (O)   |
| **b.** | Whales can sing.              | L    | Z     |
| **c.** | All sea mammals have gills.   | J    | O     |
| **d.** | Some mammals have fins.       | R    | L     |
| **e.** | Rattlesnakes are poisonous.   | E    | B     |
| **f.** | Crabs don't have legs.        | G    | C     |
| **g.** | Bass have scales.             | D    | P     |
| **h.** | Scallops and shrimp are black.| E    | I     |
| **i.** | Jellyfish look like fish.     | T    | C     |

<u>O</u>  ____  ____  ____  ____  ____  ____  ____  ____

Now unscramble the letters to find the name of an animal: _____

**Challenge** Look at page 260 in this book. Follow the instructions.

213

1. **Look in your dictionary. Write the name of the bird, insect, or arachnid.**

   a. It makes honey from flowers. Unlike the wasp, it dies after it stings.  _honeybee_

   b. It looks like a big duck and is raised for food and feathers.  _____

   c. It's very small. It drinks blood and often lives in the fur or skin
   of mammals. It can make people sick.  _____

   d. It's brown with an orange breast.  _____

   e. It's very small and red, and it has black polka dots.  _____

   f. It has sharp claws and big eyes on the front of its head.  _____

   g. It begins its life as a caterpillar.  _____

   h. It has a long bill for eating nectar from flowers.
   It moves its wings 1,000 times per second.  _____

   i. It catches insects by making holes in trees with its beak.  _____

   j. It doesn't fly, but it swims in icy water to catch fish.  _____

   k. It lives near water. It flies and bites people to drink their blood.  _____

   l. It looks like a small grasshopper and eats cloth like a moth.
   It makes music by rubbing its wings together.  _____

   m. It has beautiful blue feathers and eats insects and fruit.  _____

   n. It likes human food and causes many diseases. A spider often
   catches it in its web.  _____

   o. It's very big with long, colourful feathers.  _____

2. **Write comparisons with *than*.**

   a. fly / tick (small)  _A tick is smaller than a fly._

   b. peacock / sparrow (colourful)  _____

   c. beetle / scorpion (dangerous)  _____

   d. pigeon / eagle (large)  _____

   e. butterfly / moth (beautiful)  _____

3. **What about you? Make a list of some birds, insects, and arachnids that are common
   where you live. Use your own paper.**

**Challenge** Look up information about a bird, insect, or arachnid in your list from Exercise 3.
Where does it live? What does it eat? How does it help or hurt people?

1.  **Look in your dictionary. Write the names of the animals that fit the descriptions?**

    **a.** they eat nuts          _chipmunks_ and _____

    **b.** they are babies        _____ and _____

    **c.** they have wings        _____, _____, and _____

    **d.** they live in holes      _____ and _____

    **e.** they give us milk       _____, _____, and _____

    **f.** they carry people       _____ and _____

2.  **Look at the magazine article. Complete the sentences.**

# Care and Cost of Common Pets

- ✓✓✓ a lot of care
- ✓✓ moderate care
- ✓ not much care
- $$$ very expensive
- $$ moderately expensive
- $ not expensive

a. _____Dogs_____ need the most care. In addition to giving them food and water, you need to train them and play with them. They are also the most expensive.

b. _____ need less care than dogs. With enough water and food, they can be alone during the day. They are less expensive than dogs, but more expensive than other pets.

c. If you like _____, think about getting one or more parakeets. They aren't expensive and don't need much care. They like to climb, so give them a tall cage with a ladder.

d. Perhaps the easiest and cheapest pets are _____. They can live long and healthy lives in a big bowl of fresh water with plants and room to swim.

e. Don't be afraid of these rodents. Mice and white _____ (not the ones that live in the city!) make nice pets. They don't cost much, and they don't need a lot of care.

f. Bushy-tailed and long-eared, _____ aren't expensive, but they do need moderate care and special food. No carrots!

**Challenge** Compare a rooster and a hen, a dog and a prairie dog, and a pig and a guinea pig.
**Example**: *A hen lays eggs, but a rooster doesn't. A rooster is bigger than a hen.*

1. **Look in your dictionary. Circle the words to complete the sentences.**

   a. The lion has a <u>pouch</u> / <u>(mane)</u> and <u>hooves / paws</u>.

   b. The <u>opossum / raccoon</u> has a striped <u>tail / trunk</u>.

   c. The <u>moose / mountain lion</u> has <u>antlers / quills</u> and <u>hooves / whiskers</u>.

   d. The <u>coyote / koala</u> has a grey <u>coat / hump</u>.

   e. The <u>baboon / buffalo</u> has <u>horns / tusks</u>.

   f. The chimpanzee and the <u>orangutan / platypus</u> are in the same animal family.

   g. The <u>beaver / hyena</u> and the <u>panther / skunk</u> live in North America.

2. **Look at the bar graph. Complete the sentences.**

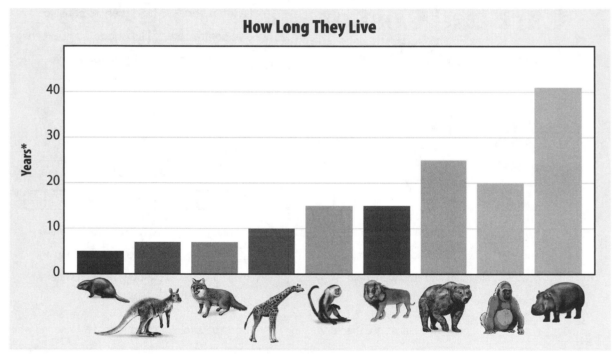

### How Long They Live

*Years = average number of years the animal can live in a zoo.

   a. The grizzly _____*bear*_____ lives 25 years.

   b. The red fox lives as long as the _____.

   c. The _____ lives as long as the lion.

   d. The gorilla lives 10 years longer than the _____.

   e. The _____ lives the longest life.

   f. The _____ lives the shortest life.

   g. The _____ lives twice as long as the beaver.

**3. Look at the maps. Make a list of endangered\* animals and the continents where they live.**

\*Endangered = there are very few of these animals and they may not continue to live.

_____wolf, North America_____    _____

_____    _____

_____    _____

_____    _____

_____    _____

**Challenge**  List reasons why some animals are endangered. Search online or in an encyclopedia for "endangered species." **Example:** _People kill elephants for their tusks_

1. **Look in your dictionary. Circle the words to complete these sentences.**

   a. Nuclear / (Solar) energy comes directly from the sun.

   b. Coal, oil, and natural gas / radiation are sources of energy.

   c. Another source of energy is acid rain / wind power.

   d. Hydroelectric power / Geothermal energy comes from water.

   e. A danger of nuclear energy is air pollution / radiation.

   f. Old batteries are examples of biomass / hazardous waste.

   g. Acid rain / Fusion damages trees.

   h. Water pollution and oil spills / smog hurt the oceans.

2. **Look at the pie chart.** *True* or *False*?

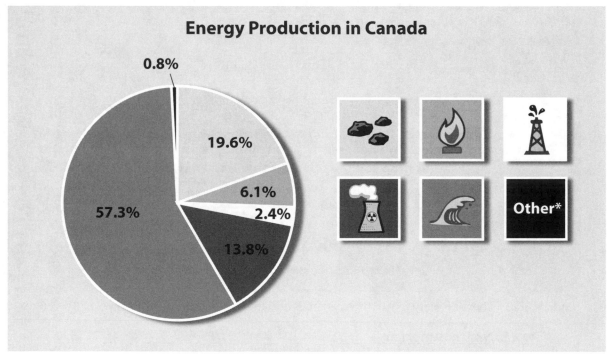

**Energy Production in Canada**

0.8%

19.6%

6.1%

2.4%

57.3%

13.8%

Other*

*Other sources include geothermal, solar, and wind.

   a. More than half of the energy produced in Canada is from hydroelectric power.  _____true_____

   b. Almost 20% of energy produced is from oil.  _____

   c. Canada produces more energy from oil than from natural gas.  _____

   d. Almost 14% of energy production is from nuclear energy.  _____

   e. More energy is produced from nuclear energy than from coal.  _____

   f. Canada doesn't produce much energy from wind power or solar energy.  _____

**3. Look in your dictionary. Complete the sentences.**

a. The streets will look better if people _don't litter_____.

b. You can _____ by using a "regular" coffee cup instead of a paper one.

c. You can _____ by turning off the faucet when you brush your teeth.

d. If you _____ bottles and cans, you help reduce garbage and improve the quality of the earth at the same time!

**4. Look at the chart. Check (✓) the correct column(s).**

| | | 💧 WATER | ⚛ ENERGY | 🌲 TREES |
|---|---|---|---|---|
| **a** | adjust the thermostat | | ✓ | |
| **b** | wash clothes in cold water | | | |
| **c** | carpool | | | |
| **d** | recycle paper | | | |
| **e** | fix leaky faucets | | | |
| **f** | reuse paper shopping bags | | | |
| **g** | plant a tree | | | |
| **h** | buy recycled paper | | | |
| **i** | turn off the faucet | | | |

**Help Save ...**

www.helpsave.ca

**5. What about you? List the things in Exercise 4 that you do.**

**Example:** *I carpool to work to save energy.*

**Challenge** List other things that people can do to help conserve energy and resources.
**Example:** *They can recycle batteries or use rechargeable batteries.*

**1. Look in your dictionary. Which brochures show the following things? Check (✓) the columns.**

|  | Glacier | Gros Morne | Wapusk |
|---|---|---|---|
| **a.** water | ✓ | ✓ |  |
| **b.** wildlife |  |  |  |
| **c.** a cave |  |  |  |
| **d.** a ferry |  |  |  |
| **e.** a park ranger |  |  |  |

**2. Look in your dictionary. *True* or *False*? Rewrite the false sentences. Make them true.**

|  | True | False |
|---|---|---|
| **a.** Canada national parks protect <u>park rangers</u>. |  | ✓ |

*Canada's national parks protect landscapes.*

|  | True | False |
|---|---|---|
| **b.** Rogers Pass is in <u>Wapusk</u> National Park. |  |  |

_____

|  | True | False |
|---|---|---|
| **c.** Gros Morne National Park is in <u>Newfoundland</u>. |  |  |

_____

|  | True | False |
|---|---|---|
| **d.** You can take a ferry to <u>Glacier</u> National Park. |  |  |

_____

|  | True | False |
|---|---|---|
| **e.** Glacier National Park is home to the Nakimu <u>Caves</u>. |  |  |

_____

|  | True | False |
|---|---|---|
| **f.** <u>Park rangers</u> give tours of national parks. |  |  |

_____

**3. What about you? Tell a partner about your experiences.**

    **a.** Have you ever visited a place that is famous for its natural beauty?

    **b.** Was it Canada or in another country?

    **c.** Was it near a river, a forest, a mountain, or a waterfall?

    **d.** Why is it famous (for example, caves, landscapes, or wildlife)?

**4. Complete the article. Use the words in the box.**

| landscape | park rangers | landmarks | wildlife |
| caves | ~~take a tour~~ | | |

## PLAN A VISIT TO A NATIONAL PARK

Banff National Park is in Alberta. You can __take a tour__ of the park in many ways: by
                                              **a.**

helicopter, by boat, by bus, or even by dogsled! The Rockies are also a great place to ski or rock

climb. Before you start out on the mountain, be sure to register with the _____.
                                                                        **b.**

They'll search for you if you are gone longer than you were supposed to be, to make sure you

are safe.

Quttinirpaaq, in Nunavut, is the most northerly national park in the world. While there, you

might have interesting encounters with the _____ — many of the polar bears and
                                            **c.**

caribou here are unafraid of humans and will approach people out of curiosity. During the

summer, Quttinirpaaq gets 24 hours of sunlight every day, which gives you lots of time to take

photographs of the _____, which includes glaciers and wildflowers.
                     **d.**

Bruce Peninsula National Park is in Ontario. There are lots of beautiful plants and animals to

see in the park, as well as _____ like the cliffs of the Niagara Escarpment, and the
                             **e.**

Grotto, the park's largest _____.
                            **f.**

**5. Match the photos with the parks. Use the information in Exercise 4.**

| Banff National Park | Quttinirpaaq National Park | Bruce Peninsula National Park |

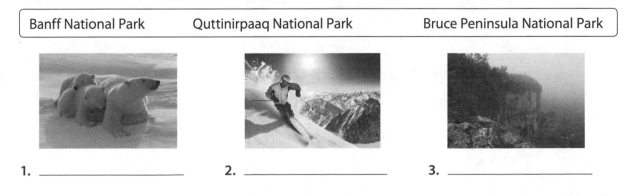

1. _____     2. _____     3. _____

**Challenge** Write a paragraph about a Canadian National Park or another park or special outdoors place
you know about.

1.  **Look in your dictionary. Where can you go to do the following things?**

    **a.** hear music      _____rock concert_____ , _____ ,

    or _____

    **b.** see sharks and starfish      _____

    **c.** see flowers, trees, and plants      _____

    **d.** hear people sing      _____ or _____

    **e.** see paintings      _____

    **f.** go on rides      _____

    **g.** dance      _____

    **h.** buy old clothes      _____

    **i.** see a film      _____

    **j.** see elephants      _____

    **k.** play alone or on a team      _____

2.  **Look in your dictionary. Recommend places where these people could go.**

    **a.** David wants to be a gardener.      ____botanical garden____

    **b.** Julia needs some things for her home.      _____

    **c.** Tina likes looking at quilts and farm animals.      _____

    **d.** Amy enjoys seeing live theatre performances.      _____

    **e.** Karl wants to be an artist. He likes paintings.      _____

3.  **What about you? Look at the places in your dictionary. Where do you go? Why? Complete the chart.**

| | Places I go . . . | Why? |
|---|---|---|
| Often | | |
| Sometimes | | |
| Never | | |
| Never, but I'd like to go. | | |

**4. Look in your dictionary. Complete the newspaper listings below.**

## WHAT'S HAPPENING

### ART

**NORTH RIDGE** _Art Gallery_
a.
Special exhibit of sculpture and paintings by local artists. Through August 25. **Tickets $5**.

### MUSIC

**CITY CENTRE**

Adriana Domingo sings the leading role in Antonio Rivera's new _____,
b.
Starry Night. 8:00 p.m., August 14 and 15.

**Tickets $10–$30**.

**PLM HALL**

Oakland Chamber Orchestra, with Lily Marksen at the piano, performs a _____
c.
featuring works by Beethoven, Bach, and Brahms. 8:00 p.m., August 15.

**Tickets $20-$30**.

### THEATRE

**CURTAINS UP**

The Downtown Players perform _The Argument_, a new _____ by J.L. Mason, starring
d.
Vanessa Thompson and Tyrone Williams as a married couple. Through August 20. **Tickets $20**.

### CHILDREN

**CROWN**_____
e.
Roller coaster, merry-go-round, and other rides provide fun for kids and adults. Open daily 10:00 a.m. to 5:00 p.m. **Free admission**.

### GENERAL INTEREST

North Ridge_____ Food, exhibitions,
f.
and prizes for best cow, best quilt, and more. August 14–15, 10:00 a.m. to 7:00 p.m. **Free**.

### SAL'S _____
g.
Dance to the music of rock band, Jumpin' Lizards. 8:00 p.m. to midnight. Must be 18 or older (ID required). **$10.00 (includes 1 beverage)**.

**5. Look at the events in Exercise 4. _True_ or _False_?**

a. The play is free. _____false_____

b. You can see an opera at City Centre. _____

c. The county fair is open until 10:00 p.m. _____

d. A seventeen-year-old can go to Sal's. _____

e. There's an evening concert at PLM Hall on August 15. _____

f. Tickets to the amusement park are expensive. _____

g. You can see the special art exhibit on August 24. _____

**Challenge** Look at a local newspaper, an online website of weekend events, or the listings in Exercise 4. Talk to two classmates and agree on a place to go. Write your decision and give a reason.

**1. Look in your dictionary. Where can you hear the following things?**

a. "I love playing in the sand." _____sandbox_____

b. "OK. Now try to hit this to left field." _____

c. "Here. Have some more chicken." _____

d. "We're the only cyclists here today." _____

e. "Push me higher, Mommy!" _____

f. "Serve the ball like this." _____

**2. Read about the children. What should they use?**

a. Toby likes to jump. _____jump rope_____

b. Jennifer is a little too young to ride a bicycle. _____

c. Jason is thirsty. _____

d. Sharzad likes to climb bars. _____

e. Shao-fen likes to play on things that go up and down. _____

f. Carlos is tired and just wants to sit down and rest. _____

**3. What about you? Look at the park in your dictionary. What would you like to do there . . .**

a. alone?

_I'd like to ride my skateboard._

b. with three of your classmates?

_____

c. with a three-year-old child?

_____

d. with a ten-year-old child?

_____

e. with a seventy-five-year-old relative?

_____

**Challenge** Design the ideal park. What does it have? Write a description.

**See page 316 for listening practice.**

1. **Look in your dictionary. Complete the sentences.**

   a. The boy with the diving mask has _____ fins _____ on his feet.

   b. There's a pink _____ hanging from the lifeguard station.

   c. The little girl in the red bathing suit is listening to a _____.

   d. A _____ is riding his surfboard.

2. **Circle the words to complete the hotel ad.**

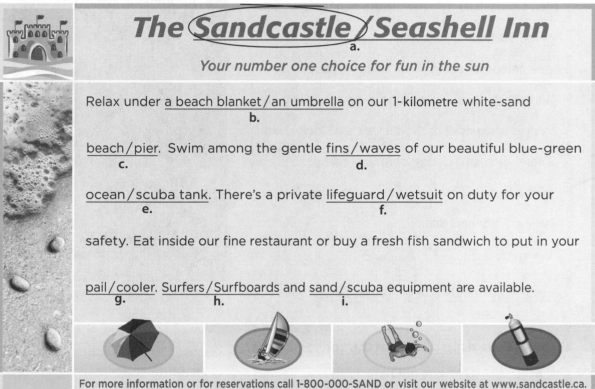

   The (Sandcastle) / Seashell Inn
   a.

   *Your number one choice for fun in the sun*

   Relax under <u>a beach blanket / an umbrella</u> on our 1-kilometre white-sand
                         b.

   <u>beach / pier</u>. Swim among the gentle <u>fins / waves</u> of our beautiful blue-green
     c.                    d.

   <u>ocean / scuba tank</u>. There's a private <u>lifeguard / wetsuit</u> on duty for your
     e.                    f.

   safety. Eat inside our fine restaurant or buy a fresh fish sandwich to put in your

   <u>pail / cooler</u>. <u>Surfers / Surfboards</u> and <u>sand / scuba</u> equipment are available.
    g.           h.           i.

   For more information or for reservations call 1-800-000-SAND or visit our website at www.sandcastle.ca.

3. **What about you? What would you take to the beach? What would you buy or rent? Check (✓) the columns.**

| | Take | Buy / Rent |
|---|---|---|
| surfboard | | |
| beach chair | | |
| beach umbrella | | |
| blanket | | |

| | Take | Buy / Rent |
|---|---|---|
| sunscreen | | |
| cooler | | |
| fins | | |
| Other: | | |

**Challenge** Imagine you are at the beach in your dictionary. Write a postcard describing it.
       **Example:** *I'm sitting . . .*

**1. Look in your dictionary. Find and correct five more mistakes in the email.**

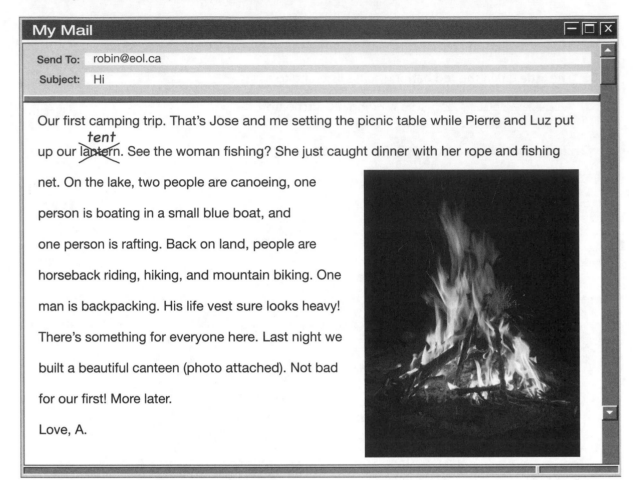

My Mail ⎯ ▢ ✕

| | |
|---|---|
| Send To: | robin@eol.ca |
| Subject: | Hi |

Our first camping trip. That's Jose and me setting the picnic table while Pierre and Luz put

up our ~~lantern~~ *tent*. See the woman fishing? She just caught dinner with her rope and fishing

net. On the lake, two people are canoeing, one

person is boating in a small blue boat, and

one person is rafting. Back on land, people are

horseback riding, hiking, and mountain biking. One

man is backpacking. His life vest sure looks heavy!

There's something for everyone here. Last night we

built a beautiful canteen (photo attached). Not bad

for our first! More later.

Love, A.

**2. Circle the words to complete the conversations.**

a. **Luke:** It's really dark out here. I can't see where I'm going.
   **Mike:** Here. Take this camping stove / (lantern) with you.

b. **Ming:** *Brrr.* It's getting cold out here.
   **Sue:** Hand me the canteen / matches. I'll light the fire.

c. **Jose:** Ow! These mosquitoes are driving me crazy.
   **Ana:** Here's some foam pad / insect repellent. That'll keep them away.

d. **Mia:** This rope is too long.
   **Tom:** You're right. What did we do with that multi-use knife / sleeping bag?

**3. What about you? Would you like to go camping? Why or why not?**

**Example:** *I'd like to go camping. I like sleeping outside.*

**Challenge** Look in your dictionary. Imagine you are on a camping trip. List the five most important items to have. Give reasons.

1. **Look in your dictionary. For which sports do you need the following equipment?**

   a. a boat ___water skiing___ and _____

   b. waves _____

   c. wind _____ and _____

   d. a mask and fins _____ and _____

2. **Look at the chart. Complete the sentences.**

## 2006 WINTER OLYMPICS IN TURIN, ITALY

|  |  | GOLD (First Place) | SILVER (Second Place) | BRONZE (Third Place) |
|---|---|---|---|---|
|  | MEN | Antoine Deneriaz<br>France 1:48.80 | Michael Walchhofer<br>Austria 1:49.52 | Bruno Kernen<br>Switzerland 1:49.82 |
|  | WOMEN | Michaela Dorfmeister<br>Austria 1:56.49 | Martina Schild<br>Switzerland 1:56.86 | Anja Paerson<br>Sweden 1:57.13 |
|  | MEN (15 km) | Andrus Veerpalu<br>Estonia 38:01.3 | Lukas Bauer<br>Czech Republic 38:15.8 | Tobias Angerer<br>Germany 38.20.5 |
|  | WOMEN (10 km) | Kristina Smigun<br>Estonia 27:51.4 | Marit Bjorgen<br>Norway 28:12.7 | Hilde G. Pedersen<br>Norway 28:14.0 |
|  | MEN | Yevgeny Plushenko<br>Russia | Stephane Lambiel<br>Switzerland | Jeffrey Buttle<br>Canada |
|  | WOMEN | Shizuka Arakawa<br>Japan | Sasha Cohen<br>United States | Irina Slutskaya<br>Russia |
|  | MEN (500 m) | Joey Cheek<br>United States 1:09.76 | Dmitry Dorofeyev<br>Russia 1:10.41 | Lee Kang Seok<br>South Korea 1:10.43 |
|  | WOMEN (500 m) | Svetlana Zhurova<br>Russia 1:16.57 | Wang Manli<br>China 1:16.78 | Ren Hui<br>China 1:16.87 |

a. China won two medals in ___speed skating___.

b. Russia won a gold and a bronze medal in _____.

c. The United States won one gold medal in _____.

d. Estonia won the gold medal in both men's and women's _____.

e. Bruno Kernen lost the silver medal in _____ by less than half a second.

f. _____ is not a timed event.

**Challenge** Which winter sports or water sports are the most popular where you live? Why?

**1. Look in your dictionary. Cross out the word that doesn't belong. Give a reason.**

a. billiards   ~~martial arts~~   table tennis   _It doesn't use a ball._

b. fencing   gymnastics   wrestling   _____

c. boxing   inline skating   skateboarding   _____

d. cycling   horse racing   badminton   _____

**2. Look at the line graph. Circle the words to complete the sentences.**

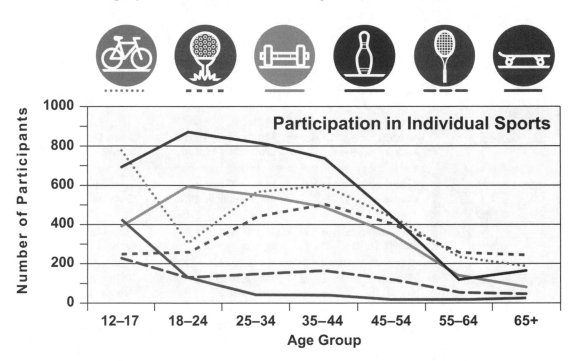

a. (Bowling) / Cycling is the most popular sport for people 18 to 24 years old.

b. Skateboarding / Tennis is the least popular sport for people over 25.

c. Golf / Cycling is the most popular sport for people over 65.

d. Participation in tennis / weightlifting decreases after the age of 24.

e. Between the ages of 64 and 65, the participation in bowling / golf goes up.

f. Participation in cycling / skateboarding goes down after the age of 12, but then it goes up again.

**3. What about you? How has your participation in sports changed? Write sentences.**

Example: _I started to play soccer more often in high school._

**Challenge** Write five more sentences using information from the line graph in Exercise 2.

1. **Look at the basketball court in your dictionary. Circle the words to complete the sentences.**

   a. There are two <u>players / teams</u> on the basketball court.

   b. The <u>coach / official</u> is on the court, too.

   c. The home <u>fan / score</u> is 83.

2. **Look at the bar graph.** *True* or *False*? **Correct the <u>underlined</u> words in the false sentences.**

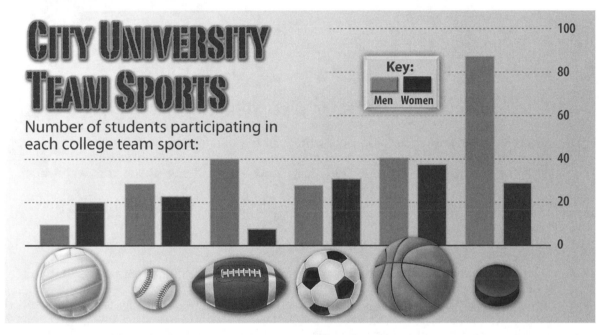

**City University Team Sports**

Number of students participating in each college team sport:

Key:
Men  Women

   *Hockey*
   a. <s>Baseball</s> is the most popular team sport among men
      at City University.                                                    *false*

   b. More women than men play <u>soccer</u>.                    _____

   c. Not many men play <u>volleyball</u>.                       _____

   d. Very few women play on the <u>football</u> team.          _____

   e. About 30 women play <u>basketball</u>.                     _____

   f. Almost as many men as women play <u>baseball</u>.         _____

   g. More students play basketball than <u>volleyball</u>.     _____

**Challenge**  Look at page 260 in this book. Follow the instructions.

1. **Look in your dictionary. Cross out the word that doesn't belong.**

   a. with your feet        ~~catch~~        kick        jump

   b. with a ball           hit              serve       bend

   c. in water              swim             skate       dive

   d. with other people     serve            tackle      pass

2. **Circle the words to complete the article.**

# Ski or Swim?
## Getting and Staying Fit for Life

There are many choices for people who want to get and stay fit. Some sports require very little special equipment. All you really need is a good pair of shoes to walk your way to good health. But you can also (dive) / dribble into a pool and ski / swim your
    a.                                          b.
way to fitness.

Want to exercise / serve with other people? Many communities have gyms that you
         c.
can join. There you can tackle / work out alone or with others. Bending / Pitching and
                        d.                                    e.
hitting / stretching help build your muscles and keep your body flexible.
     f.

For those people who enjoy competing, there are many opportunities to race / pass in
                                                                         g.
city marathons. But remember: Winning isn't everything. Even if you don't finish / start
                                                                              h.
the race, you should feel good that you participated.

It's not really important which sport you choose. You can throw / shoot a baseball
                                                            i.
or kick / swing a golf club. Just start slowly and be careful. Most of all, enjoy what you
   j.
do and do it regularly. In order to get and stay fit, sports should be a part of your
everyday life.

**Challenge** Look in your dictionary. Where else can a person swim, work out, ski, or race?
Write two sentences for each verb. **Example:** *You can swim in the ocean. You can swim in . . .*

1. **Look in your dictionary. Which pieces of equipment are customers talking about?**

   a. "These are a little too heavy for me." _____ *weights* _____

   b. "Oh, I see them now. They're under the target and next to the bow." _____

   c. "There's one. Under the volleyball." _____

   d. "They look like ice skates with wheels!" _____

   e. "Great! It's blue and white—the same as my team's colours." _____

   f. "I'd love to throw one of those around. I'd like red, or maybe pink." _____

   g. "Well, this will really protect my head." _____

   h. "Wow! These will make me look really big!" _____

   i. "Oh, there they are. Between the snowboard and the ski poles." _____

   j. "Do you have one for left-handed pitchers?" _____

   k. "I have to wear them to protect my legs during soccer games." _____

2. **Make comparisons using *than* and the words in parentheses.**

   a. volleyball / basketball (big)

   A basketball is bigger than a volleyball.

   b. golf club / hockey stick (long)

   _____

   c. ice skates / ski boots (warm)

   _____

   d. baseball / football (small)

   _____

   e. bowling ball / soccer ball (heavy)

   _____

3. **What about you? Look in your dictionary. What sports equipment would you buy from the store? Why?**

   **Example:** *I'd buy a bat for my niece because she wants to play baseball.*

   **Challenge** Look online or at a newspaper ad. Find the prices of these pieces of sports equipment.

   a baseball glove _____     a tennis racket _____

   Other: _____

**1. Look in your dictionary. Complete the crossword puzzle.**

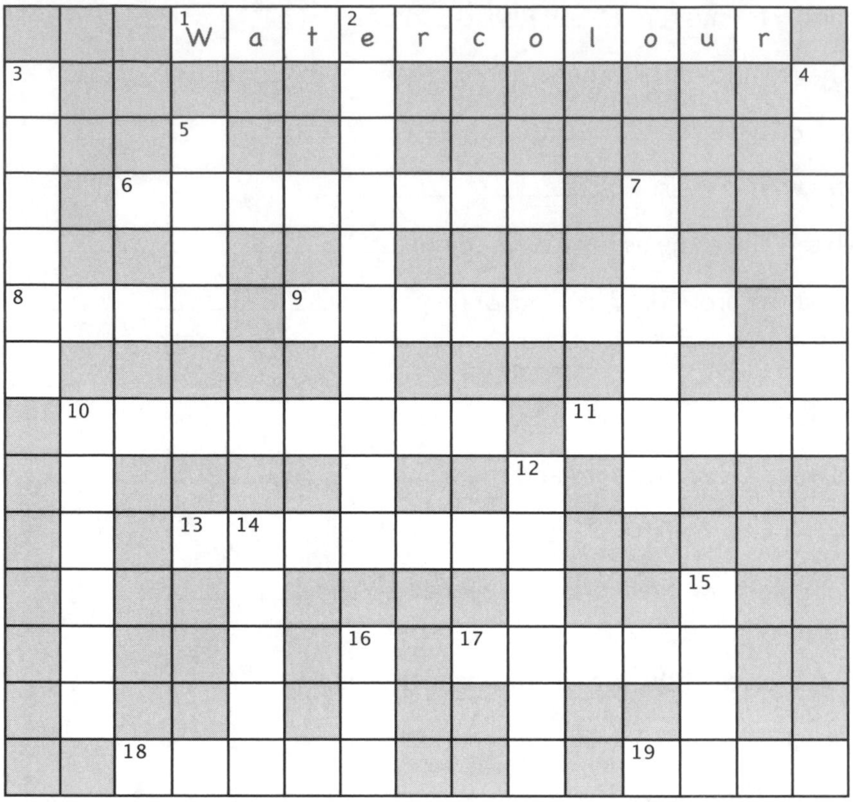

The crossword puzzle grid with 1 Across filled in: W a t e r c o l o u r

**ACROSS**

1. It's not oil paint
6. This one looks like a kitten
8. It comes in a stick
9. Red, but not hearts
10. A board game
11. Black, but not spades
13. Type of paint
17. Type of game
18. It holds a canvas
19. I like to _____ games

**DOWN**

2. It has a flower on it
3. Collect _____
4. You use them to knit
5. These are cubes
7. You can build these with a kit
10. It's on the easel
12. Type of figure
14. A board game
15. You can make one from paper
16. Type of paint

**2. Cross out the word that doesn't belong. Give a reason.**

| a. | checkers | chess | ~~crocheting~~ | _It's not a board game._ |
| b. | dolls | diamonds | clubs | _____ |
| c. | watercolour | acrylic | quilt block | _____ |

**3. Look at the bar graph. Circle the words to complete the sentences.**

# Fun and Games

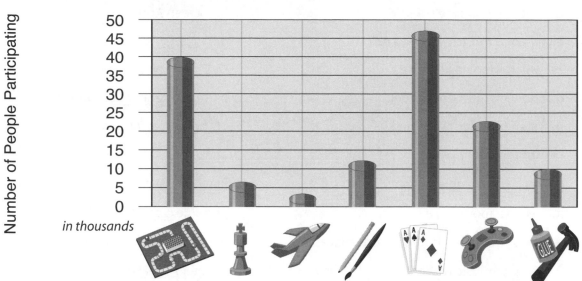

Number of People Participating

50
45
40
35
30
25
20
15
10
5
0

*in thousands*

a. Playing (cards) / video games was the most popular of the seven activities.

b. About 12 thousand people drew or <u>painted / played board games</u>.

c. Almost 10 thousand people used <u>model / woodworking</u> kits.

d. The least popular of the seven activities was <u>chess / model making</u>.

e. Playing cards was about two times as popular as playing <u>board / video</u> games.

**4. What about you? How often do you do the following things? Check (✓) the columns.**

|  | Every week | Every month | Never |
|---|---|---|---|
| play cards |  |  |  |
| play board games |  |  |  |
| use a video game console |  |  |  |
| do crafts |  |  |  |
| play with model trains |  |  |  |
| paint |  |  |  |
| quilt |  |  |  |
| Other: |  |  |  |

**Challenge** Make a list of things to collect. Compare your list with your classmates.

**1. Look in your dictionary. What can you use to do the following things? Circle the answers.**

a. watch TV outside

flat screen / (portable TV)

b. listen to music while you run

MP3 player / turntable

c. watch a movie at home

DVD / personal CD player

d. show pictures on a screen

battery charger / LCD projector

e. listen to music in the park

CD boom box / tuner

f. hold an MP3 player

dock / plug

g. keep photos on a memory card

film / digital camera

h. watch a movie on a train

portable cassette / DVD player

i. keep your paper photos in one place

photo / digital photo album

j. listen to music without headphones

adapter / speakers

k. record your own voice

battery pack / microphone

**2. Look at the chart. Complete the sentences.**

**Percentages of Homes in Thamesville with Electronic Devices**

| 54% 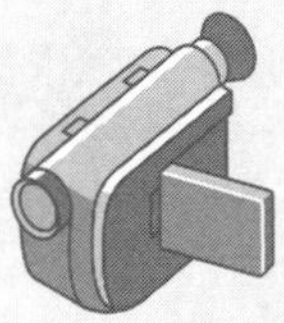 | 88% 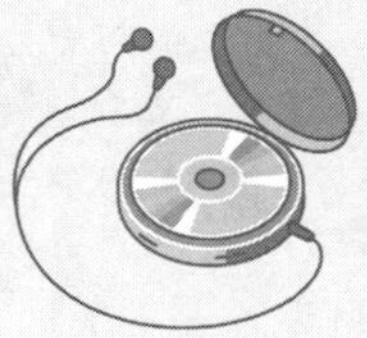 | 32% 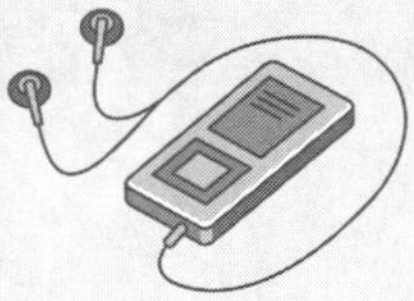 | 84% 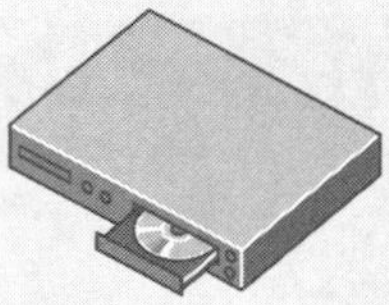 | 62% 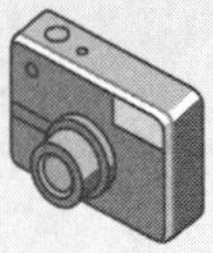 |
|-----|-----|-----|-----|-----|

a. Only a little more than half of homes in Thamesville have _____*camcorders*_____.

b. Almost 90% have _____.

c. More than 60% have _____.

d. In Thamesville, 52% more homes had _____ than _____.

3. **Look at these instructions for a universal remote. Complete the sentences.**

## Operation Buttons

**INSTRUCTIONS**

a. _____play_____ : to watch a DVD

b. _____ : to go back

c. _____ : to stop the DVD for a short time during playing or recording

d. _____ : to record a program (You must press PLAY at the same time.)

e. _____ : to go to the end quickly

4. **Look at the pictures. Circle the words to complete the sentences.**

a. The (photo)/ screen is out of focus.

b. She didn't use a camera case / tripod.

c. The photo is overexposed / underexposed.

d. He didn't use a film camera / zoom lens.

5. **What about you? Look at the electronic devices in Exercise 2.**
   **Which is the most important to you? Why?**

**Challenge** Write instructions for using a portable cassette player, a CD boombox, an MP3 player, or another electronic device.

**1. Look in your dictionary. Where can you hear these things?**

a. "And now a look at what's happening today in Europe."     <u>news program</u>

b. "Goodbye girls, goodbye boys. See you tomorrow."     _____

c. "And now, for $50,000 . . ."     _____

d. "Don't be afraid. I come from a friendly planet."     _____

e. "This beautiful dress can be yours for just $55.99!"     _____

f. "I love you and only you! Not your sister!"     _____

g. "Pandas live in the forest of central China."     _____

h. "Lopez is trying to get the ball from Jackson!"     _____

i. "I'm almost finished brushing my teeth."     _____

**2. Circle the words to complete the TV movie listings.**

# Movie Listings
## *This Week's Highlights*

| | | |
|---|---|---|
| **Titanic*****<br>(1997) | Rich girl (Kate Winslet) meets poor boy (Leonardo DiCaprio) on the historic sinking ship, and it's love at first sight. Don't miss this beautiful mystery / <u>romance.</u> (194 minutes)<br>a. | Fri<br>8:00 P.M.<br>Ch 7 |
| **Jurassic Park III***<br>(2001) | Dinosaurs attack (again) in this scary <u>horror story</u> / western with Sam Neill, William H. Macy, and Téa Leoni.<br>b.<br>You'll be scared out of your seat. (92 minutes) | Fri<br>9:00 P.M.<br>Ch 4 |
| **Spider–Man 3***<br>(2007) | Tobey Maguire stars again as the superhero Spider Man in this exciting <u>action story</u> / comedy. Great special effects.<br>(140 minutes)     c. | Fri<br>10:00 P.M.<br>SCI |
| **Romeo and Juliet****<br>(1996) | Starring Leonardo DiCaprio as Romeo and Claire Danes as Juliet, this modern version of Shakespeare's <u>mystery</u> / tragedy will bring tears to your eyes. (120 minutes)<br>d. | Sat<br>9:00 P.M.<br>ENT |
| **Mr. & Mrs. Smith*****<br>(2005) | An "average" husband (Brad Pitt) and wife (Angelina Jolie) live secret and surprising lives in this very funny <u>comedy</u> / tragedy. (120 minutes)<br>e. | Sat<br>10:00 P.M.<br>Ch 7 |

**3. Look in your dictionary. Label the CDs. Then look at the pie chart.** *True* or *False*?

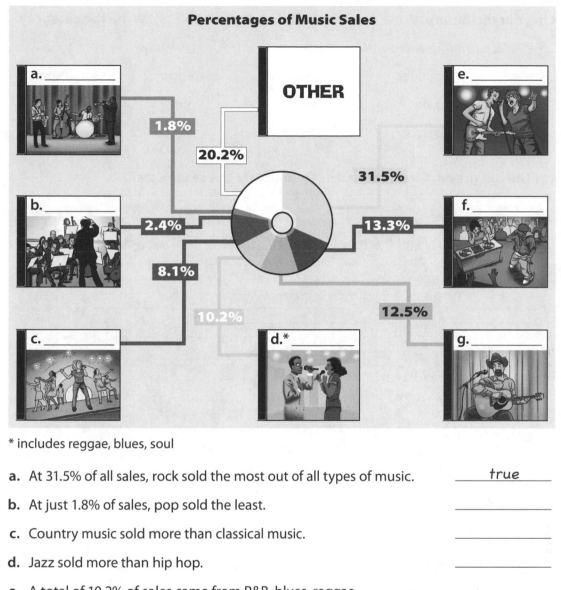

**Percentages of Music Sales**

a. _____

OTHER

e. _____

1.8%

20.2%

31.5%

b. _____

2.4%

13.3%

f. _____

8.1%

10.2%

12.5%

c. _____

d.* _____

g. _____

*includes reggae, blues, soul

**a.** At 31.5% of all sales, rock sold the most out of all types of music.  _____ *true* _____

**b.** At just 1.8% of sales, pop sold the least.  _____

**c.** Country music sold more than classical music.  _____

**d.** Jazz sold more than hip hop.  _____

**e.** A total of 10.2% of sales came from R&B, blues, reggae, and soul together.  _____

**4. What about you? How often do you listen to the following types of music? Check (✓) the column.**

|  | Often | Sometimes | Never |
|---|---|---|---|
| classical music |  |  |  |
| jazz |  |  |  |
| gospel |  |  |  |
| reggae |  |  |  |
| world music |  |  |  |

**Challenge** Write two short reviews of television programs or movies. Give them a rating from one to six stars (*).

1. **Look in your dictionary. Cross out the word that doesn't belong. Write the category.**

   a. ___brass___    French horn    ~~bass~~    trombone    tuba

   b. _____    clarinet    tambourine    xylophone    drums

   c. _____    cello    violin    guitar    organ

   d. _____    bassoon    oboe    harmonica    saxophone

2. **Look at the bar graph. Circle the words to complete the sentences.**

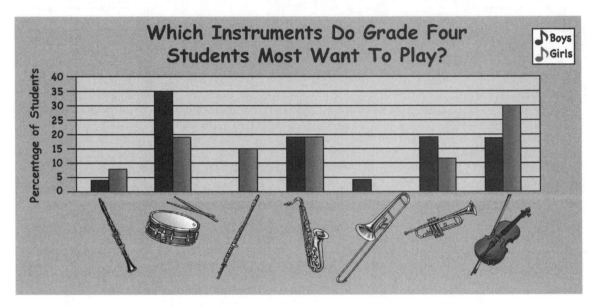

   a. The (drum) / violin is the favourite instrument among boys.

   b. Among girls, 30% chose the <u>flute / violin</u> as their favourite instrument.

   c. Among both boys and girls, 19% chose the <u>saxophone / trumpet</u>.

   d. No boys chose the <u>flute / trumpet</u> as their favourite instrument.

   e. No girls chose the <u>clarinet / trombone</u> as their favourite instrument.

   f. The graph does not include the harmonica or the <u>electric keyboard / saxophone</u>.

3. **What about you? Can you do these things? *Yes* or *No*?**

   play an instrument?   _____   If *yes*, which one?   _____

   sing a song?   _____   If *yes*, what is your favourite?   _____

   conduct an orchestra?   _____

   play or sing in a rock band?   _____

   **Challenge**   Ask your classmates about the instruments they play. Draw a bar graph like the one in Exercise 2.

**1. Look in your dictionary. Complete the holiday cards.**

a.

I looked really hard

to find this ___card___,
_a._

just to say on this special day—

that you're always a part

of my _____ .
_b._

Happy _____ .
_c._

I think we're a great _____ !
_d._

b.

Resolutions are made,

here comes the _____ .
_e._

I'm more than ready,

so throw the _____ !
_f._

The time is now near

to say Happy New _____ !
_g._

c.

As _____
_h._

light up the sky, the Canadian

_____ will proudly fly! Happy
_i._

_____ !
_j._

d.

I hope that there will always

be _____ and
_k._

candy _____ on your tree!
_l._

Merry _____ .
_m._

e.

In the fall it's time

for us all to give thanks for the

good things this year and, not the

least, a delicious _____
_n._

where _____ and stuffing
_o._

appear. Happy _____ !
_p._

f.

_____ burning bright, on a cool
_q._

October night. In scary costumes and a

_____ , for _____ treats
_r._ _s._

the children ask. Happy _____ !
_t._

**2. What about you? Check (✓) the cards you send each year. Who do you send them to?**

☐ New Year's _____

☐ Valentine's Day _____

☐ Christmas _____

☐ Other: _____

**Challenge** Make a card for one of the holidays in your dictionary or for any other event.

1. **Look in your dictionary. Match the sentence parts.**

   _5_ **a.** There are presents          **1.** wrapping Lou's gift.

   ___ **b.** Lou is making a wish for       **2.** on a long table.

   ___ **c.** There are two cakes          **3.** from the deck.

   ___ **d.** A woman is videotaping the party   **4.** a new car.

   ___ **e.** Gani is                **5.** on a round table.

   ___ **f.** Amaka is                **6.** blowing out the candles.

2. **Lou's mom videotaped birthday messages for Lou and Gani. Circle the words to complete the messages.**

   **a.** "Hi, Lou. Happy 18th birthday! Did you (make a wish)/ blow out the candles for a new car? I hope you get it. You can take me for a ride!"

   **b.** "Happy birthday, Gani. Eighty years old! Wow! You have a lot of candles to <u>wrap / blow out</u>!"

   **c.** "Hey, Lou. Have a great day. I hope you like the present I <u>videotaped / brought</u>."

   **d.** "Happy birthday, Gani. Open my present first! I <u>sang / wrapped</u> it in some pretty red paper."

   **e.** "Lou, happy birthday! I <u>hid / brought</u> your present in the yard. I hope you can find it!"

   **f.** "Enjoy the party, Lou! Your Mom did a great job with the <u>decorations / videotape</u>. They look beautiful!"

3. **What about you? How do you celebrate birthdays in your family? Compare your list with a partner's.**

   ☐ have a party

   ☐ have a cake with candles

   ☐ put up decorations

   ☐ make a wish

   ☐ videotape the party

   ☐ bring gifts

   ☐ Other: _____

**4. Look at the picture. *True* or *False*?**

a. The present isn't for Lou. _____*false*_____

b. The present is from Paul. _____

c. Someone hid the present. _____

d. The present is wrapped in polka-dotted paper. _____

e. The present isn't a new car. _____

**5. What happened first? Number the sentences *1* and *2* for each pair.**

a. __2__ I blew out the candles.     __1__ I made a wish.

b. ____ We videotaped the party.     ____ We watched the videotape.

c. ____ He gave me the present.     ____ He wrapped the present.

d. ____ I found my present on the deck.     ____ My mom hid my present.

e. ____ My dad cut the cake.     ____ We ate the cake.

**6. Complete the card. Use the words in the box.**

| hid | presents | ~~make~~ | blow | decorations | brought | wrapped |

## Happy Birthday!

_____*Make*_____ a wish, _____ the candles out,
    a.                   b.

Cut the cake, scream and shout,

Open _____ that were _____ with care.
         c.                   d.

It's your birthday, you don't have to share!

I _____ you a gift with a colourful bow.
   e.

Can you open it yet? My answer is no!

I _____ it behind a big, oak tree.
   f.

We put up _____ for you to see.
         g.

**Challenge** Write a birthday message for a greeting card. It can rhyme, but it doesn't have to.

## Picture Comparison

Write about the two classrooms. How are they the same? How are they different?
**Example:** *Both classes are ESL classes. One class is ESL 101, the other class is ESL 102. Both classes have six students. In class 101, half of the students are women, but in 102…*

**A Picture is Worth a Thousand Words**

Write about the people in the photographs.

Describe the people.

What are their relationships with the other people in the same photograph?

Where are they?

What are they doing?

How do they feel?

### Word Map

Complete the diagram. Use the words in the box.

| | | | | |
|---|---|---|---|---|
| bathroom | bathtub | bed | bedroom | blanket |
| medicine cabinet | counter | ~~stove~~ | toothbrush | drawer |
| ~~stuffed animals~~ | end table | pot | ~~rubber mat~~ | hutch |
| entertainment centre | faucet | ~~house~~ | dining area | dishes |
| ~~kids' bedroom~~ | kitchen | lamp | living room | |
| food processor | ~~pillow~~ | ~~napkin~~ | placemat | |
| ~~stereo system~~ | ~~toy chest~~ | table | dresser | |

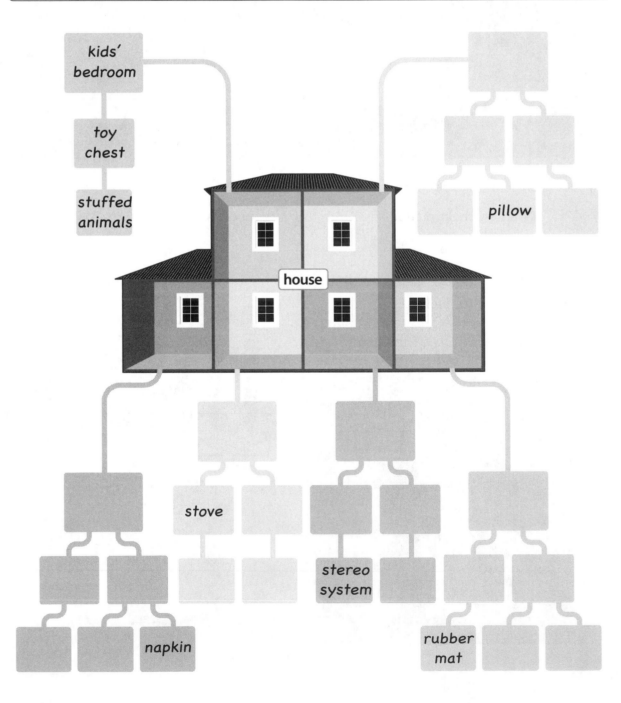

## "C" Search

Look at the picture. There are more than 15 items that begin with the letter c. Find and circle them. Then, write at least 8 sentences describing the picture. Use the circled words in your sentences.

**Example:** *One man is eating a cheeseburger.*

**Pack It Up!**

Imagine that you are going away for the weekend. What clothing and accessories will you take for each location? Put at least six items in each suitcase. Use your dictionary for help.

WEEKEND FUN IN THE SUN!

Special
2-day package
at The Sunshine Inn

2 bathing suits

NATURE CLUB OVERNIGHT TRIP

Fall Weekend

Meet Sat. Sept. 9, 7:00 a.m. Rain or Shine!

You are cordially invited to celebrate the marriage of
Heather Miller
to
Brian Johnson
at the Country Manor Hotel Ballroom
Saturday, June 29, 8:00 p.m.
R.S.V.P.

QUÉBEC
SKI WEEKEND

Come join us for
two days of fun and relaxation

For information visit us at www.ski.ca

## Crossword Puzzle

Complete the crossword puzzle.

### ACROSS

1. Identification (short form)
3. Brush and _____ your teeth
6. A hole in a tooth
9. It holds your hair in place
10. She's _____ the hospital
13. Women wear it to smell good
14. Take with milk _____ food
15. _____ smoking!
17. Your brain is inside it
19. Your throat is inside it
20. It helps you walk
23. They operate on patients
26. Throw up
28. It's part of the foot
29. It's another part of the foot
32. _____-the-counter medication
34. High temperature
35. Your eye_____ covers your eye

### DOWN

2. A serious disease
4. An eye specialist
5. You do this with your eyes
6. Cardiopulmonary resuscitation (short form)
7. These do the opposite of what *arteries* do
8. Listen _____ your heart
11. _____ not operate heavy machinery
12. One of the five senses
16. You put a bandage on this
18. Part of your face
21. *Break* (past form)
22. The dentist _____ a cavity yesterday
24. You shave with this
25. You do this with your nose
27. A doctor can look _____ your throat
30. Put _____ sunscreen
31. Intravenous (short form)
33. Registered nurse (short form)

### Things Change

Look at the maps of Middletown 50 years ago and Middletown today. What's different? What's the same? Write sentences. Use your own paper.

**Example:** *There was a bakery on the southeast corner of Elm and Grove. Now there's a coffee shop. There's still a...*

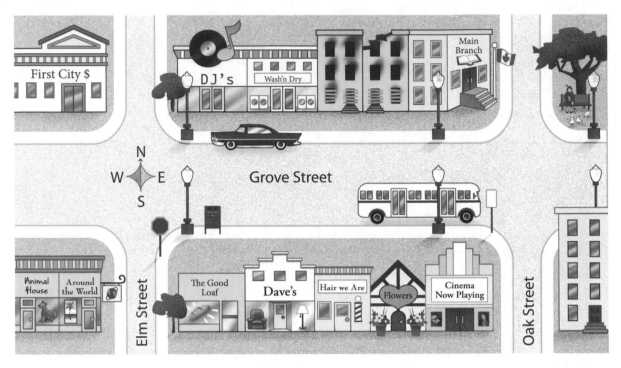

**50 Years Ago**

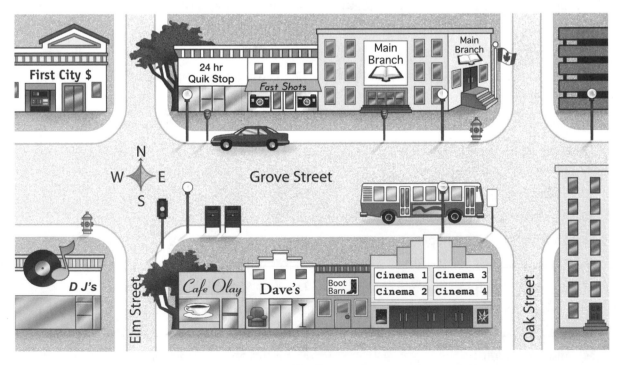

**Today**

## What's Wrong With This Picture?

Look at the picture. Describe ten more problems.

**Example:** *A subway car is going over the bridge.*

**On the Job**

Look at the pictures. Describe each photograph and answer the questions for each picture. Use your own paper.

1.

2.

3.

4.

a. Where are the people?

b. What are they doing?

c. What types of equipment are the people using?

d. Are they using safety equipment? If *yes*, what types?

e. What types of job skills do the people need to do these jobs?

f. How do you think the workers feel?

g. Compare the four jobs. How are they the same? How are they different?

h. Would you like to work in any of these places? Why or why not?

## Word Map

Complete the diagram. Use the words in the box.

| | | | | |
|---|---|---|---|---|
| ~~add~~ | astronaut | chemistry | comma | computers |
| desert | ~~DVD drive~~ | English composition | ~~essay~~ | exploration |
| geography | ~~high school~~ | ~~invention~~ | light bulb | magnet |
| ~~math~~ | mountain peak | mountain range | multiply | ocean |
| paragraph | ~~physics~~ | product | ~~sand dune~~ | science |
| sentence | ~~sum~~ | test tube | ~~tower~~ | world history |

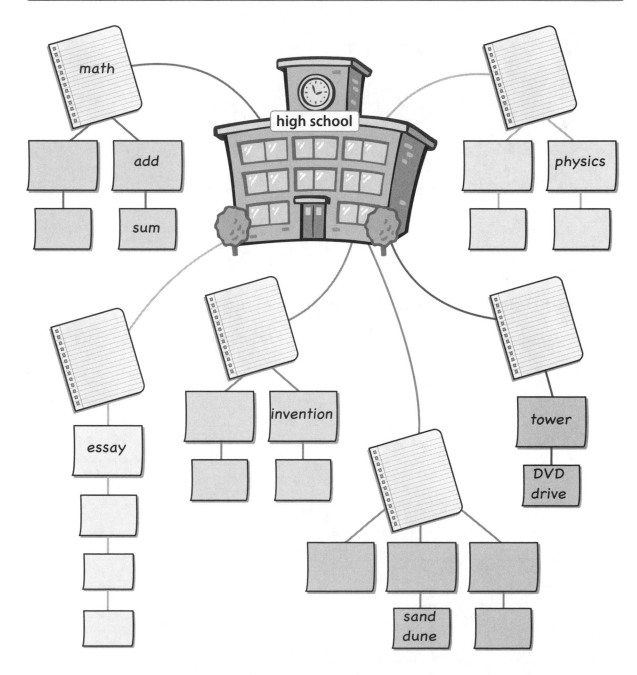

**Word Search**

1. There are 25 plant and animal words in the box. The words go → and ↓.
   Find and circle them.

```
L  I  O  N  P  A  R  O  S  E
L  C  A  T  I  R  O  O  E  L
A  D  K  O  N  A  O  C  A  E
M  O  N  K  E  Y  S  T  L  P
A  L  L  I  G  A  T  O  R  H
P  P  L  L  G  N  E  P  R  A
O  H  I  F  O  E  R  U  A  N
W  I  L  L  O  W  A  S  P  T
L  N  Y  Y  S  T  T  O  A  D
W  H  A  L  E  A  G  L  E  Y
```

2. Put each circled word from Exercise 1 into the correct category.

| Flowers | Sea Animals | Amphibians | Insects |
|---|---|---|---|
| _____ | _____ | _____ | _____ |
| _____ | _____ | _____ | _____ |

| Mammals | Sea Mammals | Trees | Birds |
|---|---|---|---|
| _llama_ | _____ | _____ | _____ |
| _lion_ | _____ | _____ | _____ |
| _____ | _____ | _____ | _____ |
| _____ | | | _____ |
| _____ | | | |

| Reptiles | Rodents |
|---|---|
| _____ | _____ |

**Complete the puzzle.**

|     |     | ²S | u | r | f | i | ³n | g |     | ⁴ |     | ⁵ |     |     |
|-----|-----|-----|-----|-----|-----|-----|-----|-----|-----|-----|-----|-----|-----|-----|

(Crossword grid with numbered cells: 1, 2(S u r f i n g), 3, 4, 5, 6, 7, 8, 9, 10, 11, 12, 13, 14, 15, 16, 17, 18, 19, 20, 21, 22, 23, 24, 25, 26, 27, 28, 29, 30)

## ACROSS

**2.** A water sport

**4.** Type of player for movies

**6.** Type of paint

**8.** It goes up and down

**11.** You can use them to light a campfire

**14.** Compact disc (short form)

**15.** Bucket

**16.** _____ and touch your toes

**17.** You see them in a theatre

**18.** Type of block for your skin

**19.** Opposite of *Yes*

**23.** A bike with three wheels

**25.** 35 _____ camera

**26.** It has three legs; you put your camera on it

**27.** _____ the ball with the bat

**29.** You can swim in it

**30.** String instrument

## DOWN

**1.** _____ a swing

**2.** A winter snow sport

**3.** _____ Year's Day

**5.** _____ crafts

**7.** _____ skating

**9.** Edmonton 5, Los Angeles 3

**10.** Track and _____

**12.** Type of park

**13.** Downhill _____

**16.** You can sit on it in the park

**20.** Type of camera

**21.** You can look at pictures and charts on it

**22.** You can see them in a theatre

**23.** You can sleep inside it

**24.** Billiards

**28.** This _____ the end of the Down clues!

# Challenge Exercises

Challenge for page 13

Use the formulas to convert the temperatures. Then describe the temperature.

| To convert Fahrenheit to Celsius: | To convert Celsius to Fahrenheit: |
|---|---|
| Subtract (−) 32, multiply (×) by 5, divide (÷) by 9 | Multiply (×) by 9, divide (÷) by 5, add (+) 32 |
| Example: 50°F = _____?_____ °C | Example: 25°C = _____?_____ °F |
| 50 − 32 = 18   18 × 5 = 90   90 ÷ 9 = 10 | 25 × 9 = 225   225 ÷ 5 = 45   45 + 32 = 77 |
| Answer: 50°F = 10°C | Answer: 25°C = 77°F |

a.  25°C = _77°_ F ___warm___

b.  41° F = ____ C _____

c.  68°F = ____ C _____

d.  95°F = ____ C _____

e.  30°C = ____ F _____

f.  −20°C = ____ F _____

Challenge for page 15

Look up the information in a phone book or online.

a.  What are the area codes for these cities?

Victoria, BC _____

Saskatoon, SK _____

St. John's, NL _____

Whitehorse, YK _____

b.  What are the city and country codes for these locations?

| | Country code | City code |
|---|---|---|
| Mexico City, Mexico | | |
| San Francisco, CA | | |
| Beijing, China | | |
| Moscow, Russia | | |

Write six sentences comparing the time in different cities. Use words, not numbers.

**Example:** *When it's five in the afternoon in Athens, it's eleven at night in Hong Kong.*

| When it's noon Eastern Standard Time, it's ... in ... . | | | | | |
|---|---|---|---|---|---|
| Athens | **7** P.M. | Hong Kong | **1** A.M.* | Riyadh | **8** P.M. |
| Baghdad | **8** P.M. | Mecca | **8** P.M. | St. Petersburg | **8** P.M. |
| Bangkok | **12** MIDNIGHT | Mexico City | **11** A.M. | San Juan | **12** NOON |
| Buenos Aires | **2** P.M. | Paris | **6** P.M. | Seoul | **2** A.M.* |
| Halifax | **1** P.M. | Rio de Janeiro | **2** P.M. | Tokyo | **2** A.M.* |

* = morning of the next day

Add to the chart. Look up the information online.
Continue on your own paper if you need more space.

| International Holidays | | |
|---|---|---|
| **Date** | **Holiday** | **Country** |
| January 26 | Republic Day | India |
| February 5 | Constitution Day | Mexico |
| May 5 | Children's Day | South Korea |
| June 20 | Flag Day | Argentina |
| July 4 | Independence Day | United States |
| July 14 | Bastille Day | France |
| | | |
| | | |

## Challenge for pages 34 and 35

**Children living with two parents and . . .**

- one or more brothers or sisters
- one or more stepbrothers or stepsisters
- one or more half brothers or half sisters
- no brothers or sisters
- other

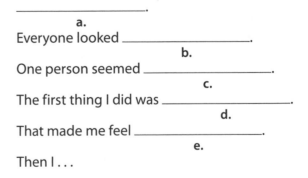

1.1%

10.7%

15.8%

71.1%

1.3%

**Look at the pie chart.** *True* or *False*?

**a.** Most children living with a mother and father also live with one or more brothers or sisters.

_____true_____

**b.** Only 10.7% of children living with two parents don't live with brothers or sisters.

_____

**c.** More than 10% of children living with two parents live with stepbrothers or stepsisters.

_____

**d.** More children living with two parents live with half-brothers and half-sisters than with stepbrothers and stepsisters.

_____

## Challenge for pages 42 and 43

**Imagine that you are the person in the far left of this picture. Complete the story.**

When I went into the room, I felt

_____.
        **a.**

Everyone looked _____.
                **b.**

One person seemed _____.
                  **c.**

The first thing I did was _____.
                    **d.**

That made me feel _____.
                **e.**

Then I . . .

**Challenge** for page 59

What's your opinion? List appropriate toys for each group. Use your dictionary for help.

| Age group | Activities | Toys |
|---|---|---|
| Babies (under 2) | looking and listening<br>holding things | *rattle* |
| Toddlers (age 2-3) | throwing, rolling, and pushing objects<br>listening to stories and songs | |
| Children over age 3 | learning stories and songs<br>drawing | |

**Challenge** for pages 72 and 73

Look at the receipts. Compare prices. Write six sentences.

**Example:** *Black beans are cheaper at Dave's.*

```
         DAVE'S
     54 CHURCH STREET
       MONCTON, NB

1 CAN BLACK BEANS        $0.60
2 L APPLE JUICE          $4.99
1 KG FLOUR               $1.69
6 FROZEN BAGELS          $1.09
1 L ICE CREAM            $3.99
1 150 ML FAT-FREE
  BANANA YOGOURT         $0.80

     THANK YOU FOR
   SHOPPING WITH US
```

```
       SHOPWELL

1 150 ML FAT-FREE
  BANANA YOGURT          $0.90
6 FROZEN BAGELS          $1.19
1 L ICE CREAM            $3.99
2 L APPLE JUICE          $4.39
1 KG FLOUR               $1.39
1 CAN BLACK BEANS        $0.80

     THANK YOU FOR
   SHOPPING WITH US
```

**Challenge** for page 75

Check the labels on the containers of four of your favourite foods.
Make a chart like the one below.

| Food | Serving Size | Calories | Calories from fat | Protein | Carbohydrate |
|---|---|---|---|---|---|
| *ice cream* | *125 mL* | *170* | *90* | *3g* | *17g* |

## Challenge for page 142

What type of punishment do you think someone should get for committing these crimes? Check (✓) the columns to complete the chart.

| Crimes | Prison | Hospitalization | Community service* | Fines** |
|---|---|---|---|---|
| assault | | | | |
| burglary | | | | |
| drunk driving | | | | |
| identity theft | | | | |
| murder | | | | |
| possessing illegal drugs | | | | |
| shoplifting | | | | |
| vandalism | | | | |

\* *Community service* is work that a person does without pay. An example is picking up garbage from the sidewalks.
\*\*A *fine* is an amount of money that a person has to pay for doing something wrong.

## Challenge for page 166

Look at the pairs of jobs. Compare them. What is the same for both jobs? Use your own paper.

Example: *A childcare worker and a babysitter both work with children.*

a. a childcare worker and a babysitter

b. an accountant and a cashier

c. a butcher and a baker

d. an auto mechanic and an appliance repair person

e. a businessperson and an administrative assistant.

## Challenge for page 170

Work with a partner. List three job skills. Check (✓) the ones you and your partner have.

| Job Skills | Your Name | Partner's Name |
|---|---|---|
| | _____ | _____ |
| _____ | ☐ | ☐ |
| _____ | ☐ | ☐ |
| _____ | ☐ | ☐ |

**Challenge** for page 173

Add to the following list of ways to find a job. What do you think are the best ways to find a job? Rank the ways. (Number 1 = the best). Explain your choices to your classmates.

**Ways to find a job**

____ networking

____ classified ads

____ employment service offices

____ Other: _____

____ school placement services

____ employment agencies

____ the Internet

____ Other: _____

**Challenge** for page 179

**Look at the worker. Write about the safety hazards. What should the worker do to protect herself?**

**Example:** *She's wearing sandals. She should wear safety boots.*

**Challenge** for page 213

Find out more information about at least two animals in Exercise 4. Look online, in an encyclopedia, or a science book and make a chart like the one below. Use your own paper.

| Name | Type | What it eats | How it protects itself |
|---|---|---|---|
| scallop | mollusk | small bits of food in the water | propels itself away from danger |

**Challenge** for page 229

Interview five or more people. Which sports do they like to play? Which sports do they like to watch? Complete the chart.

| Number of people who like to play | | | | | | | |
|---|---|---|---|---|---|---|---|
| | Basketball | Baseball | Softball | Football | Soccer | Hockey | Volleyball | Water polo |
| Play | | | | | | | | |
| Watch | | | | | | | | |

# LISTENING EXERCISES

🎧 1. Listen to the entire conversation. Answer the questions with your class.

    **a.** Where is Carlos?

    **b.** What is he doing?

🎧 2. Listen to each part of the conversation. Complete the receptionist's questions.

    **a.** Can you _____ that for me, please?

    **b.** Is there an _____ with that?

    **c.** What _____ do you live in?

    **d.** Now I need your _____.

    **e.** And what's your _____?

    **f.** Put your _____ right there.

🎧 3. Listen again. Complete the form.

## School Registration Form

| | |
|---|---|
| _____ | _____ |
| first name | last name |

| | | |
|---|---|---|
| _____ | _____ | _____ |
| address | apartment number | city |

| | | | |
|---|---|---|---|
| _____ | _____ | _____ | (___)___-____ |
| province | postal code | phone number | cellphone number |

| | | | |
|---|---|---|---|
| _____ | _____ | _____ | M   F |
| birthplace | DOB | SIN | sex |

4. Where have you had to fill out forms like this? Make a list of places.

    _____     _____

    _____     _____

    _____     _____

    _____     _____

**Oxford Picture Dictionary pp. 6–7**

🎧 **1.** Look at the picture at the top of pages 6 and 7 in the OPD. Listen to the entire conversation. Answer the questions with your class.

    **a.** What is Tom looking for?

    **b.** How many people does he ask for help?

    **c.** Does he find it?

🎧 **2.** Close your book. Listen to each part of the conversation. Complete the sentences.

> **a.** I think it's over there by the _____.
>
> **b.** Well, look in the _____.
>
> **c.** He's over there, in front of the _____.
>
> **d.** It's on her _____.
>
> **e.** It's near her _____.
>
> **f.** The teacher is at the _____.

🎧 **3.** Complete the paragraph. Then listen again and check your answers.

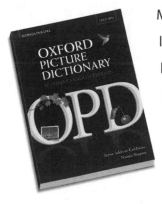

Mrs. Olsen says the _____ is by the computer, but it's not there. Tom looks in the bookcase. He sees a lot of _____, but no dictionaries. He looks under some _____ too. Albert's dictionary is on Linda's desk. Linda is _____ to the _____. Tom asks Linda for the dictionary, but she says, "Shhh! The teacher is _____." Mrs. Olsen says, "Please _____ and _____ your books to page 18." Tom never gets to look in the dictionary.

**4.** Write a paragraph describing your classroom.

_____

_____

_____

_____

_____

**Oxford Picture Dictionary p. 13**

🎧 **1.** Look at the weather map on page 13 in the OPD. Listen to the entire forecast. Answer the questions with your class.

    **a.** What five cities are mentioned in the forecast?

    **b.** Which city is hot?

    **c.** Which city is cold?

🎧 **2.** Close your dictionary. Listen to each part of the forecast. Underline *True* or *False*.

| | | |
|---|---|---|
| **a.** It's sunny, clear, and hot in Toronto. | True | False |
| **b.** It's cool in Calgary, with temperatures around 12 degrees. | True | False |
| **c.** There are low temperatures in Vancouver. | True | False |
| **d.** The rainstorm in Montreal should end this afternoon. | True | False |

🎧 **3.** Complete the sentences. Then listen again and check your answers.

In Toronto, it's a _____ day. They're having a _____.

In Regina and Calgary, it's _____ and cloudy. It isn't _____.

In Vancouver, it's _____ in many places. There could be a _____
later this afternoon.

It's _____ in Montreal. The _____ should end this afternoon.

**4.** Write a paragraph describing the current weather in your area.

_____

_____

_____

_____

_____

**Oxford Picture Dictionary p. 16**

🎧 1. Listen to the commentators on the recording. Answer the questions with your class.

   a. What event is taking place?

   b. When is it taking place?

🎧 2. Listen to each part of the conversation. Complete the sentences.

> a. What a beautiful day here — _____ degrees and sunny — just perfect weather for running.
>
> b. This morning, he placed _____ in both the 100-metre and 200-metre races.
>
> c. We'll return at _____ o'clock.

🎧 3. Complete the paragraph. Then listen again and check your answers.

The commentators are at the _____ annual Provincial Track and Field Championship. They are waiting for the _____-metre race to begin. Before the race starts, _____ runners line up. The commentators think that Stanley Cheng, who is in lane _____, will win the race because he placed _____ in the one hundred-metre and _____-metre races earlier in the day. Stanley actually finishes in _____ place because he trips over his shoelace. Oscar Anderson wins the race with a time of _____ seconds.

4. Look at the picture at the top of pages 6 and 7 in the OPD. Write a paragraph describing the classroom.

_____

_____

_____

_____

_____

🎧 **1.** Listen to the entire conversation. Answer the questions with your class.

    **a.** What is the couple talking about?

    **b.** What does the couple decide to do?

🎧 **2.** Listen to each part of the conversation. Complete the sentences.

> **a.** We should start planning our next _____ soon, dear.
>
> **b.** You mean we wouldn't be home for _____ or my birthday?
>
> **c.** We can't miss the _____!
>
> **d.** We can spend _____ there.

🎧 **3.** Complete the paragraph. Then listen again and check your answers.

The man and woman are trying to plan a _____. The woman suggests spending _____ in Ottawa. The man wants to visit British Columbia in October, but the woman doesn't want to be away from her family for _____ or her _____. The couple cannot travel in November because it is a busy month — they have to attend a _____ and a 60th-_____ party. They finally decide to fly to Cuba on _____ and return on _____.

**4.** Which Canadian holidays do you enjoy? Write a paragraph describing what you do to celebrate these days.

_____

_____

_____

_____

_____

Oxford Picture Dictionary p. 26

🎧 **1.** Listen to the conversations. Answer the questions with your class.

   **a.** Where are the conversations taking place?

   **b.** How many customers does the vendor have?

🎧 **2.** Listen to each conversation. Complete the sentences.

---

   **a.** Here's your change: a five, a _____, and a quarter.

   **b.** Three dollars and _____ cents, please.

   **c.** I've got . . . a toonie, two loonies, six _____, three nickels, and seven pennies.

   **d.** Here you go — three _____.

---

🎧 **3.** Complete the paragraph. Then listen again and check your answers.

   The first customer pays for her hot dog with a _____-dollar bill and receives a five-dollar bill, a _____, and a quarter in change. The second customer wants to give the vendor a _____-dollar bill, but pays with three loonies and a _____ instead. The third customer shows the vendor all the money he has. It includes three _____ and seven _____. The fourth customer gives the vendor three _____ and lets him keep the change, which is five _____.

**4.** Look in your purse or wallet. Make a list of the bills and coins that you have.

   _____    _____

   _____    _____

   _____    _____

   _____    _____

🎧 **1.** Listen to all four conversations between the clerk and her customers. Answer the questions with your class.

  **a.** What does this store sell?

  **b.** What are the customers doing?

🎧 **2.** Listen to each conversation. Complete the sentences.

  **a.** I want to _____ this lamp.

  **b.** I want to pay with a _____.

  **c.** The _____ for this lamp is $12.50.

  **d.** I want to _____ this lamp.

🎧 **3.** Complete the paragraph. Then listen again and check your answers.

```
----------------------------------
          LAMP SHOP
       221 QUEEN STREET
----------------------------------

ITEM                      PRICE
1 DESK LAMP @             $12.50
1 DESK LAMP @             $12.50

SUBTOTAL                 $25.00
SALES TAX                $ 2.06
TOTAL                    $27.06

PAYMENT METHOD:           CASH
```

Darla works at the returns desk at the Lamp Shop. Her first customer can't _____ his lamp because he didn't _____ it at the Lamp Shop. Darla's second customer isn't happy because she doesn't want to _____ cash or use a _____. Her third customer doesn't understand why his _____ is $27.06. He forgot about the _____ of $2.06. Darla's last customer can _____ her lamp with no problem because she has her _____.

**4.** Did you ever return something to a store? Why?

_____

_____

_____

_____

_____

**Oxford Picture Dictionary p. 32**

🎧 1. Listen to the entire conversation. Answer the questions with your class.

    **a.** What does the woman ask Nishad to do?

    **b.** How does she try to help him?

🎧 2. Listen to each part of the conversation. Complete the sentences.

> **a.** Just look for three _____ young women.
>
> **b.** Well, Meghan is short and _____.
>
> **c.** Wow, that is _____.
>
> **d.** Oh, she's _____, like me.

🎧 3. Complete the paragraph. Then listen again and check your answers.

The woman asks Nishad to pick up her friends from the airport. She describes them as

_____ and _____. Meghan is short and _____.

She has a _____ and a butterfly _____. Barbara is _____

than Nishad and she is seven months _____. Malia is heavier than the other two

friends and she is _____.

4. Imagine that someone you have never met will be picking you up from the airport. In one or two paragraphs, write a clear description of yourself so that he or she can find you.

_____

_____

_____

_____

_____

1. Look at pages 34 and 35 in the OPD. Listen to the entire conversation. Answer the questions with your class.

   a. Who is talking to Sue?

   b. What is happening tonight?

2. Close your dictionary. Listen to each part of the conversation. Complete the sentences.

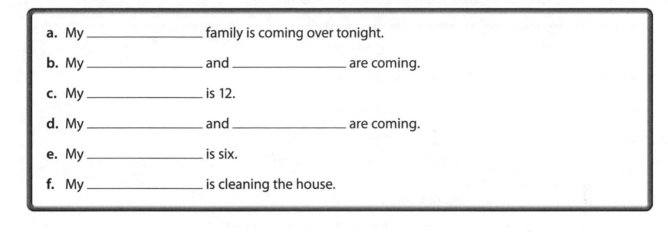

   a. My _____ family is coming over tonight.

   b. My _____ and _____ are coming.

   c. My _____ is 12.

   d. My _____ and _____ are coming.

   e. My _____ is six.

   f. My _____ is cleaning the house.

3. Complete the paragraph. Then listen again and check your answers.

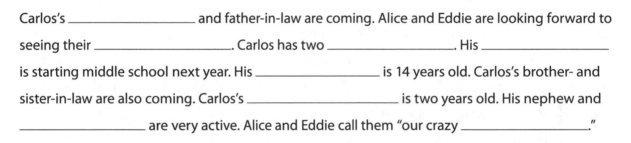

   Carlos's _____ and father-in-law are coming. Alice and Eddie are looking forward to seeing their _____. Carlos has two _____. His _____ is starting middle school next year. His _____ is 14 years old. Carlos's brother- and sister-in-law are also coming. Carlos's _____ is two years old. His nephew and _____ are very active. Alice and Eddie call them "our crazy _____."

4. Draw a family tree based on your family or a classmate's family. Name the people and write a paragraph about them.

**Oxford Picture Dictionary pp. 36–37**

🎧 1. Listen to the entire conversation between a husband and a wife. Answer the questions with your class.

    **a.** Why is the woman leaving?

    **b.** Who is staying with the baby?

    **c.** How does the mother feel? How does the father feel?

🎧 2. Listen to each part of the conversation. Complete the sentences.

> **a.** Don't forget to _____ Joey tonight.
>
> **b.** There are _____ on the table.
>
> **c.** Don't _____ him until 3:00, though.
>
> **d.** Be sure you have _____ if you take him out.
>
> **e.** Take the _____.
>
> **f.** _____ him before bed.

🎧 3. Complete the paragraph. Then listen again and check your answers.

Don's wife is going away overnight. She tells Don to _____ Joey that night. She says the extra _____ are in the cabinet. There's _____ on the shelf, and she reminds him to use the _____. Don helps take care of Joey every day, so he isn't worried. He knows there are wipes in the _____. He'll _____ in the car. He won't forget to _____ Joey before bed. But he won't _____. Don is a good father, but he's a terrible singer.

4. Imagine you are leaving your baby with a friend. Write a note. Tell your friend what to do.

1. Look at pages 38 and 39 in the OPD. Listen to the story. Point to the times you hear. Answer the question with your class.

   Who is telling the story?

2. Close your dictionary. Listen to each part of the story. Complete the sentences.

   a. At my house, we _____ together at 7:00.

   b. My parents _____ at 7:30.

   c. My mom _____ at 5:00.

   d. After dinner, usually around 7:30, my sister and I _____.

   e. At _____, I'm still working hard on my homework.

   f. About 8:30, my sister and I _____.

3. Complete the paragraph. Then listen again and check your answers.

   Jimmy's parents take him to school in the morning. Then his mother _____ to adult school and his father _____ to work. After school Jimmy, his mother, and his sister _____. In the evening, he and his sister _____. His parents _____, and his mom _____. When Jimmy and his sister go to bed, his dad _____ and his mom _____.

4. Write a paragraph about someone you know. Describe what the person does every day.

   _____

   _____

   _____

   _____

   _____

Oxford Picture Dictionary pp. 40–41

🎧 **1.** Look at pages 40 and 41 in the OPD. Listen to two people talk about family photos. Listen to the entire conversation. Answer the questions with your class.

    **a.** Who is the woman that is speaking?

    **b.** Who is the man that is speaking?

    **c.** Where was Grandfather born?

🎧 **2.** Close your dictionary. Listen to each part of the conversation. Write the verbs that you hear.

    **a.** We _____ to Egypt in 2005.

    **b.** He _____ in 1935, two years before me.

    **c.** He _____ with his parents in 1950.

    **d.** He _____ in 1953.

    **e.** He _____ his degree in 1959.

    **f.** No, we _____ this house in 1965.

🎧 **3.** Complete the paragraph. Then listen again and check your answers.

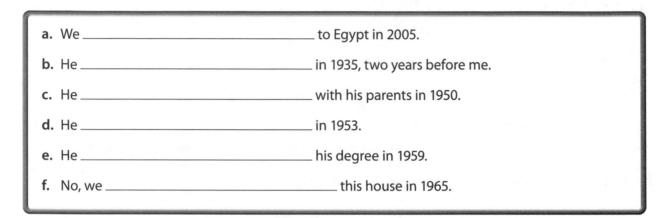

Martin _____ in Nicaragua. He _____ when he was 15 years old, and he _____ from high school three years later. Martin and Rosa met in 1955. They _____, but they didn't _____ until 1959. Six years later, they _____. Martin _____ in 2000, and he and Rosa _____ for a few years.

**4.** Write a paragraph that briefly describes your life. Use exercise 3 as a guide.

_____

_____

_____

_____

_____

**Oxford Picture Dictionary pp. 42–43**

🎧 1. Listen to the entire conversation. Answer the questions with your class.

    **a.** Why hasn't Riyaad been studying for his exam?

    **b.** What advice does Danny give Riyaad?

🎧 2. Listen to each part of the conversation. Complete the sentences.

> **a.** You always help me out when I'm _____ by the professor.
>
> **b.** I met someone last week and I think I'm _____!
>
> **c.** You're _____ over nothing.
>
> **d.** You didn't have to be _____ to ask her out.
>
> **e.** I can concentrate better when I'm _____.

🎧 3. Complete the paragraph. Then listen again and check your answers.

Riyaad started studying for his exam last night, but stopped because he was

_____. This _____ Danny, because Riyaad is usually

a good student. Riyaad explains that he could not concentrate on studying because he is

_____ with someone, but he is _____ that she doesn't

know he exists. Danny tells Riyaad that this is _____ and convinces Riyaad

to call the woman. Riyaad is _____ when she asks him out for coffee.

With Riyaad's problem solved, the two friends order some pizza and pop, because they are

_____ and _____.

4. Write a paragraph about a time you were either nervous or excited.

    _____

    _____

    _____

    _____

    _____

**Oxford Picture Dictionary pp. 48–49**

🎧 **1.** Listen to the entire conversation. Answer the questions with your class.

    **a.** What is Mrs. Denunzio doing?

    **b.** Does she mention anything that she doesn't like?

🎧 **2.** Listen to each part of the conversation. Complete the sentences.

> **1.** Your _____ said that the apartment is 800 dollars a month.
>
> **2.** Are _____ included?
>
> **3.** Hmm, I would have to _____ this room.
>
> **4.** First, I'll need you to _____.
>
> **5.** I'll start _____ today.

🎧 **3.** Complete the paragraph. Then listen again and check your answers.

**708** | Apartments for rent

**Westside Apartments**

3 bdrm 2 ba furn apt New kit
$1000/mo Util incl Call mgr

**555-1002 eves**

Mrs. Denunzio is looking at an _____ that she saw listed in a _____. She is happy when she finds out that some of the _____, water and electricity, are included. She does not like the colour of one of the rooms, though, and would have to _____. The manager asks Mrs. Denunzio to _____, and tells her that once she has been approved, she can _____. When she returns, she should bring a cheque for 1,600 dollars, then she can _____. Mrs. Denunzio is so excited that she plans to start _____ that day.

**4.** Have you ever rented an apartment? Write a paragraph about the steps you took.

_____

_____

_____

_____

1. Listen to the entire conversation between a manager and a woman looking for an apartment. Answer the questions with your class.

    **a.** What kind of apartment is the woman looking for?

    **b.** Is she going to move in?

2. Listen to each part of the conversation. Underline *True* or *False*.

| | | | |
|---|---|---|---|
| **a.** The woman saw a vacancy sign and would like to take a look around. | | True | False |
| **b.** The woman is happy about the playground because her children will enjoy it. | | True | False |
| **c.** The manager points out the fact that all of the second-floor apartments have balconies. | | True | False |
| **d.** Each tenant can use one of the six storage lockers on the first floor. | | True | False |
| **e.** Every apartment has security features including an intercom and a dead bolt lock. | | True | False |
| **f.** The woman really likes the apartment, but she thinks it's too expensive. | | True | False |

3. Complete the paragraph. Then listen again and check your answers.

Sara visits an _____. She's looking for an apartment on the _____. She likes the _____ in the courtyard. There's also a _____ with a big-screen TV. There are _____ — one on the first floor of each building. They each have six _____ and four _____. She also likes the security features. All of the doors have dead bolt locks and _____.

4. Imagine a perfect apartment. Write a paragraph about it.

_____

_____

_____

_____

_____

**Oxford Picture Dictionary p. 56**

🎧 **1.** Listen to the entire conversation. Answer the questions with your class.

    **a.** What are the son and daughter doing?

    **b.** Why aren't they happy about the carpet?

🎧 **2.** Listen to each part of the conversation. Complete the sentences.

> **a.** Put it here across from the _____.
>
> **b.** I'll put the _____ on it later.
>
> **c.** I'll bring in the _____.
>
> **d.** Put the _____ on the coffee table.
>
> **e.** Should I put the _____ by the sofa?
>
> **f.** When I get my new _____, it will be perfect.

🎧 **3.** Complete the paragraph. Then listen again and check your answers.

    Amanda and Tom are helping their mother move. They put the _____ across from the window and the _____ near the fireplace. They set up the _____ to the right of the fireplace. Amanda brought in the _____. They put the _____ in front of the sofa and put a _____ on it. There are two _____. The mother wants her _____ on the one next to the sofa. When Amanda and Tom are finished, they're tired, but their mother is happy.

**4.** Write a paragraph describing your living room.

    _____

    _____

    _____

    _____

    _____

**Oxford Picture Dictionary p. 60**

🎧 **1.** Listen to the entire conversation. Answer the questions with your class.

    **a.** What does the couple have to do?

    **b.** What does the man tell the woman not to do? Why?

🎧 **2.** Listen to each part of the conversation. Complete the sentences.

> **a.** Don't forget to _____ the floor first.
>
> **b.** I'll _____ and you can dry them.
>
> **c.** I'll tell them to _____ their toys.
>
> **d.** I'll just _____ these bags of garbage.

🎧 **3.** Complete the paragraph. Then listen again and check your answers.

The couple is cleaning the house. The man starts by _____ the kitchen floor while the woman _____ the living room carpet. In the kitchen, they _____ and dry the dishes, and then _____ the oven. The kids have to clean their own bedrooms by _____ their toys and _____ their beds. As the man's parents arrive, the couple finishes cleaning by _____ the garbage and _____ the old newspapers.

**4.** Write a paragraph about the types of housework you enjoy doing and the types you do not enjoy doing.

_____

_____

_____

_____

_____

Oxford Picture Dictionary pp. 62–63

🎧 1. Listen to the entire conversation between a husband and a wife. Answer the questions with your class.

    **a.** What did the man find?

    **b.** How does the woman feel at first? How does she feel at the end of the conversation?

🎧 2. Listen to each part of the conversation. Complete the sentences.

> **a.** One of the bedroom windows is _____.
>
> **b.** And the kitchen faucet is _____ a little bit.
>
> **c.** I think we'll need to call a _____.
>
> **d.** Are there _____?

🎧 3. Complete the paragraph. Then listen again and check your answers.

The house is cheap, but it needs a lot of repairs. One of the bedroom windows is _____,
but that's a small problem. There are also problems with the kitchen sink. The faucet is
_____, and the sink is _____. Joel and Anna might need to call a
_____. Unfortunately, they might also have to call a _____ because the
roof is _____. Finally, they probably need an _____ because there
are _____ in the basement.

4. Answer the questions.

    **a.** Which problem do you think will be the most expensive to fix? Why?

    _____

    **b.** Which problem should Joel and Anna fix first? Why?

    _____

    **c.** Should they move into this house? Why or why not?

    _____

**1.** Listen to the entire conversation about two different salads. Answer the questions with your class.

    **a.** What's the difference between the two salads?

    **b.** Which salad would you like better?

**2.** Listen to each part of the conversation. Write the words you hear.

> **a.** a head of _____
>
> **b.** yellow _____
>
> **c.** half a _____
>
> **d.** purple _____
>
> **e.** green _____
>
> **f.** _____ lettuce

**3.** Complete the paragraph. Then listen again and check your answers.

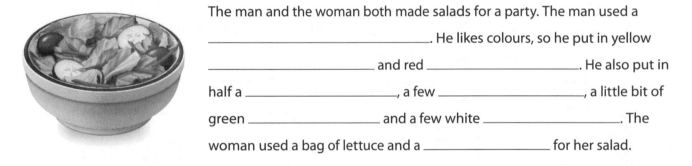

The man and the woman both made salads for a party. The man used a _____. He likes colours, so he put in yellow _____ and red _____. He also put in half a _____, a few _____, a little bit of green _____ and a few white _____. The woman used a bag of lettuce and a _____ for her salad.

**4.** Write a paragraph about the vegetables you like in salads and the vegetables you prefer cooked.

_____

_____

_____

_____

**Oxford Picture Dictionary pp. 72–73**

1. Listen to the entire conversation between the customer and the clerk. Answer the questions with your class.

   **a.** Is the clerk a man or a woman?

   **b.** Why is the customer confused?

2. Listen again. Complete the sentences.

   **a.** I'm looking for the _____.

   **b.** Oh, I also need _____ and oil.

   **c.** And I need _____.

   **d.** Maybe I should buy a _____.

   **e.** Do you like _____?

   **f.** Where are the _____?

3. Complete the paragraph. Then listen again and check your answers.

   Mrs. Mills wants to bake a _____, so the grocery clerk takes her to the _____ aisle. Then he tells her that the _____ section is at the back of the store. If Mrs. Mills wants to buy a cake, the store has lots of them in the _____, and she can find ice cream in _____ 2B in the _____ section. Fortunately, they didn't move the _____. The _____ are still working at the front of the store.

4. Imagine you are shopping for a party. Make a shopping list. Organize it so that items from the same section of the grocery store are listed together.

   _____     _____

   _____     _____

   _____     _____

   _____     _____

**Oxford Picture Dictionary p. 74**

1. Listen to the entire conversation between a husband and a wife. Answer the questions with your class.

   **a.** Where is the man going? Why?

   **b.** What does he forget?

2. Listen to each part of the conversation. Underline *True* or *False*.

| | | |
|---|---|---|
| **a.** He's going to the grocery store for a six-pack of pop. | True | False |
| **b.** She thinks some strawberry juice would be nice. | True | False |
| **c.** She wants two jars of peanut butter and some cookies. | True | False |
| **d.** She wants him to get two boxes of cereal. | True | False |
| **e.** They have a carton of eggs in the refrigerator. | True | False |
| **f.** She wants a carton of non-fat milk. | True | False |

3. Write the man's shopping list. Then listen again and check your answers.

4. Write a paragraph describing the foods you currently have in your kitchen.

_____

_____

_____

_____

_____

Oxford Picture Dictionary pp. 76–77

🎧 **1.** Listen to the entire conversation. Answer the questions with your class.

    **a.** Why is Chef Zamora on the show?

    **b.** Is the show's host happy with what Chef Zamora makes?

🎧 **2.** Listen to each part of the conversation. Complete the sentences.

> **a.** Would you like me to _____ the oven?
>
> **b.** We're going to _____ the onions and garlic.
>
> **c.** Now add in that cheese that I _____ earlier.
>
> **d.** I'll probably just _____ them; that's much faster.

🎧 **3.** Complete the recipe. Then listen again and check your answers.

### CHILES RELLENO

| | |
|---|---|
| **Step 1:** | Broil the peppers. |
| **Step 2:** | _____ the onions and _____ the garlic. |
| **Step 3:** | _____ the onions and garlic. Add the ground beef. |
| **Step 4:** | Add spices and tomato paste and _____ everything together. |
| **Step 5:** | _____ in the raisins, almonds, and olives. Add some _____ cheese. |
| **Step 6:** | _____ the peppers open and stuff them with the beef mixture. |
| **Step 7:** | Batter and fry the stuffed peppers. |
| **Step 8:** | _____ some sauce over top and serve. |

**4.** Name something that you enjoy cooking. How is it prepared? Write the recipe.

_____

_____

_____

_____

**1.** Look at the menu on pages 80 and 81 in the OPD. Listen to the entire conversation between the server and the customer. Answer the questions with your class.

   **a.** Does the man have the spaghetti dinner? Why?

   **b.** What is the customer's final order?

**2.** Close your dictionary. Listen to each part of the conversation. Underline *True* or *False*.

| | | | |
|---|---|---|---|
| **a.** The customer orders a cup of regular coffee and a dessert. | True | False |
| **b.** He's going to eat dessert before he eats lunch. | True | False |
| **c.** He changes his order from coffee to tea. | True | False |
| **d.** He's going to have a club sandwich with soup. | True | False |

**3.** Complete the paragraph. Then listen again and check your answers.

Menu ****

The customer can't decide what he wants. At first, he orders a slice of

_____. Then he asks for a _____. He also

orders a _____ with _____. Then he orders

a cup of _____ with _____. In the end, he changes his

order again. He gets a _____ with _____ instead.

**4.** Write a conversation between a server and a customer. Write at least eight lines. Read the conversation with a partner.

*Server: How can I help you?*

*Customer: I'd like . . .*

_____

_____

_____

_____

_____

_____

_____

**Oxford Picture Dictionary pp. 88–89**

🎧 1.  Look at pages 88 and 89 in the OPD. Listen to the entire conversation. Point to the people who are described. Then answer the questions with your class.

   a.  What are the women doing in the hotel lobby?

   b.  Does the woman prefer the evening gown or cocktail dress?

   c.  How do they know the two people are working?

🎧 2.  Close your dictionary. Listen to each part of the conversation. Underline *True* or *False*.

| | | |
|---|---|---|
| a.  They think the little girl wearing overalls is cute. | True | False |
| b.  They think the evening gown is pretty, but they prefer the cocktail dress. | True | False |
| c.  They think that the bellhop looks uncomfortable in his uniform. | True | False |
| d.  Both women think the man's tie looks nice with his suit. | True | False |

🎧 3.  Complete the paragraph. Then listen again and check your answers.

Michelle and Amy are sitting in a hotel lobby. There's a cute little girl wearing _____.

They see a woman on a sofa. She's wearing a _____. There are two women

who are probably going to the prom. One of them is wearing an _____.

The other one is wearing a _____ and carrying a _____.

There's another woman talking to a bellhop. She's wearing _____ and sandals.

There are two people wearing _____. Amy doesn't like the man's

_____, but Michelle does.

4.  Write a paragraph describing the people in your classroom. What are they wearing?

_____

_____

_____

_____

_____

🎧 **1.** Listen to the entire conversation between Tom and his friend at the store. Answer the questions with your class.

    **a.** What is Tom looking for?

    **b.** What will he get his wife?

🎧 **2.** Listen to each part of the conversation. Complete the sentences.

> **a.** I'm just looking at the _____.
>
> **b.** Well, how about those plastic _____?
>
> **c.** Maybe I'll get her some _____.
>
> **d.** I don't like _____.
>
> **e.** I'm going to look at the _____.
>
> **f.** These _____ are nice.

🎧 **3.** Complete the paragraph. Then listen again and check your answers.

Tom thinks about buying a _____, but the _____ is too expensive. The store has _____, but it doesn't have any _____. He thinks about the _____, but he doesn't know what colours she likes. Tom wants to get her a _____, but Joe says that's not a good idea. Finally, Tom sees some _____ in a _____. He decides to buy one for himself and a gift card for his wife.

**4.** What kinds of jewellery, shoes, and accessories do you like? Write a paragraph.

_____

_____

_____

_____

_____

Oxford Picture Dictionary p. 101

🎧 1. Listen to the entire conversation between a mother and her son. Answer the questions with your class.

   a. Who is doing the laundry?

   b. What does Billy need to do first?

   c. Why must Billy take out the red T-shirt?

🎧 2. Listen to each part of the conversation. Complete the sentences.

   a. Do you want to wear _____ clothes?

   b. First, you need to _____ the clothes.

   c. Now _____ the washer.

   d. Now you have to put the clothes in the _____.

   e. You need to _____ the clothes.

   f. The _____ is right there.

🎧 3. Complete the paragraph. Then listen again and check your answers.

Billy's mom wants him to help with the _____. He has to set the washer to use hot water and add _____. Then he has to _____ the washer with white clothes. When the clothes are clean, Billy puts them in the _____ and puts in a _____. When the dryer stops, he needs to _____ the clothes. One of his shirts is _____, but he doesn't want to _____ it.

4. Write a paragraph about doing the laundry.

   _____

   _____

   _____

   _____

   _____

🎧 **1.** Listen to the woman and her daughter in the store. Answer the questions with your class.

    **a.** What does the girl want?

    **b.** Which items won't the mother buy for her daughter?

🎧 **2.** Listen to each part of the conversation. Complete the sentences.

    **a.** We need _____.

    **b.** We don't need _____.

    **c.** Look at this _____.

    **d.** Let's get some _____.

    **e.** Let's get some _____.

    **f.** Look, there's the _____.

🎧 **3.** Complete the paragraph. Then listen again and check your answers.

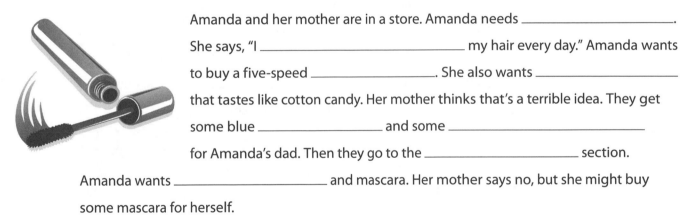

Amanda and her mother are in a store. Amanda needs _____. She says, "I _____ my hair every day." Amanda wants to buy a five-speed _____. She also wants _____ that tastes like cotton candy. Her mother thinks that's a terrible idea. They get some blue _____ and some _____ for Amanda's dad. Then they go to the _____ section. Amanda wants _____ and mascara. Her mother says no, but she might buy some mascara for herself.

**4.** How often do you buy the items mentioned in exercise 3?

_____

_____

_____

_____

_____

**Oxford Picture Dictionary p. 110**

🎧 **1.** Mandy is a receptionist at a doctor's office. Listen to her telephone conversations. Answer the questions with your class.

    **a.** Which caller is coming in first?

    **b.** Which caller is not coming in?

🎧 **2.** Listen to each part of the conversation. Underline *True* or *False*.

| | | |
|---|---|---|
| **a.** Mr. Han wants a morning appointment, but he gets an afternoon appointment. | True | False |
| **b.** Annie Jackson is far away from the doctor's office. | True | False |
| **c.** The man hangs up before Mandy can ask his name. | True | False |
| **d.** Mandy gives Brian an appointment for later in the afternoon. | True | False |

🎧 **3.** Complete the paragraph. Then listen again and check your answers.

Mandy works in Dr. Shin's office. Her first call today is from Mr. Han. He has a bad _____.
Her second call is from Annie Jackson. Annie's baby has a _____ of 39 and a
_____. She's very worried. Another caller has had a _____
for a week. Yesterday he started to _____, and now he has the
_____. Then Brian calls. He says he has an _____, but his
finger isn't red or _____. He just wants to talk to Mandy.

**4.** Write a conversation between Mandy and a new patient. Practise the conversation with a partner.

Mandy: _____*Good morning. Dr. Shin's office.*_____

Patient: _____

Mandy: _____

Patient: _____

Mandy: _____

🎧 **1.** Listen to the conversations at the pharmacy. Answer the questions with your class.

    **a.** What will the customer take for back pain?

    **b.** What things does the pharmacist tell customers not to do?

🎧 **2.** Listen to each conversation. Underline *True* or *False*.

| | | |
|---|---|---|
| **1.** Mr. Randall is dropping off his prescription. | True | False |
| **2.** He's getting tablets for back pain. | True | False |
| **3.** The correct dosage for Mr. Tam is two pills every four hours. | True | False |
| **4.** This customer knows a lot about cold medicine. | True | False |

🎧 **3.** Complete the paragraphs. Then listen again and check your answers.

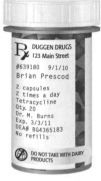

The pharmacist talks to Mr. Randall about a _____. The medication is a _____. Mr. Randall should _____ two tablets every four hours. He can't drive.

The pharmacist explains the correct _____ for Mr. Tam's medication. He is getting _____. He can't drink alcohol.

The last customer has a cold. He wants an _____. He doesn't want _____ because they're too big. He can buy tablets or _____.

    **4.** Look at pages 110 and 111 in the OPD. List 10 symptoms or health problems and the medications people take for them.

**Oxford Picture Dictionary pp. 114–115**

🎧 1. Listen to the conversations. Answer the questions with your class.

    **a.** What does Dr. Ohja tell the second patient to do?

    **b.** Which patient does Dr. Ohja send to the hospital?

🎧 2. Listen to each conversation. Complete the sentences.

> **a.** If you stay fit and _____, you should have more energy.
>
> **b.** Have you been having any _____?
>
> **c.** Didn't you _____ before you left?
>
> **d.** I can recommend a _____ for you.

🎧 3. Complete the paragraph. Then listen again and check your answers.

Dr. Ohja's first patient says she always feels tired. The doctor thinks this is due to _____. He recommends staying fit and _____. The second patient complains of headaches. Dr. Ohja thinks these might be due to _____, and he recommends an _____. The third patient is sick because she didn't get _____ before her vacation. Dr. Ohja gives her some medicine and advises her to get some _____. The fourth patient says he has chest _____. Dr. Ohja believes that this is due to the fact that the patient smokes; he advises the patient to _____ at the hospital right away.

4. Look at page 114 in the OPD. What things do you do to get well when you are sick? What things do you do to stay well when you are healthy? Write a paragraph.

_____

_____

_____

_____

_____

**Oxford Picture Dictionary p. 118**

🎧 1. Listen to the entire conversation. Answer the questions with your class.

    **a.** Why does the patient visit Dr. Willis?

    **b.** Why does Dr. Willis decide to do more tests?

🎧 2. Listen to each part of the conversation. Complete the sentences.

> **a.** I see you've filled out your _____.
>
> **b.** Please have a seat on the _____.
>
> **c.** I'm going to _____ your eyes, ears, and throat.
>
> **d.** Yes, I'm going to use this _____ to draw some of your blood.
>
> **e.** Check with my _____.

🎧 3. Complete the paragraph. Then listen again and check your answers.

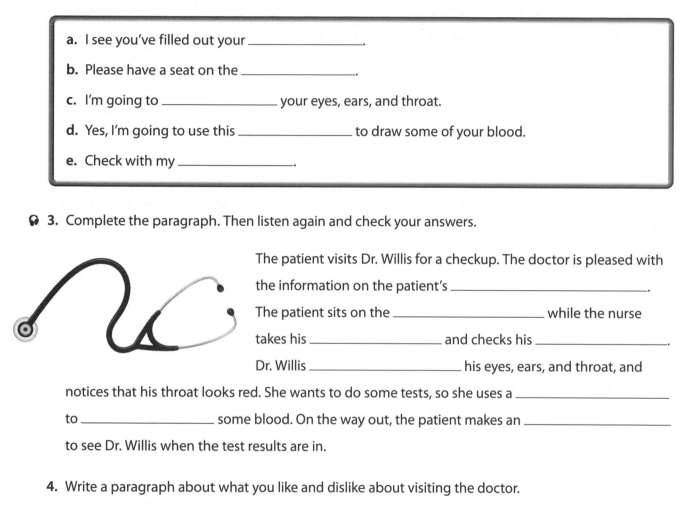

The patient visits Dr. Willis for a checkup. The doctor is pleased with the information on the patient's _____. The patient sits on the _____ while the nurse takes his _____ and checks his _____. Dr. Willis _____ his eyes, ears, and throat, and notices that his throat looks red. She wants to do some tests, so she uses a _____ to _____ some blood. On the way out, the patient makes an _____ to see Dr. Willis when the test results are in.

    **4.** Write a paragraph about what you like and dislike about visiting the doctor.

_____

_____

_____

_____

_____

**Oxford Picture Dictionary pp. 120–121**

🎧 **1.** Listen to the conversations at the hospital. Answer the questions with your class.

    **a.** Why is Mrs. Morales at the hospital?

    **b.** When can Mrs. Morales eat?

🎧 **2.** Listen to each conversation. List the hospital employees that Mrs. Morales sees. Check your dictionary for the correct spellings.

> **a.** _____
>
> **b.** _____
>
> **c.** _____
>
> **d.** _____
>
> **e.** _____

🎧 **3.** Complete the paragraph. Then listen again and check your answers.

Rosa Morales is a _____ at a hospital. First, a _____ comes into her room and gives her a _____. The nurse tells Mrs. Morales how to use the _____ and to push the _____ if she needs help. A _____ comes in because Mrs. Morales needs a _____. The last person to come in is the _____.

**4.** What would be the best job in a hospital? Why? Write a paragraph.

_____

_____

_____

_____

_____

1. Listen to the entire conversation. Answer the questions with your class.

   a. Why is the man asking for directions?

   b. Which places does he ask for directions to?

2. Listen to each part of the conversation. Complete the sentences.

   a. It's across the street from the _____.

   b. Do you know how to get to the _____?

   c. Is that on the same street as the _____?

   d. It's on Maple Street, between the bakery and the _____.

   e. Here's the _____.

3. Complete the paragraph. Then listen again and check your answers.

   The man asks the woman where the _____ is located, and she informs him that it is across the street from the _____. He then asks for directions to the _____. He needs to go to the _____ tomorrow, so the woman tells him that it is beside the _____, near the _____. Finally, he asks her for directions to someplace to eat and she suggests a _____. They walk there together, and pass a _____ along the way.

4. Choose a location in your town or city. Write a paragraph explaining how to get there from your home. Use the buildings along the way to help describe where to turn, how far to walk, etc.

   _____

   _____

   _____

   _____

   _____

**Oxford Picture Dictionary pp. 128–129**

🎧 1. Look at pages 128 and 129 in the OPD. Listen to the phone call between two friends. Answer the question with your class.

Where are they going to meet?

🎧 2. Close your dictionary. Listen to each part of the conversation. Complete the sentences.

> **a.** The _____ opens at 8:00.
>
> **b.** What time does the_____ open?
>
> **c.** The _____ opens at 9:00.
>
> **d.** It's near the _____.
>
> **e.** There's a _____ across from Burger Queen.
>
> **f.** It's across from the _____.

🎧 3. Complete the paragraph. Then listen again and check your answers.

Sue and May are going downtown this morning. May is going to drop off her daughter at the

_____. After that, she's going to pick up her jacket at the _____.

Sue is going to the _____ first. She's also going to buy some soap at the

_____. May needs to buy some magazines and mail a letter. There's a newsstand

next to the _____ and a _____ next to the newsstand. At 10:00,

the women are going to meet at the _____ on the _____.

4. Imagine that you visited the intersection shown on pages 128 and 129. Write a paragraph about what you did there.

_____

_____

_____

_____

_____

**Oxford Picture Dictionary p. 132**

🎧 **1.** Listen to the entire conversation. Answer the questions with your class.

    **a.** Why is the woman at the bank?

    **b.** What does the account manager give to the woman right away?

    **c.** What is he going to send to her in a few weeks?

🎧 **2.** Listen to each part of the conversation. Complete the sentences.

> **a.** I'm the _____ here, so I can help you open your account.
>
> **b.** No, you'll just have to carry your _____ and remember your PIN.
>
> **c.** Finally, would you like to rent a _____?
>
> **d.** You'll just need to fill out a _____.
>
> **e.** If you'd like, you can _____ instead.

🎧 **3.** Complete the paragraph. Then listen again and check your answers.

Tom Miller
17 Third Ave.
Brandon MB
R7A 6M9
Date _____
Pay to the
Order of _____ $ [_____]
_____ Dollars
For _____ _____
⑆000000000⑆ 00000000000000⑆ ⑇000

The woman is a new _____ at the bank. She meets with the _____ to open her bank accounts. He tells her that she doesn't need to memorize her account numbers, as long as she carries her _____ and remembers her PIN. She doesn't receive her _____ right away — the bank will send it to her in a few weeks. She does, however, want to make a _____ that day. The manager tells the woman that one of the _____ can help her do this if she fills out a _____. The lineups are too long, though, so the woman decides to _____ instead.

    **4.** Write a paragraph describing your last trip to the bank.

_____

_____

_____

_____

_____

**Oxford Picture Dictionary p. 133**

🎧 1. Listen to the library information line. Listen to all the messages. Answer the questions with your class.

    **a.** What is the name of the library?

    **b.** When is the library open?

🎧 2. Listen to each message. Underline *True* or *False*.

| | | |
|---|---|---|
| **a.** To get a library card, you need photo ID and a utility bill. | True | False |
| **b.** You can access the online catalogue at www.suncitylibrary.org. | True | False |
| **c.** The late fine for DVDs is $1.00 each week. | True | False |
| **d.** You must put books in the box and return DVDs to the circulation desk. | True | False |

🎧 3. Complete the paragraph. Then listen again and check your answers.

Tom takes his daughter to the Sun City library. Suzie is four years old. Next year, she can

_____ a library card. First, they _____ books in the online

catalogue. On the first floor, they get _____ for Suzie. They go upstairs to get

_____ for Suzie's mom. They go downstairs to get _____.

Suzie likes to _____ books, but not at the circulation desk. She likes to go to

the _____. She also likes to _____ books because she can

put them in the box.

4. Write a conversation between a reference librarian and a library patron. Write at least six lines.
Read the conversation with a partner.

Library Patron: *Excuse me. How can I* _____?

Librarian: _____

Library Patron: _____

Librarian: _____

Library Patron: _____

Librarian: _____

Library Patron: _____

🎧 **1.** Look at pages 136 and 137 in the OPD. Listen to the conversations between the licensing clerk and the customers. Answer the questions with your class.

    **a.** How many customers are there?

    **b.** What is the second customer's problem?

🎧 **2.** Close your book. Listen to each conversation. Complete the sentences.

> **a.** I'm ready to take my _____.
>
> **b.** I want to get my _____.
>
> **c.** I'd like to get a _____.
>
> **d.** What kind of _____ do you need?

🎧 **3.** Complete the paragraphs. Then listen again and check your answers.

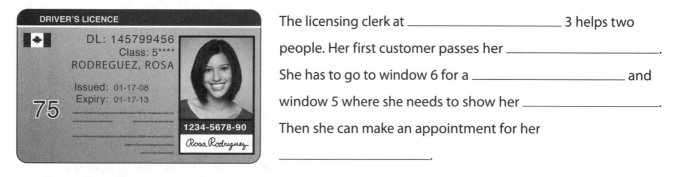

The licensing clerk at _____ 3 helps two people. Her first customer passes her _____. She has to go to window 6 for a _____ and window 5 where she needs to show her _____. Then she can make an appointment for her _____.

The second customer wants to get a _____. He has to _____ his passport, and he's ready to _____ the application fee, but the clerk says no. She'll see him next year.

**4.** Write a paragraph about how to apply for a driver's licence in your province.

_____

_____

_____

_____

_____

**Oxford Picture Dictionary pp. 138–139**

🎧 **1.** Listen to the entire conversation. Answer the questions with your class.

    **a.** What job does the woman have?

    **b.** What other jobs has she had in the past?

🎧 **2.** Listen to each part of the conversation. Complete the sentences.

> **a.** Earlier today, our new _____ was sworn in.
>
> **b.** I worked in the _____ for almost ten years.
>
> **c.** And what did you do before becoming a _____?
>
> **d.** My _____ in the riding were very experienced and were excellent speakers.
>
> **e.** I don't know, maybe I'll become a _____!

🎧 **3.** Complete the paragraph. Then listen again and check your answers.

The reporter is talking to the new _____, who has just been sworn in. He asks about her experience in government. She explains that she used to be a _____, working in the _____ for almost 10 years. At the beginning of her political career she was on _____. After this, she ran for office in the provincial government, where she had to _____ some very experienced _____. Now she wants to _____ as prime minister as well as she can. She jokes that her next job might be as a _____.

**4.** Would you ever consider running for a government office? Write a paragraph that gives reasons for your answer.

_____

_____

_____

_____

_____

🎧 **1.** Listen to the entire conversation. Answer the questions with your class.

    **a.** What is Mustafa doing today?

    **b.** Why does he want to do this?

🎧 **2.** Listen to each part of the conversation. Complete the sentences.

---

    **a.** I'm on my way to _____.

    **b.** You must _____.

    **c.** In Canada, I can use my writing to express my opinions because I have the freedom

       of _____.

    **d.** We were able to do that because of our right to _____.

    **e.** For example, they should obey the country's laws and _____.

    **f.** Once I'm a citizen, it will also be my responsibility to _____.

---

🎧 **3.** Complete the paragraph. Then listen again and check your answers.

## Citizenship Test

Mustafa is on his way to take his _____. He was not able to take it before now

because he hadn't _____ in Canada for three of the last four years —

this is one of the requirements for citizenship. There is also an age requirement: he must be

_____. Mustafa wants to become a citizen because he enjoys the freedoms

that Canadians have, such as the freedom of _____ and the right to

_____. Mustafa is also aware of his responsibilities as a Canadian citizen, which

include _____ the country's laws and _____ others in his

community. It will also be his responsibility to _____ once he becomes a citizen.

**4.** Look at page 140 in the OPD. Which responsibility of Canadian citizens do you think is the most important? Write a paragraph explaining why you think it is important.

_____

_____

_____

**Oxford Picture Dictionary p. 143**

🎧 1. Listen to the entire conversation. Answer the questions with your class.

   **a.** Why does Sabrina take Paula's purse?

   **b.** What advice does Paula give to Sabrina?

🎧 2. Listen to each part of the conversation. Complete the sentences.

> **a.** You didn't _____ your apartment door.
>
> **b.** You should _____ by keeping it close to your body.
>
> **c.** You should always _____ in the evening so you're not alone.
>
> **d.** We should stay on this street — it's _____.
>
> **e.** Always _____ your PIN when you're at the ATM.

🎧 3. Complete the paragraph. Then listen again and check your answers.

Sabrina and Paula are going to a movie. Paula leaves her apartment without _____ her door. Sabrina decides to test Paula on her safety knowledge — she asks whether Paula is always _____, and advises her to _____ by keeping it close to her body. She also tells Paula that she should _____ so that she's not alone. She won't let Paula take a shortcut through the alley because they should _____. Sabrina finally gets a lesson from Paula, who tells her to _____ at the ATM.

4. Look at page 143 in the OPD. Write a paragraph about the public safety advice that you think is the most important.

_____

_____

_____

_____

_____

**Oxford Picture Dictionary pp. 146–147**

🎧 **1.** Listen to the guest speaker talk with the class. Listen to the entire conversation. Answer the questions with your class.

    **a.** What committee is Ms Thomas from?

    **b.** What is she talking about?

🎧 **2.** Listen to each part of the conversation. Complete the sentences.

    **a.** We need to _____ for an emergency.

    **b.** You need _____.

    **c.** You should have _____.

    **d.** Don't forget the extra _____.

    **e.** What about a _____?

    **f.** Include _____.

🎧 **3.** Complete the paragraph. Then listen again and check your answers.

People need to _____ for an emergency. One way is to _____ a disaster kit. You should put in _____ and canned food because stores may be closed. Don't forget a _____ for your food. You need warm things because you may have to _____ shelter. Put in a _____ and extra batteries. It's a good idea to include a _____ in case someone is injured. You should also have _____. You don't want them to get lost.

**4.** Write a paragraph about other items you might put in a disaster kit. Why would you include those items?

_____

_____

_____

_____

_____

**Oxford Picture Dictionary p. 152**

🎧 1. Look at page 152 in the OPD. Listen to the conversations. Point to the locations as you listen.

🎧 2. Close your book. Listen to each conversation. List the locations that are mentioned.

a. _____

b. _____

c. _____

d. _____

e. _____

🎧 3. Complete the sentences. Then listen again and check your answers.

   a. The man is buying a round trip _____ to Churchill.

   b. The girl doesn't have any _____. She doesn't have to go to the _____ because the boy gives his token to her. He'll use his _____.

   c. The man is looking at the wrong _____.

   d. The passenger thinks the _____ isn't working because the ride is so expensive. Next time she's going to take the _____.

   e. The passenger doesn't know how much the fare is, and he doesn't have the exact change. He's not usually a bus _____.

4. Write a paragraph about your experience with public transportation.

   *When I lived in Korea, I took the subway everywhere...*

   _____

   _____

   _____

   _____

🎧 1. Look at the map at the bottom left of page 155 in the OPD. Listen to the conversations. Point to the streets as you listen.

🎧 2. Close your dictionary. Listen to each conversation. Underline *True* or *False*.

| | | | |
|---|---|---|---|
| **a.** Tara is at 19th Street and 1st Avenue. | | True | False |
| **b.** Sal is near Friendship Park. | | True | False |
| **c.** Mary is on 1st Avenue North at 25th Street East. | | True | False |
| **d.** Edgar is on 22nd Street West in the Central Business District. | | True | False |
| **e.** Jin is on Idylwyld Drive North. | | True | False |

🎧 3. Listen again. Complete the sentences.

a. Cindy: _____ north through the Central Business District.

   Then turn _____. The park is on the left, just before the river.

b. Ted: Go _____ until you cross the _____. Turn left at the next street.

c. Donna: _____ on 22nd Street West.

d. Diego: _____ on 3rd Avenue South, make a right at the next street, and then

   make another right. You need to go _____.

e. Jin: I'll get an _____.

4. Look at the map on page 155 again. Choose a starting place and an ending place. Write directions. Then ask a partner to follow the directions.

   _____

   _____

   _____

   _____

   _____

Oxford Picture Dictionary pp. 160–161

🎧 1. Listen to the entire conversation. Answer the questions with your class.

    **a.** How does Scott know that the flight will be on-time?

    **b.** Why does Scott's father put Scott's bag in the overhead compartment?

🎧 2. Listen to each part of the conversation. Complete the sentences.

> **a.** Do you see any _____?
>
> **b.** It'll be faster if we _____.
>
> **c.** There's the _____ for our gate.
>
> **d.** Do you have your _____?
>
> **e.** Hey, they just called us to _____.
>
> **f.** Be sure to _____.

🎧 3. Complete the paragraph. Then listen again and check your answers.

Scott and his dad arrive at the airport, and Scott's dad looks for a _____ to take his luggage. Scott's dad wants to go to a _____, but Scott suggests _____ to save time. They wait in the _____ for a short time before they are called to _____. Once on the plane, Scott's dad _____ Scott's bag in the overhead compartment, _____ his cellphone, and they get ready to _____.

4. Do you enjoy travelling by plane? Write a paragraph explaining why or why not.

_____

_____

_____

_____

_____

🎧 **1.** Listen to the entire conversation. Answer the question with your class.

What tasks does Ms Chang ask Donald to do?

🎧 **2.** Listen to each part of the conversation. Complete the sentences.

---

**a.** First, I'll need you to _____.

**b.** Can you _____ with Mr. Goldstein so I can discuss my notes with him?

**c.** Please _____ twenty copies of these sales reports and staple them.

**d.** Should I _____ to you?

**e.** Did Mr. Goldstein _____ for me?

---

🎧 **3.** Complete the paragraph. Then listen again and check your answers.

Ms Chang needs help preparing for a meeting, so she asks Donald to _____ some notes for her. Then she asks him to _____ with Mr. Goldstein. Donald's next task is to make 20 _____ of the sales reports and _____ them. Donald receives a call from Mr. Goldstein. Instead of _____ the call to her, Ms Chang asks Donald to _____. Donald finds out that Mr. Goldstein is missing a report, so he _____ a copy of it and _____ it to Mr. Goldstein.

**4.** Look at page 171 in the OPD. Which of the office skills do you have experience with?

_____

_____

_____

_____

**Oxford Picture Dictionary p. 172**

🎧 1. Look at page 172 in the OPD. Listen to the conversations at the Job Resource Centre. Answer the questions with your class.

   **a.** What does the man want?

   **b.** How does Mrs. Alvarez feel at the end?

🎧 2. Close your dictionary. Listen to each conversation. Complete the sentences.

> **a.** Welcome to the _____.
>
> **b.** I'm interested in finding a _____.
>
> **c.** After that, you can complete the _____.
>
> **d.** Do you offer _____ here?
>
> **e.** Yes, we have a _____.

🎧 3. Complete the paragraph. Then listen again and check your answers.

Albert is talking to a _____, Mrs. Alvarez. She's going to give him an _____ to help him get ideas for jobs. Then she'll give him a _____ so he can see which skills he has and which skills he'll need. Mrs. Alvarez knows which schools offer _____ and which companies have _____. The Resource Centre also has a _____, and Mrs. Alvarez knows about several _____ where Albert can meet _____ from local companies. Albert is glad he came to the Resource Centre.

4. What are your interests? What are your skills? Make two lists.

| Interests | Skills |
|---|---|
|  |  |
|  |  |
|  |  |
|  |  |
|  |  |
|  |  |
|  |  |
|  |  |

1. Look at page 174 in the OPD. Listen to the radio show. Answer the questions with your class.

   a. What is Jill Thurman giving advice about?

   b. What should you not do in an interview?

2. Close your dictionary. Listen to each part of the show. Write the suggestions you hear.

   a. First, _____.

   b. Second, _____.

   c. Third, _____.

   d. And fourth, _____.

3. Answer the questions. Then listen again and check your answers.

   a. What will the employer think if you are late for the interview?

   _____

   b. Is it OK to dress casually for some interviews? Why or why not?

   _____

   c. What might an interviewer think if you don't look him or her in the eye?

   _____

   d. According to Jill Thurman, what is a good question to ask an interviewer?

   _____

4. Write another suggestion for a good job interview. Explain your suggestion.

   _____

   _____

   _____

   _____

   _____

**Oxford Picture Dictionary pp. 180–181**

🎧 **1.** Look at page 181 in the OPD. Listen to the entire conversation. Answer the questions with your class.

    **a.** What is the woman going to paint?

    **b.** What colour does she like?

🎧 **2.** Close your dictionary. Listen to each part of the conversation. Complete the sentences.

    **a.** You'll need a _____ .

    **b.** The _____ are on that wall.

    **c.** This is a good _____ .

    **d.** The _____ is right here.

🎧 **3.** Complete the paragraph. Then listen again and check your answers.

The customer needs a lot of supplies for painting. She needs to buy a _____ and a _____ to use with it. She also needs _____ to protect her furniture and some _____ to hold them in place. The sales clerk reminds her to take off the _____ . Her windowsills have old, chipped paint. She needs to buy a _____ and _____ to get the old paint off. She's going to put a _____ on the windowsills.

**4.** Write short answers about your opinions.

    **a.** What is the best colour for a living room?

    _____

    **b.** Do you like to do home repairs?

    _____

    **c.** If yes, which ones?

    _____

    **d.** If you could change anything about your living room, what would you change?

    _____

🎧 **1.** Look at the office on page 182 of the OPD. Listen to the conversations. Answer the questions with your class.

    **a.** How many phone calls does the receptionist get?

    **b.** Where is Mrs. Tam?

    **c.** What is the office manager's problem?

🎧 **2.** Close your dictionary. Listen to each conversation. Complete the sentences.

    **a.** Well, how about her _____?

    **b.** I'd like to speak to the _____.

    **c.** And please find the _____ for me.

    **d.** Do you mean Roland, the _____?

🎧 **3.** Complete the paragraph. Then listen again and check your answers.

Melissa is the _____ at Green Energy Corporation. A caller asks for Mrs. Tam, but she's in the _____ watching a _____. Then Lucinda Majors calls. She wants to talk to the _____. He is at his _____, but he can't talk to Ms. Majors because he's busy. His _____ isn't working. He wants to talk to Mark, the new _____, but Mark is making copies. The office manager is not happy. The _____ are at the presentation while he's doing all the work.

**4.** Write a phone conversation between Melissa and another caller.

Melissa: _Green Energy Corporation. How can I help you?_ _____

Caller: _____

Melissa: _____

Caller: _____

Melissa: _____

Caller: _____

**Oxford Picture Dictionary p. 197**

🎧 **1.** Look at page 197 in the OPD. Listen to the entire conversation between the mother and the daughter. Answer the questions with your class.

    **a.** What is the woman trying to find?

    **b.** What was the girl using the computer for?

🎧 **2.** Close your dictionary. Listen to each part of the conversation. Complete the sentences.

> **a.** I think the _____ is www.TV101.ca.
>
> **b.** You have to put your _____ over the box.
>
> **c.** Type your _____ and your _____.
>
> **d.** Don't forget to _____ a subject.
>
> **e.** Just click the _____ button.

🎧 **3.** Complete the paragraph. Then listen again and check your answers.

Hana wants to look at a _____ on the Internet, but she's having some problems. She tries to _____ "cat video" in the _____, but nothing happens. Then a _____ appears on her screen. After Hana sees the video, she wants to _____ it to Guillermo, but she can't find the button. She has to use the _____ to scroll down. Then she wants to watch the video again, but she can't find the _____. So she clicks History in the _____.

**4.** What do you use the Internet for? Make a list.

_____    _____

_____    _____

_____    _____

_____    _____

🎧 1. Look at page 198 in the OPD. Listen to the teacher and the students. Answer the questions with your class.

    **a.** What kind of class is this?

    **b.** Do the students know the answers?

🎧 2. Close your dictionary. Listen to each part of the conversation. Write the correct answers.

> **a.** How many provinces were there at Confederation? _____
>
> **b.** Who lived in Northern Canada before the settlers came? _____
>
> **c.** What was created during Confederation? _____
>
> **d.** What do we call the group of people who created the British North America Act?
>
>     _____
>
> **e.** Who was Canada's first prime minister? _____

🎧 3. Complete the paragraphs. Then listen again and check your answers.

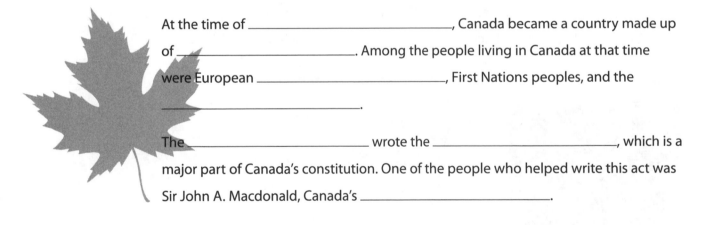

At the time of _____, Canada became a country made up of _____. Among the people living in Canada at that time were European _____, First Nations peoples, and the _____.

The _____ wrote the _____, which is a major part of Canada's constitution. One of the people who helped write this act was Sir John A. Macdonald, Canada's _____.

4. How many Canadian prime ministers can you name? Make a list.

_____      _____

_____      _____

_____      _____

_____      _____

**Oxford Picture Dictionary pp. 200–201**

1. Look at pages 200–201 in the OPD. Listen to Gina talk about her trip. As you listen, point to the provinces you hear.

2. Close your dictionary. Listen to each part of the conversation. Complete the sentences.

> **a.** We drove to _____ and saw the Anne of Green Gables farmhouse.
>
> **b.** Then we went east to _____.
>
> **c.** After that we went through _____ again, and we stayed in Quebec City.
>
> **d.** Maybe we'll go to _____.

3. Complete the paragraph. Then listen again and check your answers.

   Gina went on a long road trip last summer. She drove through the _____.

   She kept going _____, passing through _____

   then Newfoundland and Labrador. Gina didn't go to _____. She drove

   _____ through Quebec and Ontario. Then she went west all the way to

   _____. After she left Alberta, Gina drove through _____

   to Ontario. She's happy to be back _____. She's tired of driving.

4. How many Canadian provinces and territories can you name? Write them in the chart.

| | |
|---|---|
| **Northern Canada** | |
| **the West Coast** | |
| **the Prairie Provinces** | |
| **Central Canada** | |
| **the Atlantic Provinces** | |

**Oxford Picture Dictionary pp. 218–219**

🎧 1. Look at pages 218–219 in the OPD. Listen to the teacher and the students. Answer the questions with your class.

    **a.** What's the problem with oil?

    **b.** What's another big problem?

🎧 2. Close your book. Listen to each part of the conversation. Complete the sentences.

> **a.** We use _____ for most of our energy needs.
>
> **b.** We can save energy by _____ lights.
>
> **c.** We can _____ bottles, cans, paper, and plastic.
>
> **d.** Don't _____.

🎧 3. Complete the paragraphs. Then listen again and check your answers.

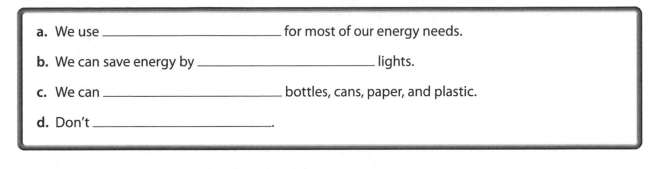

The class is talking about ways to _____ _____ and help the environment. We can turn off lights and _____ energy-efficient bulbs in lamps. We can _____ trash, too.

The class also talks about ways to help with _____. We can recycle and _____ recycled products. Another good idea is to _____ shopping bags. And of course we should never _____.

4. How do you save energy? Make a list.

    _____    _____

    _____    _____

    _____    _____

    _____    _____

**Oxford Picture Dictionary p. 224**

1. Look at page 224 in the OPD. Listen to the little girl and her father. Answer the questions with your class.

    a. How does the girl feel at the park?

    b. What does she want to do?

    c. How does the father feel?

2. Close your book. Listen to each part of the conversation. Complete the sentences.

    a. I want to go on the _____.

    b. I want to _____.

    c. Did you bring the _____?

    d. I want to go in the _____.

    e. Can I get a _____?

3. Complete the paragraph. Then listen again and check your answers.

    Beto's daughter rides around on her _____. Then she does a lot of things at the _____. She asks Beto to _____ her on the swings. She can _____ to the top of the bars, but Beto tells her not to go too high. Then she wants the _____. She wants Beto to go on the _____, but Beto wants to go to the _____ and look at the ducks. Beto is happy when his wife arrives and they can _____.

4. What did you like to do when you were a child? If you have children, what do your children like to do? Write complete sentences.

    _____

    _____

    _____

    _____

    _____